The Complete Book of Gambits

Raymond Keene

An Owl Book
Henry Holt and Company
New York

Henry Holt and Company, Inc.
Publishers since 1866
115 West 18th Street
New York, New York 10011

Henry Holt® is a registered trademark
of Henry Holt and Company, Inc.

First published in the United States in 1993 by
Henry Holt and Company, Inc.
Originally published in Great Britain in 1992 by
B. T. Batsford Ltd.

Library of Congress Catalog Card Number: 92-56739

ISBN 0-8050-2635-5 (An Owl Book: pbk.)

First American Edition—1993

Printed in the United Kingdom
All first editions are printed on acid-free paper. ∞

10   9   8   7   6   5   4   3   2   1

To Thelma Milner-Barry and Sir Stuart, a great gambit
knight.

Acknowledgements
I would like to thank Andrew Kinsman for an excellent
editing job, Byron Jacobs for his speedy and efficient
typesetting, and the two Annettes: Keene for typing
and Hardman for delivering.

Adviser: R. D. Keene, GM, OBE
Technical Editor: Andrew Kinsman

Algebraic Notation

The moves contained in this book are given in what is known as 'Figurine Algebraic Notation'. This somewhat complicated sounding term actually describes a very simple way of writing down the moves. Readers familiar with the system can jump ahead to the games themselves, but those who are comparatively new to the game or who have only learned the older English Descriptive notation will find what follows helpful. It is assumed that the reader already knows how to *play* chess.

Each piece is represented by a symbol, called a 'Figurine', as follows:

Pawn	♙
Knight	♘
Bishop	♗
Rook	♖
Queen	♕
King	♔

The squares on the chessboard are described by coordinates, consisting of a letter followed by a number (see diagram). For instance the square marked with a cross is called 'e4'. This follows exactly the same principle as reading off a reference on an A–Z street guide or road map. Everybody can pick this up in a matter of minutes. There is no mystery to it at all!

Symbols

+	Check
++	Double check
!	Good move
!!	Excellent move
?	Bad move
??	Blunder
!?	Interesting move
?!	Dubious move
(!)	Best move in difficult circumstances
±	Small advantage for White
∓	Small advantage for Black
±	Clear advantage for White
∓	Clear advantage for Black
+−	Winning advantage for White
−+	Winning advantage for Black
1−0	White wins
0−1	Black wins
½−½	Draw
=	The position is equal
∞	The position is unclear
⧜	With counterplay
Ch.	Championship
Ol.	Olympiad
Izt.	Interzonal
Zt.	Zonal
corr.	Correspondence
aka	also known as
qv	refer elsewhere

Introduction

The notion of the gambit is one of the most exciting in chess. Gambits have always appealed to the most aggressive players and, indeed, the word itself has passed powerfully into popular vocabulary. Political gambits, military gambits, even economic gambits have become part of the common linguistic heritage of confrontational situations in the English language.

What does the word - gambit - actually mean? If one refers to a dictionary one finds the following definition: The offer of a sacrifice for the sake of an advantage in timing or position in the opening stages of a game of chess. An initial move in anything, especially one with an element of trickery. From the Italian *Gambetto*, a tripping-up in wrestling from *Gamba*, leg.

Gambit, as a word, was first used in its chess sense by Ruy Lopez in 1561. Ruy Lopez was a Spanish priest, a great writer and theoretician of the game, and his very own opening, the Ruy Lopez or Spanish Opening, as it is known on the continent, is replete with gambit ideas. This will become clear as we advance further into the text of this book.

What does this book contain? For me, it is essentially A THOUSAND WAYS TO DARE AND WIN! a manual of risk, for those players, the boldest, prepared to renounce material for the attack, for the initiative and for the spirit of the game. Dull materialists should also take note, and prepare to add a new dimension to their game, becoming converted to the faith of the gambiteer, for whom the initiative is alpha and omega.

This volume contains up-to-the-minute designer gambits to smash your opponents in the most sophisticated of modern openings, plus revivals of forgotten 19th Century gambits to bowl over your unsuspecting victims -

with both White and Black.

Too often the chess reader associates the word gambit with those semi-dinosaurs of the Victorian era, the Evans, the Kings, the Two Knights etc., in their various manifestations. In this book I have, of course, sought to do justice to these venerable examples of the gambiteers' art. Indeed, games by Anderssen, Staunton and their illustrious contemporaries abound. What I have also tried to show, though, is that gambits can be present in every opening; they are continually appearing in the most modern and sophisticated of chess openings, as Kasparov, Alekhine and Tal have repeatedly demonstrated. I have tried to be as complete as possible with this book, and I have also tried to push forward the frontiers of gambit research, but like the physical universe, the discovery of gambits is continually expanding. Who knows, the readers of this book may invent their own, armed with the techniques for seizing the initiative, which I have expounded here!

I have evolved, and publish here for the first time, what I regard as an economical and revolutionary method of defining the playability of each gambit examined. It is as follows: a unique Star System evaluates risk in every gambit.

Verdict ✳✳✳✳✳   Absolutely reliable for the gambiteer.

Verdict ✳✳✳✳   The gambit is a good bet! Go for it!

Verdict ✳✳✳   Playable for both sides.

Verdict ✳✳   The gambit is doubtful.

Verdict ✳   The gambit is unsound.

I wish my readers good luck in their quest for the initiative, for the attack and for checkmate.

Ray Keene.

A

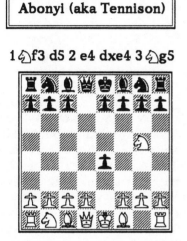

Abonyi (aka Tennison)

1 ♘f3 d5 2 e4 dxe4 3 ♘g5

Istvan Abonyi was a Hungarian master (1886 - 1942), while Otto Tennison (1834 - 1909) was a New Orleans amateur. Both of them favoured the above gambit. Nevertheless, after 3 ...♘f6 White can only aspire at the very best to the recovery of his gambit pawn. This line cannot be recommended. A comparison can be made with the Budapest Gambit (qv) with colours reversed. But the fact that Black has not yet committed his c-pawn is probably an advantage for him.

Verdict ✶✶

Adorjan

1 d4 ♘f6 2 c4 g6 3 d5 b5

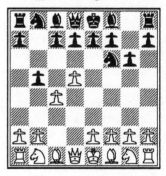

This gambit first saw the light of day in the game Spassov - Adorjan, Camaguey 1974. After 4 cxb5 a6 5 bxa6 c6 6 dxc6 ♘xc6 Black had excellent play. The only problem is that almost nobody nowadays plays the over-extending 3 d5.

Verdict ✶✶✶✶

Albin

1 d4 d5 2 c4 e5 3 dxe5 d4

The Albin is a shock weapon which has never been refuted. But unlike the Benko Gambit (qv), which has established itself as a respectable black defence in international tournament play, the Albin has never really caught on at the highest levels. Part of the explanation for this must be that it does not offer Black permanent structural compensation for his invested pawn. Instead, Black acquires a development lead (which may be eventually neutralised) and various tactical chances, often directed against White's king. If White survives Black's early burst of activity, and there is no compelling reason to believe that he should not, he can look forward to a middle-game with extra material and/or distinct counter-chances against the black king.

Korchnoi - Veinger
Beersheva 1978

1	d4	d5
2	c4	e5
3	dxe5	d4
4	♘f3	♘c6
5	g3	♗g4

Sensible alternatives are:
a) 5 ... ♗e6 6 ♘bd2! ♕d7 7 ♗g2 0-0-0 (7 ... ♘ge7 8 0-0 ♘g6 9 ♘g5 ♘gxe5 10 ♘xe6 ♕xe6 11 ♘f3 and White has the two bishops and attacking chances, Hort - Gazic, Sarajevo 1972) 8 0-0 h5!? 9 b4 ♗xb4 10 ♖b1 h4 11 ♕a4 with complicated play, Vladimirov - Volfson, USSR 1969. The simple 9 h4 merits attention.

b) 5 ... ♗f5!? 6 a3 ♕d7 7 ♗g2 0-0-0 8 0-0 ♗h3 9 b4 h5 10 b5 ♘ce7 when Black has compensation for the pawn in a complicated position, typical of the Albin. This line occurred in Chigorin - Albin, Nuremberg 1896.

6	♗g2	♕d7
7	0-0	0-0-0
8	♕b3!	

An excellent move, striking directly at Black's most sensitive point, the b7-

square. Possibilities now are:

a) 8 ... ♗h3. This natural looking move stumbles into an ambush - 9 e6! ♗xe6 10 ♘e5 ♕d6 11 ♘xc6 bxc6 12 ♕a4 ♕c5 13 ♘a3 ♕b6 14 ♗xc6 ♗xa3 15 bxa3± Spassky - Forintos, Sochi 1964.

b) 8 ... h5 9 ♖d1 b6 10 ♗f4 h4 11 ♘c3! ♗xf3 12 ♗xf3 g5 13 ♕b5!±.

c) 8 ... ♗c5 9 ♘bd2 ♗h3? 10 e6! ♗xe6 and 11 ♘e5 again confers great advantage on White.

d) 8 ... ♘a5 9 ♕d3 ♗f5 10 e4 dxe3 11 ♕xe3±.

e) 8 ... ♕f5 9 ♖d1 ♘ge7 - this may be Black's best chance but it looks artificial.

8	...	♘ge7
9	♖d1 ·	♗xf3

If, innocently, 9 ... ♘g6? 10 ♘xd4 ♗xe2 (10 ... ♘xd4?? 11 ♕xb7 mate) 11 ♖d2+-. It is quite obvious, though, that this exchange of bishop for knight is an unwelcome one for Black, whose sensitivity along the h1-a8 diagonal is now accentuated.

10	♕xf3	♘g6
11	♕h5	♔b8
12	♗f4	♘xf4

Renouncing any thought of regaining the 'Albin' pawn, Veinger strives for counterplay by fracturing the pawns around White's king.

13	gxf4	g6
14	♕f3	f6
15	exf6	♕f5
16	♘d2	♕xf6
17	♘e4	♕f5
18	b4!	

A move thoroughly conforming to the whole pattern of White's attack - namely, a breakthrough at b7. If now 18 ... ♘xb4 19 ♘d6+- or 18 ... ♗xb4 19 ♖ab1 and Black is clearly finished. The black bishop on b4 can be nudged away with a3, when there would follow moves like ♖b5 and ♘g3, intensifying the pressure against b7, on the b-file and from the white queen and bishop to intolerable levels.

18	...	d3
19	♖xd3	♗xb4
20	♖b1	♖xd3
21	♕xd3	♗e7
22	c5	♕xf4

He might as well. There is no good defence to the white attack. If 22 ... ♗xc5

23 ♕c3 ♗d4 24 ♕xc6+-.
23   ♖xb7+!
The logical culmination of White's strategy - a sacrificial bomb-blast on his theme square, b7.

23   ...   ♔xb7
24   ♕b5+   ♔c8
25   ♗h3+   1-0

If 25 ... ♔d8 26 ♕xc6+-.

Verdict   ✳✳✳

Alekhine-Chatard Attack

1 e4 e6 2 d4 d5 3 ♘c3 ♘f6
4 ♗g5 ♗e7 5 e5 ♘fd7 6 h4

See Chatard-Alekhine Attack.

Alekhine's Defence

Alekhine's Defence has never been particularly noted for its gambit variations. However, there are some interesting possibilities in both the sharp Four Pawns Attack and the solid Modern Variation.

Peacock - Williams
SCCU Jamboree 1970

1   e4   ♘f6
2   e5   ♘d5
3   d4   d6

4   c4   ♘b6
5   f4   g5?!

This gambit is enterprising, but probably not sound. It was dreadfully punished in Durao - Pomar, Madrid 1982: 6 ♕h5! dxe5 7 c5! ♘d5 8 fxe5 ♘f4 9 ♗xf4 gxf4 10 ♗c4 e6 11 ♘e2 and 0-0-0+-.

After the normal 5 ... dxe5 6 fxe5 there are some interesting gambit lines for both Black and White.

a) 6 ... c5 7 d5 e6 8 ♘c3 exd5 9 exd5 c4 10 ♘f3 ♗g4 11 ♕d4 ♗xf3 12 gxf3 ♗b4 13 ♗xc4 0-0 14 ♖g1 g6 15 ♗g5 ♕c7 16 ♗b3 ♗c5 17 ♕f4 ♗xg1 Grünfeld - Ljubojevic, Riga Izt 1979.

b) 6 ... ♘c6 7 ♗e3 ♗f5 8 ♘c3 e6 9 ♘f3 ♗e7 10 d5 exd5 11 cxd5 ♘b4 12 ♘d4 ♗d7 13 e6 fxe6 14 dxe6 ♗c6 15 ♕g4 ♗h4+ 16 g3 ♗xh1 17 ♗b5+ c6 18 0-0-0 0-0 Velimirovic - Kovacevic, Yugoslav Ch 1984.

6   ♗e2
Clearly bad for White is 6 fxg5 dxe5 7 dxe5 ♕xd1+ 8 ♔xd1 ♘c6. Most other moves seem playable.

6   ...   dxe5
The only logical continuation is 6 ... gxf4 but Black feared White's pressure on the f-file.

7   fxe5   ♘c6
8   ♗e3

8 e6, now or on move 9

or 10 is adequately met by capturing on d4 with the biggest piece available. White's lack of pawns compensates for Black's active king.

8	...	♗g7
9	♘c3	♗f5
10	a3	

Presumably directed against 10 ... ♘b4 and 11 ... c5, this move proves useful later.

10	...	♛d7
11	♘f3	0-0-0
12	♖c1	

12 ♘xg5, which Black was hoping for, loses to 12 ... ♗h6 13 ♛d2 ♘a5. After the text 13 c5 ♘d5 14 ♘xd5 ♛xd5 15 ♗c4 was worrying.

12	...	h6
13	0-0	e6
14	b4	♛e7
15	♛b3?	

15 ♛e1 to meet 15 ... g4 with 16 ♘h4.

15	...	g4
16	♘e1	♘xd4
17	♗xd4	♖xd4
18	c5	♘d7

18 ... ♘d5 loses to 19 ♘xd5 ♖xd5 20 ♖xf5.

19	♘b5	

(*see following diagram*)

19	...	♗xe5!

Forced, but quite good, as 19 ... ♖e4 loses to 20 ♘d6+!.

20	c6!	♘b6!
21	cxb7+	♔xb7
22	♘xd4	♗xd4+

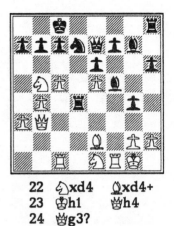

22	♘xd4	♗xd4+
23	♔h1	♛h4
24	♛g3?	

The losing move. The exchange of queens gives Black a winning attack. 24 ♘c2 is forced, when after 24 ... ♗e5 Black has a clear edge.

24	...	♛xg3
25	hxg3	♖g8
26	♖d1	♗e3!
27	♘d3	♖g5
28	♘f2	♘d5
29	♗c4	♘c3
30	♖de1	♗b6
31	♖e5	♘e4
32	♔g1	♖h5
33	♗d3	♘xg3
	0-1	

Notes based on those by Howard Williams.

Verdict ✳✳

Alekhine - Reshevsky
Kemeri 1937

1	e4	♘f6
2	e5	♘d5
3	♘f3	d6

4	d4	♗g4
5	c4	♘b6
6	♗e2	

6	...	dxe5

Black can decline the gambit by 6 ... c6, 6 ... e6 or 6 ... ♘c6 transposing to normal Alekhine positions but Reshevsky takes up the challenge.

7	♘xe5	♗xe2
8	♕xe2	♕xd4
9	0-0	♘8d7
10	♘xd7	♘xd7

Alekhine's risky pawn sacrifice has given him chances for a pawn, but after this recapture Black's queen becomes subject to molestation and White succeeds in building up a promising attacking formation. A better recapture would have been 10 ... ♕xd7 though after 11 a4 ♕c6 12 ♘a3 e6 13 a5 ♘d7 14 ♘b5 White still maintains prospects of aggression.

11	♘c3	c6
12	♗e3	♕e5
13	♖ad1	e6

14	♕f3	0-0-0
15	♗xa7	♕a5
16	♗d4	♕f5
17	♕g3	

17 ♕xf5 exf5 18 ♖fe1 would have made life extremely difficult for Black but White would probably have had to try to win a long endgame based on his better pawn structure. Alekhine wrote about this "The final attack of this game gave me much more pleasure than a scientifically correct but purely technical exploitation of a pawn majority on the queenside would do. After all, chess is not only knowledge and logic!"

17	...	e5
18	♗e3	♗b4
19	♘a4	♗a5
20	f4	♗c7
21	b3	f6
22	fxe5	♕e6
23	h3	

There is a tendency for lesser players to deify the champions and Alekhine wrote a humourous debunking of this notion in his book of best games "A good positional move which is however, neither particularly deep nor difficult to find. I was, therefore, not a little surprised to read all the compliments addressed by the critics to the modest text move and also to be questioned in all seriousness after the game was over, whether by 23 h3, I already planned to play my queen to h2 on the 33rd move."

23	...	♖hg8
24	♗d4	♘xe5
25	♕c3	♘d7
26	c5	♖ge8
27	b4	

Launching a blitzkrieg.

27	...	♘b8
28	♘b6+	♗xb6
29	cxb6	♕xa2
30	♕g3	♖d7
31	♗c5	♕f7
32	♖a1	♕g6
33	♕h2	♖e5
34	♖a8	♖d2

From the diagram position Alekhine launches one of my favourite combinations. One of the impressive elements is that Black's pieces seem so powerfully centralised while White's are strewn around the edge of the board and yet they suddenly come together with cataclysmic fury.

| 35 | ♖xb8+ | ♔xb8 |
| 36 | ♕xe5+ | 1-0 |

After 36 ... fxe5 37 ♖f8+ Black has to give up all his pieces but still cannot avert mate.

Verdict ✷✷✷✷

Alekhine's Gambit
(Closed Ruy Lopez)

---

1 e4 e5 2 ♘f3 ♘c6 3 ♗b5 a6 4 ♗a4 ♘f6 5 0-0 ♗e7 6 ♖e1 b5 7 ♗b3 d6 8 c3 ♘a5 9 ♗c2 c5 10 d4 ♕c7 11 ♘bd2 0-0 12 ♘f1 ♗g4 13 ♘e3 ♗xf3 14 ♕xf3 cxd4

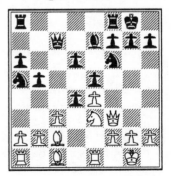

This gambit was introduced in the game Alekhine – Fine, Hastings 1936/37. The idea of sacrificing White's d4-pawn is an interesting and typical Ruy Lopez strategy. Alekhine now played 15 ♘f5 but later recommended 15 cxd4 exd4 16 ♘f5, ♛xc2 17 ♘xe7+ ♔h8 18 ♘f5 already with the threat of ♘xg7 followed by ♗h6+.

Verdict ✳ ✳ ✳

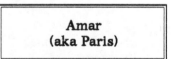

Aleppo

(Alternative name for Queen's Gambit)

1 d4 d5 2 c4

Named after Phillip Stamma of Aleppo in Syria, translator of Oriental languages to the court of George II, who introduced the Queen's Gambit in the 18th Century.

Verdict ✳ ✳ ✳ ✳ ✳

Allgaier
(King's Gambit)

1 e4 e5 2 f4 exf4 3 ♘f3 g5 4 h4 g4 5 ♘g5 h6 6 ♘xf7 ♔xf7

For long considered a byway of the King's Gambit. Keres, no less, has suggested that both sides have chances after 7 ♘c3 f3 (or 7 ... ♘f6 8 d4 d5 9 ♗xf4) 8 gxf3 ♗e7 9 ♗c4+ d5 10 ♘xd5 ♗xh4+ 11 ♔f1 ♔g7 12 f4.

Verdict ✳ ✳ ✳

Amar
(aka Paris)

1 ♘h3 d5 2 g3 e5 3 f4 ♗xh3 4 ♗xh3 exf4 5 0-0 fxg3 6 hxg3 ♘f6

An eccentric gambit fa-
voured by the 1930's Parisian amateur Charles Amar.
The starting position is
given above and although
White won the only extant
grandmaster game, the
gambit is clearly not sound.
White is a pawn down with
an exposed king's position.
Nevertheless, Tartakower – Lilienthal, Paris 1933 continued: 7 d3 ♘c6 8 ♘c3 ♗d6
9 ♗g5 ♗xg3 10 ♗xf6 gxf6 11
e4 ♖g8 12 ♘xd5 ♗e5+ 13 ♔h1
♕d6 14 c3 ♖g3 15 ♕h5 ♖xd3
16 ♖ad1 ♖xd1 17 ♖xd1 ♘e7 18
♘e3 ♕c5 19 ♕xh7 ♘c8 20
♕g8+ 1-0. Even the simple 8
... ♗e7 would have been ∓.

Verdict ✳

B

Balogh
(Budapest)

1 d4 ♞f6 2 c4 e5 3 dxe5 ♞g4 4 e4 d6

A dubious line given by the Hungarian master Balogh. White has two alternatives, the strategical 5 ♗e2 ♞xe5 6 f4 ♞g4 7 ♞f3 ♗e7 8 ♞c3 0-0 9 0-0 ♞c6 10 h3 or the tactical 5 exd6 ♗xd6 6 ♗e2 f5 7 exf5 ♛e7 8 c5 ♗xc5 9 ♛a4+ ♞c6 10 ♛xg4. Here Black has the option between 10 ... 0-0 or investing a second piece with 10 ... ♗xf5. I prefer the former cautious option for White.

Instead of 4 ... d6, Black should simply play 4 ... ♞xe5 when material equality is restored.

Verdict ✳✳

Basmaniac

Agdestein - Hodgson
Hastings 1991/92

1	c4	c5
2	♞f3	h6

The introduction to an unorthodox defence, a version of the Basmaniac Defence 1 ... g5. Hodgson has played this before in grandmaster chess, e.g Mednis - Hodgson, New York 1990 (1 c4 g5). Psychologically, Hodgson seems to resort to this defence against players whom he considers super-solid strategists.

3	d4	g5

This move offers a gambit - one of the weirdest in this collection!

4	dxc5	♗g7
5	♘c3	♗xc3+
6	bxc3	♕a5

Black's kingside is a mess but so is White's queenside. What Black really has to watch out for are problems on the dark squares occasioned by the absence of his king's bishop.

| 7 | h4 | |

This is a theoretical novelty, 7 ♕d4 having been played in the game Szekely – Hodgson, Barbican Open 1991.

7	...	g4
8	♕d4	♘f6
9	♘d2	g3

A probably necessary further gambit, since White was threatening to consolidate with g3 and ♗g2. Now if White captures on g3 his whole structure would be terribly unsound, so Black's g-pawn lives to fight another day.

10	f3	♘c6
11	♕e3	b6
12	h5!	

A very fine move, the point of which is either to fix Black's h6-pawn as a weakness or to deprive the far-flung pawn on g3 of support. If now 12 ... ♕xc5 13 ♕xc5 bxc5 14 ♘b3 d6 15 ♗f4 ♗a6 16 e4 wins an important pawn.

| 12 | ... | bxc5 |
| 13 | ♘b3 | ♕a4 |

14	♕xc5	♖b8
15	♘d4	♘xd4
16	♕xd4	d6
17	c5!	

White disrupts the central zone and dissolves his doubled pawns just in time. In the coming play White will lose back his extra pawn but his dark-squared bishop develops ferocious activity.

17	...	♕xd4
18	cxd4	dxc5
19	♗f4	♖b4
20	♗xg3	cxd4
21	♗e5	

This sounds the death knell of Black's d-pawn which can no longer be protected against moves such as ♖d1 and ♖h4.

21	...	0-0
22	a3	♖a4
23	♖h4	♗a6
24	♗xd4	e5
25	♗f2	

The only move but quite adequate.

| 25 | ... | e4 |
| 26 | ♖d1! | |

A very important move. Now 26 ... ♖xa3 fails to 27 ♗c5 and meanwhile the white queen's bishop can regain its post on d4.

26	...	♖e8
27	♗d4	exf3
28	gxf3	

Of course White cannot allow a capture on e2.

| 28 | ... | ♘h7 |

29 ♖g4+ ♘g5

29 ... ♔f8 loses to 30 ♗c5+ ♖e7 31 ♖d8 mate. Now Black must seemingly lose a piece and in seeking to prevent this worse befalls.

30 f4   ♖e4
31 fxg5!! ♖xg4
32 ♗f6   1-0

Amazingly, with White's king and his king's bishop still on their starting square, Black has no sensible way of preventing checkmate.

Verdict ✳✳

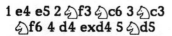

Belgrade
(Four Knights)

1 e4 e5 2 ♘f3 ♘c6 3 ♘c3 ♘f6 4 d4 exd4 5 ♘d5

This can become quite exciting after 5 ... ♘xe4 6 ♕e2 or 6 ♗c4. The drawback to the Belgrade Gambit is that 5 ... ♗e7 6 ♗f4 d6 7 ♘xd4 ♘xd5 8 exd5 ♘xd4 9 ♕xd4 ♗f6 leads to dead equality.

Verdict ✳✳✳

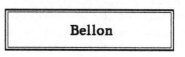

Bellon

1 c4 e5 2 ♘c3 ♘f6 3 ♘f3 e4 4 ♘g5 b5

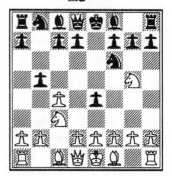

An invention of the Spanish Grandmaster, Juan Manuel Bellon. After 5 cxb5 d5 Black has good play, especially since White's king's knight is out on a limb. However ...

Keene - Wockenfuss
Bad Lauterberg 1977

1   c4   e5
2   ♘c3   ♘f6
3   ♘f3   e4!?
4   ♘g5   b5
5   d3

I prefer this to acceptance of the pawn.

5	...	bxc4
6	dxe4	♘c6

If 6 ... h6 7 ♘xf7! ♚xf7 8 e5.

7	e3	♗b4
8	♗xc4	0-0
9	0-0	♗xc3?

Premature. Correct is 9 ... h6!.

10	bxc3	h6
11	f4!!	hxg5
12	fxg5	♘h7
13	g6	♘g5

Or 13 ... ♘f6 14 ♖xf6 ♕xf6 15 ♕h5.

14	♗a3	♘e5
15	♗xf8	♘xc4
16	gxf7+	

If now 16 ... ♘xf7 17 ♖xf7! ♚xf7 18 ♕d5+ ♚e8 19 ♕g8; or 16 gxf7+ ♘xf7 17 ♖xf7 ♚xf7 18 ♕d5+ ♚g6 19 ♖f1; finally 16 gxf7+ ♘xf7 17 ♖xf7 ♚xf7 18 ♕d5+ ♚xf8 19 ♖f1+ ♚e7 20 ♕g5+ ♚e8 21 ♕g6+.

16	...	♚xf8
17	♕h5	♗b7
18	♕h8+	♚e7
19	♕xg7	♕f8
20	♕f6 mate	

A case of the biter bitten.

Verdict ✱✱

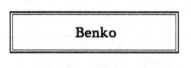

Benko

1 d4 ♘f6 2 c4 c5 3 d5 b5

This gambit is totally reliable in the main acceptance line: 1 d4 ♘f6 2 c4 c5 3 d5 b5 4 cxb5 a6 5 bxa6 ♗xa6; Black has too much play for the pawn. Nowadays, white players try to take the fight more directly to Black.

Martin del Campo - Fedorowicz Mexico City 1991

1	d4	♘f6
2	c4	c5
3	d5	b5
4	cxb5	

Refusing the gambit pawn is fashionable, e.g. 4 ♘f3 g6 5 cxb5 a6 6 ♘c3

axb5 7 e4 b4 8 ♘b5 d6 9 e5
dxe5 10 ♘xe5 ♗g7 11 ♗c4
0-0 12 0-0 ♗b7 Ftacnik -
Plachetka, Czechoslovakia
1985.

| 4 | ... | a6 |
| 5 | e3 |

White tries not to lose
castling rights, as in the
line 5 bxa6 ♗xa6 6 ♘c3 g6
7 e4 ♗xf1. By sacrificing a
tempo (e3 - e4) he hopes to
develop unhindered.

5	...	g6
6	♘c3	♗g7
7	a4	0-0
8	♘f3	♗b7
9	♖a3	e6

Here there is nothing to
be gained by opening the
queenside so Black looks
for play in the centre and
kingside while White's
pieces are underdeveloped.

10	dxe6	fxe6
11	♕d6	♕c8
12	♗e2	♘e8
13	♕g3	axb5!
14	♗xb5	♗xf3
15	gxf3	♘c6
16	0-0	♘e5
17	♗e2	d5
18	♗d2

Hereabouts f4 had to be
tried. White's passive
pieces allow his king to be
gradually overrun.

18	...	♘d6
19	b3	♘f5
20	♕h3	g5!

White is now helpless
against the threats.

21	♖a2	♖f6
22	♖c1	♖h6
23	♕g2	♘h4
24	♕g3	♕f8
25	f4	gxf4
26	exf4	♖g6
27	fxe5	♗xe5
28	f4	♗d4+
29	♔h1	♖xg3
30	hxg3	♘f5
	0-1

A game of some theore-
tical importance.

Martin - Hodgson
London Haringey 1989

1	d4	♘f6
2	c4	c5
3	d5	b5
4	cxb5	a6
5	e3	axb5

An interesting alterna-
tive treatment to the previous game.

| 6 | ♗xb5 | ♕a5+ |
| 7 | ♘c3 | ♗b7 |

If White were now to
choose to break the pin on
his queen's knight with 8
♗d2, Black would gain

counterplay by an inge-
nious method: 8 ... ♛b6 9
♛b3 e6 10 e4 ♘xe4 11 ♘xe4
♗xd5 12 ♛d3 ♛b7 13 f3 c4 14
♗xc4 ♗xc4 15 ♛xc4 d5 16
♛c2 dxe4 17 ♖c1 ♘d7.

| 8 | ♘ge2 | ♗xd5 |

If 8 ... ♘xd5 9 0-0 ♘c7 10
♗c4 leads to White's
advantage.

| 9 | 0-0 | ♗c6 |
| 10 | ♛d3 | e6 |

This move is an improve-
ment over 10 ... ♗xb5 11
♘xb5 ♘c6 12 ♗d2 ♛b6 13 a4
which was markedly in
White's favour in the game
Farago – Stangl, Altensteig
1987.

11	e4	♗e7
12	♗f4	0-0
13	♗xc6	♘xc6
14	e5	c4

A powerful riposte which
is a complete answer to
White's 14th move. Black
now obtains a majority of
pawns in the centre.

15	♛xc4	♘xe5
16	♛d4	♘c6
17	♛d2	d5
18	♖fc1	♖ac8
19	a3	♖fd8
20	b4	♛a8
21	♛d1	d4
22	♘a4	♘d5
23	♗d2	♗f6
24	♖ab1	d3
25	♘ec3	♘xc3
26	♗xc3	♘d4

White's next move errs
in attempting to cash in on
his queenside plus. In-
stead he should have elimi-
nated Black's dangerous
knight with 27 ♗xd4. Black
now obtains a decisive attack when he drives home
with superb elan.

27	♘b6	♘e2+
28	♔f1	♛b8
29	♗xf6	♛xh2
30	♔e1	♛h1+
31	♔d2	♛h6+
32	♔e1	♖xc1
33	♖xc1	d2+

0-1

The brilliant point of
Black's play is that
although 33 ... d2+ 34 ♔xe2
dxc1♛ allows 35 ♛xd8+
checkmate, Black can, ne-
vertheless, avail himself of
the rare opportunity to un-
derpromote to a knight in
actual play. Thus 34 ♔xe2
dxc1♘+ and White is help-
less.

A fine game, demons-
trating Black's opportun-
ities for counterplay.

Verdict ✳✳✳✳✳

Benoni (Modern)

1 d4 ♘f6 2 c4 c5 3 d5 e6 4 ♘c3 exd5 5 cxd5 d6 6 ♘f3 g6 7 ♗g5 ♗g7 8 e4 h6 9 ♗h4 g5 10 ♗g3 ♘h5 11 ♗b5+ ♔f8 12 e5!

This is perhaps the most powerful gambit in the Modern Benoni. It was introduced into international practice by my game against Jan Timman at Vlissingen 1975.

Hartston – Wahlbom
Clare Benedict 1977

1	d4	♘f6
2	c4	c5
3	d5	e6
4	♘c3	exd5
5	cxd5	d6
6	♘f3	g6
7	e4	♗g7
8	♗g5	h6
9	♗h4	g5
10	♗g3	♘h5

11	♗b5+	♔f8
12	e5!	

At the time, this pawn sacrifice was the latest attempt to refute the modern Benoni. In the preceding year it had become very popular with English players, but it seems from Black's response that the move was still virtually unknown in Sweden.

	12	...	g4?

Stronger is 12 ... a6 or 12 ... ♗g4.

	13	0-0

Also good is the intermezzo 13 ♗h4.

	13	...	dxe5

If 13 ... gxf3 14 ♕xf3 ♘xg3 15 fxg3! ♕e7 16 exd6 winning. White's assault on the open f-file lends this variation some similarity to the King's Gambit (e.g. the Muzio variation) which was one of Hartston's favourites as a junior some thirteen years previously.

	14	♗h4	♗f6
	15	♗xf6	♕xf6
	16	♘d2	♕g6?

Criticized after the game, but Black's prospects are already compromised. For his pawn White has achieved two important thematic advantages: he has dislocated his opponent's pawn structure and also displaced his king. In practice it is almost impossible to defend such positions.

17	♕e2	f6
18	♘de4	b6
19	♘d6	♘f4
20	♕e3	♗d7
21	♗c4	♖h7
22	g3	♘h3+
23	♔h1	♖e7
24	f3	♔g7
25	fxg4	♗xg4
26	♗e2	♗d7
27	g4	♘g5
28	h4	♘f7
29	♘de4	1-0

He cannot defend his f-pawn and after that goes his positions crumbles into ruins.

Miles - Wedberg
Stockholm 1976

1	d4	♘f6
2	c4	c5
3	d5	e6
4	♘c3	exd5
5	cxd5	d6
6	♘f3	g6
7	e4	♗g7
8	♗g5	h6

9	♗h4	g5
10	♗g3	♘h5
11	♗b5+	♔f8
12	e5	♘xg3

If 12 ... a6 then not 13 ♗d3? as Keene - Timman, England vs Holland 1975, but 13 ♗e2 ♘xg3 14 fxg3 g4 15 ♘h4. 12 ... ♗g4, played in a Hartston - Nunn 5-minute game, may be Black's best chance.

| 13 | fxg3 | a6 |
| 14 | ♗d3 | |

14 ♗e2 dxe5 15 0-0 ♖a7 16 a4 Stean - Nunn, Birmingham 1976 is also good (see the next game).

| 14 | ... | ♕b6? |

Weak. Black should try 14 ... dxe5 or 14 ... b5 or 14 ... ♗g4.

| 15 | ♘d2! | ♗xe5 |

Now Black discovers that if 15 ... ♕xb2 16 0-0 ♕xc3 17 ♕f3.

16	♘c4	♗xc3+
17	bxc3	♕c7
18	0-0	

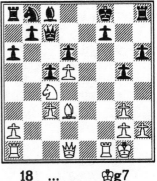

| 18 | ... | ♔g7 |

More natural is 18 ... b5

when Miles had planned the winning line 19 ♗g6 bxc4 20 ♖xf7+ ♕xf7 21 ♗xf7 ♚xf7 22 ♕f3+ ♚g7 23 ♖f1 ♖a7 24 ♕f6+ ♚h7 25 ♖b1 ♗g4 26 ♕xd6 ♘d7 27 ♕e7+ ♚g8 28 h3 ♗f5 29 ♖b8+ ♘xb8 30 ♕xa7. After 18 ... ♚g7 White has basically five pieces in action to Black's one (and that one is the king!).

19 ♕h5! ♖d8
Or 19 ... ♖f8 20 ♖f6.
20 ♖f6 ♚xf6
21 ♕xh6+ ♚e7
22 ♖e1+ 1-0

Just in time to avoid 22 ... ♗e6 23 ♖xe6+ fxe6 24 ♕g7+ ♚e8 25 ♗g6 mate.

Stean - Nunn
Birmingham 1976

1	d4	♘f6
2	c4	c5
3	d5	e6
4	♘c3	exd5
5	cxd5	d6
6	♘f3	g6
7	e4	♗g7
8	♗g5	h6
9	♗h4	g5
10	♗g3	♘h5
11	♗b5+	♚f8
12	e5!	♘xg3
13	fxg3	dxe5
14	0-0	a6
15	♗e2	♖a7
16	a4	b6
17	♕b3	f5
18	♘d2?	

Stronger is 18 ♖ad1!.

18	...	e4
19	g4	♗d4+
20	♚h1	e3
21	♘c4	f4
22	♘xb6	♖b7
23	a5	h5!

Black starts a kingside counter-offensive, while his queenside is left to its own devices.

24	gxh5	♘d7
25	♗xa6	

Nunn later published a lengthy analysis, proving that 25 ... ♖xh5! would now have given him good chances, e.g. 26 ♗xb7 ♚g7, with the terrible threat of 27 ... ♕h8.

25	...	♘f6?
26	♗xb7	♘xh5
27	♘e2	♗g4
28	♘xd4	♘g3+
29	♚g1	♖xh2
30	♚xh2	♕e8
31	♘e6+	♗xe6
32	♕xe3	♕h5+
33	♚g1	1-0

Verdict ✳ ✳ ✳ ✳ ✳

Benoni Format

The gambit described here
is not a specific variation,
but a standard plan. In certain situations, exemplified
here, White can gambit a
pawn, based on his big
pawn centre, with e5 followed swiftly by f5.

Khalifman – Larsen
London (WFW) 1991

1	d4	♘f6
2	♘f3	d6
3	c4	♗g4

A Larsen favourite,
which often leads to un-
charted positions. In this
case, however, there is
soon a transposition to a
Benoni/King's Indian for-
mation.

4	♘c3	g6
5	e4	♗g7
6	♗e2	♘fd7
7	♗e3	c5
8	d5	♘a6

Another Nordic free
thinker, Finnish grandma-
ster Heikki Westerinen,
has tried 8 ... ♗xc3+!? and 9
... ♕a5 with reasonable success here.

9	0-0	0-0
10	♘g5	♗xe2
11	♕xe2	♘c7
12	a4	a6
13	f4	♖b8

White has several the-
matic plans in such struc-
tures: attacking on the
kingside with the pawn
storm e5/f5; breaking up
Black's queenside play with
a timely b2 - b4 advance; or
a central pawn break-
through on d6. The re-
markable thing about this
game is that Khalifman
achieves all of them!

| 14 | e5! | dxe5 |
| 15 | f5 | |

The kingside assault is in
motion. The gambit of a
pawn clears the e4-square
for cavalry manoeuvres,
activates the rook on f1 and
stifles the bishop on g7 and
the knight on d7 - good value for a pawn.

| 15 | ... | b5 |

Larsen counters with one
of Black's thematic breaks
and creates the chance to
use the rook on b8 to de-
fend the kingside, by coming forwards to b6.

| 16 | axb5 | axb5 |
| 17 | ♕g4 | ♖b6 |

18 b4!

The exposed situation of the rook on b6 allows Khalifman to strike out on the opposite flank as well. The b-pawn sets out to join in the attack.

18 ...   gxf5
19 ♕xf5   ♖g6
20 bxc5   bxc4
21 d6!

Khalifman achieves standard breakthrough number three - an unusual hat-trick.

21 ...   exd6
22 cxd6   ♘e6

The d-pawn is immune from capture, as the rook must block ♕h7. 22 ... ♘e8 23 ♘xf7 ♘xd6 24 ♕xg6 hxg6 25 ♘xd8 ♖xd8 26 ♖ad1 should win for White.

23 ♘xf7

After the game, Khalifman indicated that 23 ♘d5!? may be the most accurate.

23 ...   ♕f6

23 ... ♕e8 looks more critical, but meets with an elegant refutation, as follows: 24 ♘d5! ♖xf7 25 ♕xf7+ ♕xf7 26 ♘e7+ ♕xe7 27 dxe7 ♘c7 28 ♖a8+ and the pawn which began life on b2 promotes!

24 ♕xf6   ♖xf6
25 ♖xf6   ♗xf6?

After long and resourceful defiance, Larsen falters. Better was 25 ... ♘xf6! and

it is not clear how large White's advantage is.

26 ♘h6+   ♔g7
27 ♖a7

White's attack, aided by the powerful passed d-pawn, continues into the ending.

27 ...   ♖d8
28 ♘f5+!

The last difficult move of the game. White must avoid the temptation to play the apparently decisive 28 ♗b6 when ... ♖b8 will enable Black to escape from the pressure.

28 ...   ♔g6
29 ♘e7+   ♔f7
30 ♘c6   ♖c8
31 ♖xd7+   ♔e8
32 ♘xe5   ♗xe5
33 ♖e7+   ♔d8

If 33 ... ♔f8 34 ♘h6+ ♔g8 35 ♖xe6 ♗xc3 36 d7 wins.

34 ♗b6+   1-0

Verdict ✳✳✳✳✳

Bertin
(King's Gambit)

1 e4 e5 2 f4 exf4 3 ♘f3 ♗e7 4 ♗c4 ♗h4+ 5 g3

Bertin's 5 g3 is speculative compared with 5 ♔f1 d5 6 ♗xd5 ♘f6 7 ♗b3. But after 5 g3 fxg3 6 0-0 gxh2+ 7 ♔h1 White has an enormous lead in development for his three-pawn deficit. The conclusion must be that the concept of disrupting White's king position with ... ♗h4+ is too time-consuming.

This variation of the King's Gambit was originated by the historian Alexander Cunningham in or around 1707 and first published by Joseph Bertin in 1735. Bertin's book *The Noble Game of Chess*, was according to *The Oxford Companion*, the "first worthwhile text book in the English language."

Verdict ✳✳✳

Bird's Defence
(Ruy Lopez)

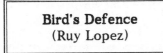

This relatively uncom-

mon line of the Ruy Lopez does not normally involve any gambit play – but one interesting and typical gambit has been contributed by the ingenious brain of the powerful Ukranian Vassily Ivanchuk.

Short - Ivanchuk
Linares 1989

1	e4	e5
2	♘f3	♘c6
3	♗b5	♘d4
4	♘xd4	exd4

Bird's Defence, as chosen by Black in this game, is antiquated, but has never been refuted.

5	♗c4	♘f6
6	♕e2	♗c5

White's next move 7 e5 is an error, overlooking that after 7 ... 0-0 8 exf6 ♖e8 wins the white queen.

7	e5	0-0
8	0-0	d5
9	exf6	dxc4
10	♕h5	

If instead, 10 ♕xc4 ♗d6 followed by ... ♗e6 when Black has an overwhelming lead in development.

    10 ...   **b6**

Now the black kingside is broken up and White takes a gambit pawn in slightly different fashion, but Ivanchuk obtains over-powering pressure against White's centre.

11	fxg7	♖e8
12	d3	cxd3
13	cxd3	♗a6
14	♕f3	♕e7
15	♗f4	♕e2
16	♘d2	♕xf3
17	♘xf3	♗xd3
18	♖fe1	♗e2
19	♗xc7	d3
20	a3	a5
21	♗f4	♖e4
22	♗d2	♖ae8
23	♗c3	a4
24	♘g5	♖c4

Short has made a tremendous fight of it, with such poor weapons as he has left, but ultimately his case is hopeless.

25	♖ad1	♖c8
26	♖a1	♖d8
27	♘f3	♖xc3
28	bxc3	d2
29	♖xe2	d1♕+
30	♖xd1	♖xd1+
31	♘e1	♖c1
32	♖e4	f5
33	♖e8+	♔xg7
34	♔f1	♖xc3
35	♔e2	♖xa3
36	♘d3	♖a2+
37	♔f3	♖a3
38	♖d8	♖c3
39	♔f4	a3
40	♖d7+	♔f8
41	♘e5	a2
42	♔xf5	a1♕
43	♖d8+	♔g7
44	♖d7+	♔g8
	0-1	

Verdict ✳✳✳✳✳

Bird's Opening

1 f4

There are two major gambits in Bird's Opening. See sections on From's Gambit 1 f4 e5 and the Swiss Gambit 1 f4 f5 2 e4!?.

Bishop's Opening

1 e4 e5 2 ♗c4

The Bishop's Opening occurs regularly throughout this book, offering ample opportunities for gambit play - consult the index for other ideas.

Cochrane - Staunton
London 1842

1	e4	e5
2	♗c4	♗c5
3	d4	♗xd4
4	♘f3	♘c6!

In a previous game Staunton tried the weaker 4 ... ♕f6 and was attractively beaten after 5 0-0 ♗b6 6 ♘c3 c6 7 ♗g5 ♕g6 8 ♘xe5! ♕xg5 9 ♘xf7 ♕c5 10 ♗b3 d5 11 ♘xh8 ♘f6 12 exd5 cxd5 13 ♘xd5 ♘bd7 14 ♕e2+ ♔f8 15 ♖ae1 a6 16 ♘xf6 ♘xf6 17 ♘f7 ♗d7 18 ♘g5 ♖e8 19 ♕xe8+! ♘xe8 (19 ... ♗xe8 20 ♘e6+) 20 ♘xh7 mate.

5	0-0	♘f6
6	♘xd4	♘xd4
7	f4	d6
8	fxe5	dxe5
9	♗g5	♗e6!
10	♗xe6	♘xe6
11	♕xd8+	♖xd8
12	♗xf6	gxf6
13	♖xf6	♘f4!

Classic refutation of gambit play by Staunton, who happily returns his pawn for an endgame advantage.

This sort of play reminds one of Lasker (e.g his defence to the Evans Gambit) rather than the miserly Steinitz who always clung to his spoils and sometimes came unstuck because of it!

| 14 | ♘c3 | ♖d2 |
| 15 | ♖d1 | |

15 g3 is forced even though it is a rotten move.

15	...	♖xg2+
16	♔h1	♖hg8
17	♖f5	f6!

Neatly protecting his king from check.

18	♖xf6	♘h3
19	♖ff1	♖g1+!
20	♖xg1	♘f2 mate

A fine revenge for the earlier loss quoted in the note to move four.

Verdict ✳✳

Blackmar-Diemer

1 d4 d5 2 e4 dxe4 3 ♘c3 ♘f6 4 f3

Black could play the spoil-sport in this position and simply give back the pawn with 4 ... e3. However, 4 ... exf3 is also perfectly possible, e.g. 5 ♕xf3 g6! 6 ♗e3 c6 7 ♗c4 ♗g7 8 ♘ge2 ♘bd7 9 0-0-0 ♘b6 10 ♗b3 a5 11 a3 ♗g4 with advantage to Black. The main line is 4 ... exf3 5 ♘xf3 ♗g4 6 h3 ♗xf3 7 ♕xf3 c6 8 ♗e3 e6 9 ♗d3 ♘bd7 10 0-0 ♗e7 when White has some compensation for the pawn.

Verdict ✳✳✳

Blumenfeld

1 d4 ♘f6 2 ♘f3 e6 3 c4 c5 4 d5 b5

The Blumenfeld Counter-Gambit has certain similarities with the Benko Gambit in that Black strikes out with an early ... b5. How-

ever, the strategic motivation is quite different as Black wishes to establish a strong pawn centre.

Tarrasch - Alekhine
Pistyan 1922

1	d4	♘f6
2	♘f3	e6
3	c4	c5
4	d5	b5

Black gives up a pawn, obtaining in exchange a very strong pawn centre. The impression made by the present game was so strong that it put many players off accepting the dangerous gift.

    5 dxe6

Nowadays, White tends to refuse the gift, e.g. 5 ♗g5 h6 6 ♗xf6 ♕xf6 7 ♘c3 b4 8 ♘b5 ♘a6 9 e4 g5 10 e5 ♕f4 11 ♗d3! g4 12 ♕d2 ♕xd2+ 13 ♘xd2± Polugayevsky – Ljubojevic, Manila 1975.

5	...	fxe6
6	cxb5	d5

Black's centre is mena- cing and invulnerable, while in addition he has the open f-file and good diag- onals for his bishops. Alek- hine exploits these factors with great skill.

7	e3	♗d6
8	♘c3	0-0
9	♗e2	♗b7
10	b3	♘bd7
11	♗b2	♕e7
12	0-0	♖ad8
13	♕c2	e5
14	♖fe1	e4
15	♘d2	♘e5
16	♘d1	♘fg4
17	♗xg4	♘xg4
18	♘f1	

It appears that White has everything in order, but Alekhine spots a weakness in his opponent's king po- sition.

18	...	♕g5
19	h3	♘h6
20	♔h1	♘f5
21	♘h2	d4
22	♗c1	d3
23	♕c4+	♔h8
24	♗b2	♘g3+!

The decisive stroke. Al- though the g3-square is covered by a white pawn, Black is the master of it.

25	♔g1	♗d5
26	♕a4	♘e2+
27	♔h1	♖f7
28	♕a6	h5

Black takes away the g4- square from White's knight and at the same time pre-

pares the concluding blow.

29	b6	♘g3+
30	♔g1	axb6
31	♕xb6	d2
32	♖f1	♘xf1
33	♘xf1	♗e6
34	♔h1	♗xh3!

White has no defence to this.

35	gxh3	♖f3
36	♘g3	h4
37	♗f6	♕xf6
38	♘xe4	♖xh3+
	1-0	

Nikolic - Miles
Tunis Interzonal 1985

1	d4	♘f6
2	c4	e6
3	♘f3	c5
4	d5	b5
5	♗g5	h6
6	♗xf6	♕xf6
7	♕c2	b4

This is an improvement on the game Chernin - Miles from an earlier round where Miles had been wiped out after 7 ... exd5? 8 cxd5 d6 9 e4 a6 10 a4 b4 11 ♘bd2 ♗g4 12 e5 dxe5 13 ♘e4 ♕f4 14 ♘fd2 ♗f5 15 ♗d3 with a huge plus to White. This kind of light-squared domination is exactly what Black must avoid in the Blumenfeld.

8	♘bd2	g5
9	e4	g4
10	♘g1	♗g7
11	♖b1	h5

12	♗d3	d6
13	♘e2	♘d7
14	f4	gxf3
15	♘xf3	♘e5
16	0-0	♕h6
17	♘xe5	♗xe5
18	♔h1	♗d7
19	♘g1	h4
20	♘f3	♗g3

This is a clumsy square for the bishop but of course it is immune from capture here.

21	e5	dxe5
22	dxe6	♗xe6
23	♗f5	♗xf5
24	♕xf5	♕f4
25	♕h3	♔e7
26	♖bd1	♖ad8

When we looked at this game after the round Miles told me that he had originally intended 26 ... f5 but then 27 ♘d4 is most unpleasant.

27	♖xd8	♖xd8
28	hxg3	hxg3
29	♕h7	

The situation is confusing and under the tension White goes seriously astray. Correct would have been 29 ♕h5 f6 when Black has counterplay and threatens ... ♕xc4.

29	...	♖d6
	0-1	

There is no defence to a fothcoming check on the h-file.

Verdict   ✳ ✳ ✳

Boden-Kieseritzky

1 e4 e5 2 ♘f3 ♘c6 3 ♗c4 ♘f6 4 ♘c3 ♘xe4 5 0-0 ♘xc3 6 dxc3

White has opened lines for his gambit pawn but after 6 ... f6 7 ♘h4 g6 Black's position is practically impregnable, e.g. 8 f4 f5 9 ♘f3 (not 9 ♘xf5? d5) 9 ... e4 10 ♘g5 ♗c5+ 11 ♔h1 ♕e7 12 ♗f7+ ♔f8.

Verdict   ✳ ✳

Breyer
(King's Gambit)

1 e4 e5 2 f4 exf4 3 ♕f3

An extravagant line of the King's Gambit. After 3 ... d5! 4 exd5 c6 5 dxc6 ♘xc6 6 ♗b5 ♕b6 it is Black who is prepared to offer material for the initiative. Alternatively, 3 ... d5! 4 exd5 ♘f6 5 ♗b5+ c6 6 dxc6 ♘xc6 7 d4 ♗g4, which is absolutely no worse for Black, Spielmann – Nimzowitsch, Carlsbad 1907.

Bringing White's queen out so early, usurping the best square for White's king's knight, is asking for trouble. White should not stray from the tried and tested 3 ♘f3.

Verdict ✳✳

Bryan
(King's Bishop's Gambit)

1 e4 e5 2 f4 exf4 3 ♗c4 ♕h4+ 4 ♔f1 b5

The most famous example of this gambit is "The Immortal Game", played at London in 1851.

Anderssen – Kieseritzky
London 1851

1	e4	e5
2	f4	exf4
3	♗c4	♕h4+
4	♔f1	b5?!

Bryan's Counter-Gambit, and to modern eyes a very dubious idea. For his pawn Black temporarily lures White's king's bishop from its attacking post on the a2-g8 diagonal, gains the possibility of protecting b5 and d5 with tempo (... c6) and creates an alternative avenue of development for his queen's bishop. In 1851 all this could be regarded, even by masters, as sufficient compensation for a pawn, in spite of the fact that Black also wrecks his queenside pawn structure with this rash move.

5 ♗xb5 ♘f6

A game Anderssen – Löwenthal, also played at London in 1851 (outside the tournament), varied from this with 5 ... g5, and Anderssen scored another smashing sacrificial victory: 6 ♘c3 ♗g7 7 d4 ♘e7 8 ♘f3 ♕h5 9 h4 h6 10 e5 ♘f5 11 ♔g1 ♘g3 12 ♖h2 ♕g6 13 ♘d5 ♔d8 14 hxg5 hxg5 15 ♖xh8+ ♗xh8 16 ♘xg5! ♕xg5 17 ♗xf4 ♕h4 18 ♗xg3 ♕xg3 19 ♕h5 ♕g7 20 ♕h4+.

| 6 | ♘f3 | ♕h6 |
| 7 | d3 | ♘h5? |

A transparent threat which is easily parried: 7 ... ♗b7! is best.

8	♘h4	♕g5
9	♘f5	c6
10	g4	♘f6?

Better would have been 10 ... cxb5 11 gxh5, but Kieseritzsky obviously expected to win White's g4-pawn (11 ♗c4 ♕xg4). Instead of this Anderssen offers a positional sacrifice of his bishop.

11	♖g1!	cxb5
12	h4	♕g6
13	h5	♕g5
14	♕f3	

With the terrible threat of ♗xf4, netting the Black's queen. In view of this Black is obliged to reverse his developmental process.

14	...	♘g8
15	♗xf4	♕f6
16	♘c3	

White clearly has sufficient positional compensation for his piece, since Black's development is non-existent, his king is exposed and his pawn-structure is full of holes. Black's best defence is 16 ... ... ♗b7 but after 17 ♘xb5 White also enjoys a virtual material equivalent.

| 16 | ... | ♗c5? |
| 17 | ♘d5!? | |

Anderssen translates his positional superiority into a grandiose combination and he must already have envisaged the fantastic mate at move 23 when he played his move. However, in view of the numerous sub-variations en route to the desired beautiful conclusion (in one of which Black can escape into an ending only one pawn down), a purely objective player might have rejected the romantic 17 ♘d5!? in favour of the bulldozer-like 17 d4 ♗e7 (or 17 ... ♗b6) 18 ♘d5 when Black is prosaically crushed.

| 17 | ... | ♕xb2 |

18 ♗d6   ♕xa1+

It should be noted than some sources give the move order as 18 ... ♗xg1 19 e5 ♕xa1+ 20 ♔e2.

19 ♔e2   ♗xg1?

Defence by acceptance once again. After 19 ... ♕b2 the situation is still obscure.

20 e5   ♘a6

The final mistake which allows Anderssen to bring matters to a sparkling, forced conclusion. It is typical for the times that Kieseritzsky should fail to prevent the brilliancy by missing the toughest defence, 20 ... ♗a6! which limits White to a winning ending: 21 ♘c7+ ♔d8 22 ♘xa6 ♗b6 23 ♕xa8 ♕c3 24 ♕xb8+ ♕c8 25 ♕xc8+ ♔xc8 26 ♗f8 h6 27 ♘d6+ ♔d8 28 ♘xf7+ ♔e8 29 ♘xh8 ♔xf8 30 ♘g6+ ♔f7 31 c3 ♔e6 32 d4 and White should win with his extra pawn. If, instead, 20 ... ♗a6 21 ♘c7+ ♔d8 22 ♘xa6 ♕c3 23 ♗c7+

♕xc7 24 ♘xc7 ♔xc7 25 ♕xa8 ♘a6 26 ♘d6 and Black is too badly tied up to offer effective resistance.

21 ♘xg7+   ♔d8
22 ♕f6+!   ♘xf6
23 ♗e7 mate

Verdict ✳✳

Budapest

---

1 d4 ♘f6 2 c4 e5 3 dxe5 ♘g4

In the main lines the Budapest tends not to constitute a real gambit, since White swiftly returns the pawn, e.g. by 4 ♘f3 ♗c5 5 e3 ♘c6 6 ♗e2 ♘gxe5. Our first game shows White, exceptionally, trying desperately to cling on to his extra gambit pawn. The second game shows the more positional treatment by White. (See also 1 d4 ♘f6 2 c4 e5 3 dxe5 ♘e4, the Fajarowicz).

Beliavsky - Epishin
Reggio Emilia 1990/91

1	d4	♘f6
2	c4	e5
3	dxe5	♘g4
4	♕d4	

A suspect method of clinging to the extra pawn. 4 ♘f3 is more sensible.

4	...	d6

Black decides to make a real gambit of the opening in the interests of hounding white's exposed queen.

5	exd6	♗xd6
6	♕e4+	

The queen's peregrinations continue. If 6 ♕xg7? ♗e5 wins.

6	...	♗e6
7	♘c3	

The gluttonous 7 ♕xb7 would grant Black an overwhelming advantage in development after 7 ... ♘d7.

7	...	0-0
8	♘f3	♕d7
9	♘d4	

In this position 9 ♕xb7 would now be parried by 9 ... ♘c6 10 a3 ♗xc4 followed by ... ♖fb8.

9	...	♗xc4
10	♘f5	♗e6
11	♘xd6	cxd6
12	g3	

White is seeking to complete his development with ♗g2 and 0-0 but Black's active forces harry White to such an extent that he can never complete this manoeuvre.

12	...	d5
13	♕f4	d4
14	♘e4	♗d5
15	f3	f5
16	♘c5	♕e7
17	♘d3	♘c6
18	h3	

If 18 ♗g2 ♖ae8 19 0-0 ♕xe2 20 ♖e1 ♕xd3 21 ♖xe8 ♖xe8 22 fxg4 ♖e1+ 23 ♗f1 ♗c4.

18	...	♘ge5
19	♘xe5	♘xe5
20	♔f2	d3
21	♗d2	dxe2
22	♗xe2	

22	...	♗xf3!

This sacrifice definitively exposes the artificiality of the white set-up. Of course White cannot capture on f3 with his bishop on account of ... ♘d3+. However, Black's calculations had to go somewhat deeper than that.

23 ♗b4   ♕e6

If now 24 ♗xf8 ♗xe2 25 ♔xe2 ♕a6+ 26 ♔d2 ♖d8+ 27 ♔c3 ♕d3+ 28 ♔b4 ♘c6+ mates. Alternatively if 26 ♔e3 ♖e8 wins.

24 ♖he1   ♗xe2
25 ♕e3

There is no way out, thus 25 ♖xe2 ♘d3+ 26 ♔f1 ♘xf4 27 ♖xe6 ♘xe6 28 ♗xf8 ♔xf8 winning.

25 ...   f4
0-1

Demoralised, Beliavsky resigned but his position is quite hopeless after 26 gxf4 ♖xf4+ 27 ♔g2 ♕d5+ or 26 ♕xe2 ♕b6+ 27 ♔f1 fxg3+ 28 ♔g2 ♖f2+.

Keene - Haugli
Gausdal 1983

1	d4	♘f6
2	c4	e5
3	dxe5	♘g4
4	♘f3	

The dubious 4 e4 d6?! is considered in a separate section under 'Balogh'.

4 ...   ♗c5

After 4 ... d6?! 5 exd6 ♗xd6 6 ♘c3 leaves Black without compensation (but don't fall into the trap 6 g3? ♘xf2! 7 ♔xf2 ♗xg3+-+). Alternatively, 4 ... ♘c6 5 e3 ♗b4+ 6 ♗d2 ♗xd2+ 7 ♕xd2 ♘gxe5 8 ♘xe5 ♘xe5 9 ♗e2 0-0 10 ♘c3 d6 11 0-0 b6 12 f4 ♘g4 13 ♗f3 ♖b8 14 ♘b5 a6 15 ♘d4± due to the holes in Black's queenside, Knezevic - Mestrovic, Yugoslavia 1980.

5	e3	♘c6
6	♗e2	♘gxe5
7	0-0	

White can also delay committing his king to this of the board, although there is no need to be nervous about it, as we shall see. The alternative is 7 ♘c3 d6 8 a3 a5 9 b3 ♘xf3+ 10 gxf3 ♘e5 11 ♗b2 ♗d7 12 ♘e4 ♕e7 13 ♕c2 f6 14 0-0-0 ♗c6 15 ♖hg1 0-0-0 16 ♘c3± Franco - Aguila, Argentina 1982.

7	...	♘xf3+
8	♗xf3	♕h4

A bold attacking try, quite in the style of those who are attracted to the Budapest. However, such adventures should make little impression on the white position.

9 ♗e2   h5

Continuing in the risky style exemplified by his previous move, but if he does not, ... ♕h4 will be pointless.

10	♘c3	♘e5
11	♘d5	

As so often in the Budapest, the occupation of this square by a white piece spells positional disaster for Black.

11	...	♗g4
12	h3	♗d6

To my total amazement, my opponent informed me after the game that this was a known theoretical position. It had actually been recommended as winning for Black in a 1982 monograph on the Budapest, written by a three-man team comprising Staker, Glasscoe and Stayart.

White, however, has committed no detectable error so far, but has developed his pieces calmly and efficiently. Over the board, it did not take me long to spot the refutation of Black's scheme.

13 f4!

Now White threatens to capture the knight, but if 13 ... ♘h6 14 c5!+-. Or 13 ... ♘f6 14 c5! ♘xd5 15 cxd6 c6 16 e4 with an overwhelming advantage. Black cannot develop his queenside pieces, his kingside is riddled with weaknesses and White dominates the centre.

13	...	c6
14	♘c3	♗e7
15	hxg4	hxg4
16	♗xg4	♕h2+
17	♔f2	♗h4+
18	♔e2	♕xg2+
19	♔d3	b5
20	cxb5	♗f6
21	♗f3	♕g6+
22	♗e4	♕g3
	1-0	

Verdict ✳ ✳ ✳

C

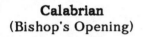

Calabrian
(Bishop's Opening)

1 e4 e5 2 ♗c4 f5

If White accepts the gambit (3 exf5? ♘f6 and ... d5) Black may overrun the centre. However, the unpretentious 3 d3 ♘f6 4 f4! d6 5 ♘f3 causes Black unexpected problems.

Verdict ✳✳

Caro-Kann Defence

The Caro-Kann is more renowned for its solid qualities than gambit variations. However, there are some possibilities worth exploring for both White and Black.

Mestel – K Arkell
British Ch. 1988

1	e4	c6
2	♘c3	d5
3	d4	

A gambit which is playable for Black arises after 3 ♘f3 ♗g4 4 h3 ♗h5 5 exd5 cxd5 6 ♗b5+ ♘c6 7 g4 ♗g6 8 ♘e5 ♖c8 9 d4 e6 10 ♕e2 ♗b4 11 h4 ♘e7 12 h5 ♗e4 13 f3 0-0 14 ♘xc6 ♘xc6 15 ♗xc6 ♖xc6 16 0-0 ♗xc3 17 bxc3 ♖xc3 18 ♗d2 ♖xc2 19 fxe4 dxe4 20 ♖fc1 Bobkov – Shakarov, corr. 1982.

3	...	dxe4
4	♘xe4	♘d7

Karpov's favourite variation. It used to be considered a quiet attempt to equalise, but now black practitioners are obliged to know reams of opening theory if they wish to employ it safely.

5	♗c4	♘gf6
6	♘g5	e6
7	♕e2	♘b6
8	♗d3	h6

Black cannot afford to play 8 ... ♕xd4 when 9 ♘1f3 grants White an overpowering lead in development.

9	♘5f3	c5
10	dxc5	♘bd7

This looks a somewhat artificial gambit, but the natural way to regain the pawn 10 ... ♗xc5 also has its disadvantages, e.g. 11 ♘e5 ♘bd7 12 ♘gf3 ♕c7 13 0-0 0-0 14 ♗f4 with a slight edge to White or, more excitingly, 10 ... ♗xc5 11 ♘e5 ♘bd7 12 ♘gf3 ♘xe5 13 ♘xe5 0-0 14 ♗d2 ♕d5 15 0-0-0 ♕xa2 16 c3 b5 17 ♗b1 ♕a4 18 ♕f3 implementing a dangerous attack for the sacrificed pawn.

11	b4	♘d5

Here Black must avoid a devilish trap 11 ... b6 12 ♘d4 bxc5 13 ♘c6 ♕c7 14 ♕xe6+ fxe6 15 ♗g6+ checkmate. However, Black may have a stronger possibility on move 11, namely 11 ... a5 12 c3 ♗e7 13 ♗c4 0-0 14 ♘h3 axb4 15 cxb4 and only now 15 ... b6, seeking to undermine White's queenside pawns.

12	♗d2	♕f6
13	♖b1	a5
14	a3	g5

15	♗e4	♘c3
16	♗xc3	♕xc3+
17	♕d2	♕xa3
18	♕d4	e5

Surprisingly, up to this point, all is opening theory. The text is an attempt to improve on the game A Rodriguez-Tal, Subotica Izt. 1987, where 18 ... ♖g8 led to a lost position for Black, though the ingenious Tal later escaped with a draw. The move chosen here offers a queen sacrifice in order to create a menacing passed a-pawn.

19	♘xe5	♗g7
20	♖a1	axb4
21	♖xa3	bxa3
22	♘gf3	0-0

This is an inaccuracy which permits White to consolidate his position. Black must fight to maintain the initiative at all costs by means of 22 ... a2 23 ♔e2 0-0 threatening to intensify the pressure against White's pinned knight with ... ♖e8.

23	♗d5	g4
24	♗xf7+	♖xf7
25	♕d5	♘xe5
26	♘xe5	♗xe5
27	♕xe5	♖a6
28	0-0	a2

This advance comes too late. Although in the further course of the game Black generates some tactical threats, White can now blockade the passed pawn and prepare to infiltrate the scattered black position with the white queen.

29	♖a1	♗e6
30	♕e2	♖f4
31	♕d2	♖aa4
32	c3	♔f7
33	♕c2	♖fc4
34	f3	gxf3
35	gxf3	♖h4
36	♔g2	♖a8
37	♕h7+	♔f6
38	♕xb7	♖g8+
39	♔h1	♖h5
40	♕e4	♖hg5

Black's final trick. He threatens to sacrifice his rook on g1 in order to promote the a-pawn. White's next move frustrates this.

41	♕d4+	♔f7
42	c4	♖g2
43	♖e1	♖8g6
44	c6	♖c2
45	c7	♗h3
46	♕d5+	♔f6
47	♕d6+	1-0

Verdict ✳ ✳ ✳

Tal - Botvinnik
USSR Team Ch. 1966

1	e4	c6
2	d4	d5
3	exd5	

3 f3 dxe4 4 fxe4 e5 5 ♘f3 exd4 6 ♗c4 ♗b4+ 7 c3 dxc3 8 ♗xf7+ ♔e7 9 ♕b3± is a successful gambit for White, but Black can play solidly with 3 ... e6 or 3 ... g6 when the f3-pawn may block White's development.

3	...	cxd5
4	c4	♘f6
5	♘c3	g6!?

5 ... e6 provides a more solid defence, e.g. 6 ♘f3 ♗b4 7 exd5 ♘xd5 8 ♕c2 ♘c6 9 ♗d3 ♘xc3 10 bxc3 ♘xd4 11 ♘xd4 ♕xd4 12 0-0 ♕xc3 13 ♗b5+ Nunn - Lobron, Biel 1982. This gambit is very risky for White.

5 ... ♘c6 can also lead to gambit play after 6 ♗g5 ♕b6 7 cxd5 ♘xd4 8 ♗e3 e5 9 dxe6 ♗c5 10 exf7+ ♔e7 11 ♗c4.

6	♕b3	♗g7
7	cxd5	0-0
8	♘ge2	♘a6
9	g3	♕b6
10	♕xb6	axb6
11	♗g2	♘b4
12	0-0	♖d8
13	d6!	

Returning the gambit pawn at the right moment.

All this was well known in 1966. Spassky-Petrosian,

World Ch (5) 1966, had continued 13 ... ♖xd6 14 ♗f4 ♖d7 15 ♖fd1 ♘bd5 16 ♗e5 with a clear advantage for White. Botvinnik attempts to improve upon Petrosian's conduct of the defence.

| 13 | ... | exd6 |
| 14 | ♗g5!! | |

A brilliant positional move which, surprisingly, decides the game. The exchange of White's queen's bishop for Black's king's knight leaves Black helplessly exposed on the light squares in the centre.

14	...	♖e8
15	a3	♘c6
16	♖fe1	♗g4
17	♗xf6	♗xf6
18	♘d5	♗d8
19	♘ec3	♖xe1+
20	♖xe1	♖a5

Also inadequate is 20 ... ♘xd4 21 ♖e8+ ♔g7 22 ♘xb6 ♖b8 23 ♘c4.

(*see following diagram*)

| 21 | ♘e3 | |

Tal was criticised for this move, but it leaves

Black in a deadly vice. It is notoriously difficult to judge positions with two minor pieces for a rook, and the alternative of 21 ♖e8+ ♔g7 22 ♘e3 ♗d7 23 ♗xc6 ♗xe8 24 ♗xe8 ♗f6 is not necessarily any more decisive than the line chosen by Tal.

21	...	♗d7
22	♘c4	♖a8
23	d5	♘d4
24	♘xd6	♖b8

White's position here is overwhelming, but Botvinnik fights on until just after the adjournment.

25	♘c4	f6
26	♘e4	♔f8
27	h3	♘b3
28	♗f1	b5
29	♘cd6	f5
30	♖e3	fxe4
31	♖xb3	♔e7
32	♘xe4	♖c8
33	g4	♖c1
34	♔g2	♖e1
35	f3	♖d1
36	d6+	♔f7
37	♗xb5	♗e6

38	♖c3	♖d4
39	♖d3	♖xd3
40	♘xd3	♗d5
41	♘c5	b6
42	♗e4	♗e6
43	♘d3	♗b3
44	f4	♔e6
45	f5+	1-0

Verdict ✳✳

Catalan

1 d4 ♘f6 2 c4 e6 3 g3 d5
4 ♗g2 dxc4 5 ♘f3

Even in the strategically-inclined fianchetto openings there is plenty of scope for gambit play, normally of White's pawn on c4. White's strategic goal is to somehow activate the king's bishop.

Tal - A Sokolov
Brussels 1988

1	d4	♘f6

2	c4	e6
3	g3	

The distinctive move of the Catalan formation, so named after its introduction by the Polish grandmaster Savielly Tartakower at the 1929 Barcelona Tournament.

3	...	d5
4	♗g2	dxc4

The traditional method of gaining equality in this opening. Black hopes to clear the centre entirely by exchanging the pawns on the c- and d- files.

5	♘f3	c5
6	0-0	♘c6
7	♘e5	

A vigorous continuation which poses Black a number of serious problems. Thus, for example, 7 ... ♘xd4 would fail to 8 e3 ♘f5 9 ♕xd8+ ♔xd8 10 ♘xf7+ winning.

7	...	♗d7
8	♘a3	

Tal could have regained his sacrificed pawn in several ways. He prefers, however, to turn the opening into a gambit.

8	...	cxd4
9	♘axc4	♗c5
10	♕b3	0-0
11	♗f4	

White gains nothing by 11 ♕xb7 ♘xe5 12 ♘xe5 ♖b8. Now, however, after White's 11th move, 12 ♕xb7 is a serious threat which Black hastens to parry.

11	...	♕c8
12	♖fd1	♖d8
13	♖ac1	♘d5
14	♘xf7	

An alarming sacrifice, quite typical of Tal at his adventurous best. It is difficult to prove that this move wins but White creates an attack so dangerous and confusing for the defence that the task of holding on becomes almost impossible.

14	...	♔xf7
15	♘e5+	

It is very tempting to play 15 ♗d6 but Black has an adequate riposte in 15 ... ♗b6.

15	...	♘xe5
16	♗xe5	b6
17	♕f3+	♔g8
18	♕g4	g6
19	♗e4	

The threat of ♗xg6 now forces Black to remove one of the guards of his pawn on e6. It was later esta-

blished that 19 ... ♗c6 would now be the correct defence.

19	...	♗e8
20	b4	

With this pawn thrust, Tal's attack reaches its climax. Sokolov now has no choice but to give back all of the material that he has won, and more.

20	...	♘xb4
21	♗xa8	♕xa8
22	♕xe6+	♗f7
23	♕f6	♗f8
24	♕h8+	♔e7
25	♗f6+	♔d7
26	♗xd8	

The final point of Tal's brilliant combination which commenced on the 14th move. If Black now recaptures the bishop with 26 ... ♕xd8 there would follow 27 ♖xd4+ ♗xd4 28 ♕xd4+ ♘d5 29 e4 with decisive gain of material. An alternative is 26 ... ♕xd8 27 ♖xd4+ ♘d5 28 ♕xd8+ ♔xd8 29 ♖xd5+ ♗xd5 30 ♖d1 and White wins. Black's choice in the game leaves him with only bishop and knight against White's two rooks. Although some technical problems remain in the conversion of his advantage, Tal solves these with consummate ease.

26	...	♘c6
27	♗f6	♕xh8
28	♗xh8	♗xa2
29	e3	a5
30	♗xd4	♘xd4
31	exd4	♗d6
32	d5	a4
33	♖c6	♗c5
34	♖c1	♗d4
35	♖6c4	

A fine move whch breaks Black's resistance. Sokolov undertakes one last desperate throw with his passed pawn.

35	...	♗xc4
36	♖xc4	b5
37	♖xd4	a3
38	♖d1	b4
39	♖a1	♔d6
40	♔f1	♔xd5
41	♔e2	1-0

After 41 ... ♔c4 42 ♔d2 ♔b3 43 ♖b1+ ♔a4 44 ♔c2 a2 45 ♖e1 ♔a3 46 ♖e3+ ♔a4 47 ♔b2 Black is hopelessly lost.

Verdict ✳✳✳✳✳

Sosonko - Hübner
Tilburg 1979

1	d4	♘f6
2	c4	e6
3	g3	d5
4	♗g2	dxc4
5	♘f3	a6
6	0-0	b5

It is relatively unusual for the sedate Catalan Opening to metamorphose into a gambit, most commonly White quickly recaptures the c-pawn with ♕c2 (or ♕a4) xc4 but here Black plays in uncompromising fashion.

7	♘e5	♘d5
8	♘c3	c6

This is too passive. Black should defend with 8 ... ♗b7 9 ♘xd5 exd5 10 e4 dxe4 11 ♕h5 g6 12 ♘xg6 fxg6 13 ♕e5+ ♕e7 14 ♕xh8 ♘d7 with serious compensation for the lost material, as in the game Sosonko - Korchnoi, Bad Kissingen 1981.

9	♘xd5	exd5
10	e4	♗e6
11	a4	b4
12	exd5	♗xd5
13	♕g4	h5

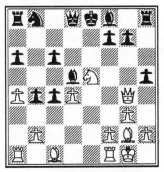

14	♗xd5!!	cxd5

Hubner had clearly overlooked White's delightful queen sacrifice. If instead 14 ... hxg4 15 ♗xf7+ ♔e7 16 ♗g5+ when Black's position is a wreck.

15	♕f5	♖a7
16	♖e1	♖e7
17	♗g5	g6
18	♗xe7	1-0

Verdict ✳ ✳ ✳ ✳ ✳

**Centre-Counter
(aka Scandinavian)**

1 e4 d5 2 exd5 ♘f6 3 c4 e6

The Centre-Counter is a time-hallowed defence, but this section deals primarily with the exciting and newly developed "Icelandic Gambit".

**A Sokolov - Speelman
Madrid 1988**

| 1 | e4 | d5 |
| 2 | exd5 | ♘f6 |

3 c4

It is remarkable that so many white players, faced by 2 ... ♘f6 in the Centre-Counter, steer immediately for the Panov-Botvinnik Caro-Kann transposition by 3 c4, instead of staying in the main lines of Black's chosen defence. Instead, White can opt to cling to his d5-pawn by means of 3 ♗b5+ though after 3 ... ♗d7 4 ♗c4 ♗g4 5 f3 ♗f5 6 ♘c3 ♘bd7 7 ♕e2 ♘b6 8 ♗b3 ♕d7 9 d6 ♕xd6 10 ♘b5 ♕d7 11 ♕e5 0-0-0 12 ♘xa7+ ♔b8 13 ♘b5 ♘fd5 14 a4, Black can establish excellent counter-chances with 14 ... e6 15 ♘e2 f6 16 ♕d4 e5 17 ♕f2 ♘b4 18 d3 ♗xd3, gaining just the kind of hyper-active play to which Black aspires in the Centre-Counter. Black should, however, avoid the continuation of Shagalovich - Roizman, USSR 1961: 14 ... f6 15 ♕e2 ♘f4 16 ♕f2 e5 17 ♘e2, when White is successfully consolidating.

As it is, White can probably keep an edge, if not his extra pawn, by playing the seemingly more modest 3 d4 ♘xd5 4 ♘f3 ♗g4 5 ♗e2 (if 5 c4 ♘b6 6 c5 ♘6d7! followed by ... e6 and ... ♗e7 and ... 0-0 with fighting chances for Black against White's extended centre) 5

... ♘c6 6 c4 ♘b6 7 0-0 e6 8 ♘c3! ♗xf3 9 ♗xf3 ♘xc4 10 d5! exd5 11 ♖e1+ ♗e7 12 ♘xd5 ♘d6 13 ♗f4 Whitehead - Peters, USA 1978. Black's position is precarious, e.g. 13 ... 0-0 14 ♖c1 or even 14 ♘xe7+ ♘xe7 15 ♗xb7 ♖b8 16 ♗f3.

3 c4 e6!?

The normal continuation here is 3 ... c6 4 d4 cxd5 5 ♘c3, transposing to the Panov-Botvinnik variation of the Caro-Kann. The text constitutes a highly unusual gambit idea, recently introduced by young Icelandic masters. It evidently came as a complete surprise to Sokolov.

4 dxe6 ♗xe6

Black has a free development for his pawn, but the white position has no apparent weaknesses and it seems that he has few problems. Nevertheless, Black whips up considerable counterplay over the coming moves.

5 d4 ♗b4+
6 ♗d2 ♕e7

A trap for White to avoid now is 7 ♕a4+, when 7 ... ♗d7+ wins White's queen. The line adopted by the Russian grandmaster, although an improvement on the accident just cited, permits the black queen to assume a dominating post.

Speelman intends to complete his mobilisation by castling on the queen's wing, thus maximising the pressure on the hostile pawn centre. It should also be mentioned that 7 ♕e2 ♘c6 8 d5 ♘d4! is excellent for Black, while 8 ♘f3 ♗xd2+ 9 ♘bxd2 ♘b4 10 ♘b3 ♗f5 11 ♕xe7+ ♔xe7 12 ♖c1 ♘xa2 is also fine.

7 ♗xb4 ♕xb4+

In the game Marinas Kuijf - Hodgson, Wijk aan Zee 1989, White now tried to trade queens to reduce Black's pressure, viz. 8 ♕d2 but after 8 ... ♘c6 it became apparent that 9 ♕xb4 ♘xb4 10 ♘a3 0-0-0 11 d5 ♗g4 would give Black plenty of compensation for the pawn. Instead the game continued 9 ♘c3 0-0-0 10 d5 ♗g4 11 f3 ♖he8+ 12 ♗e2 ♗f5 13 0-0-0 ♘a5 14 g4 ♗g6 15 ♘h3 ♘d7 (threatening ... ♘c5 and ... ♘b3+) 16 ♘b1 ♕b3!!. Now Hodgson has a very serious attack for his pawn. Ob-

viously 17 axb3 fails directly to 17 ... ♘xb3 mate. The
game went on 17 ♗d3 ♕xa2
18 ♕b4 ♖e2!! 19 ♗xe2 ♘b3+
20 ♕xb3 ♕xb3 21 ♖d2 ♕e3
and White resigned, for if
22 ♖hd1 ♘c5 is murderous.

8 ♘d2 ♘c6

The key question here is,
what happens if White
seeks to win a piece by forking Black's bishop and
knight by d5? This question
recurs after move ten. If
White goes for this option
he must run the gauntlet
of Black's amazingly efficient mobilisation, while
his own king is still lan-
guishing in the centre.

For example, if now 9 d5
0-0-0 10 dxc6 ♘e4 11 cxb7+
♔b8 12 ♘gf3 ♘xd2 13 ♘xd2
♖he8 14 ♗e2 ♗xc4 with a
terrible attack. Alterna-
tively 10 dxe6 (this has the
advantage of closing the e-
file) 10 ... ♘e4 11 ♘gf3 ♘e5
12 a3 ♕xb2 or 12 ♗e2 ♘xf3+
13 ♗xf3 ♖xd2.

9 ♘gf3 0-0-0
10 d5 ♗g4

After 11 dxc6, snapping
up the Black piece sacrifice
11 ... ♖he8+ pins down the
white king in the centre,
while 11 ... ♘e4 would transpose into one of the variations I gave after the
possibility of 9 d5. Nevertheless, Sokolov's choice
also leaves his king stuck

in the middle of the board.

11 ♗e2 ♗xf3
12 ♗xf3 ♖he8+

White is forced to re-
nounce castling, for 13
♗e2 fails outright to 13 ...
♘d4. White's position is
now dreadfully bad and his
sole ray of hope is the
extra pawn. He must, the-
refore, try to conserve it at
all costs. This rationale
explains some of Sokolov's
rather contorted subse-
quent moves.

13 ♔f1 ♘d4
14 ♕c1 ♘xf3
15 ♘xf3 ♖e4
16 b3 ♖de8

One threat now is ...
♘g4, which White hastens
to prevent with his next
move. If instead 17 g3 ♖e2
18 ♔g1 ♕c5 19 ♕f1 ♘g4 and
the f2-pawn falls, with disastrous consequences.

17 h3 ♘h5

17 ... ♖e2 18 ♔g1 ♕c5 19
♕f1 is here less pathetic for
White, since Black cannot
continue with either ... ♘g4
or ... ♘e4.

18 g3 ♘xg3+

A very fine piece sacri-
fice. Quieter continuations
would permit Sokolov to
consolidate, but the sacrifice strips away the pawn
protection around the
white king and ensures that
Black retains a permanent
initiative.

19 fxg3   ♖e3

If now 20 ♔g2 ♖e2+ 21 ♔f1 ♕c5 or 20 ♕d1 ♕c3 21 ♔f2 ♖d3.

20 ♘g1   ♕d6
21 ♖h2   ♖xg3
22 ♕b2   ♕g6

If 23 ♖g2 ♕d3+ 24 ♖e2 ♖xg1+ or 24 ♘e2 ♖xg2 or 24 ♔f2 ♖ge3 and ... ♕f5+. 23 ♕f2 ♕d3+ wins White's queen.

23 ♔f2   ♖ee3

Seizing White's king in a vice-like grip.

24 ♘e2   ♖gf3+

Not that it really matters, but 24 ... ♕f5+ 25 ♔e1 ♖g1+ 26 ♔d2 ♕d3+ is a faster win.

25 ♔e1   ♕g1+
26 ♔d2   ♕xh2
27 ♖e1   ♕f2
0-1

A rook check on d3 will inevitably win White's remaining rook, when mate can only be deferred for a few more painful moves.

Verdict ✳✳✳

Charlick-Englund

1 d4 e5

This flies in the face of all opening principles. 2 dxe5 ♘c6 3 ♘f3 ♕e7 4 ♘c3 ♘xe5 5 ♘d5 ♘xf3+ 6 gxf3 ♕d8 7 ♕d4! d6 8 ♗g5 is one way to defeat it.

Verdict ✳

Chatard-Alekhine Attack

1 e4 e6 2 d4 d5 3 ♘c3 ♘f6 4 ♗g5 ♗e7 5 e5 ♘fd7 6 h4

This variation had already been played in the 1890s by one of England's top female players, Mrs. Fagan!

After 6 ... ♗xg5 7 hxg5 ♕xg5 8 ♘h3 ♕e7 9 ♘f4 ♘c6 10 ♕g4 ♘xd4 11 0-0-0 ♘f5

12 ♘fxd5 White has good compensation. Black probably does best to decline the gambit with 6 ... a6 or 6 ... 0-0.

Verdict ✳✳✳✳

Cochrane
(Petroff)

---

1 e4 e5 2 ♘f3 ♘f6 3 ♘xe5 d6
4 ♘xf7

Free spirits may feel that this is worth a try against the solid Petroff. For star-

ters, there is the trap: 4 ... ♔xf7 5 d4 ♘xe4 6 ♕h5+ winning, while best play: 5 ... g6 6 ♘c3 ♕e8 7 ♗c4+ ♗e6 8 d5 ♗c8 9 0-0 ♗g7 10 ♖e1 ♖f8 11 e5 dxe5 12 d6+ ♗e6 13 ♖xe5 ♗xc4 14 ♖xe8 ♖xe8 15 dxc7 ♘c6 16 ♗f4 Vitolins - Anikaev, USSR 1982 is by no means clear. White always has chances!

Verdict ✳✳✳

Cordel
(Ruy Lopez)

---

1 e4 e5 2 ♘f3 ♘c6 3 ♗b5
♗c5 4 c3 f5

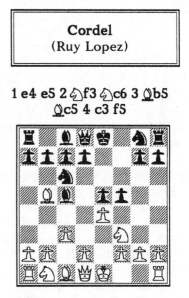

This is one ... f5 based gambit White can safely accept, e.g. 5 exf5 e4 6 d4 exf3 7 dxc5 ♕e7+ 8 ♗e3 fxg2 9 ♖g1 ♘f6 10 ♖xg2 0-0 11 ♘d2 d5 12 cxd6 cxd6 13 ♕c2± Unzicker - Campora, Berne 1987. Alternatively, 5 d4 fxe4 6 ♗xc6 dxc6 7 ♘xe5

♘d6 8 ♕h5+ g6 9 ♕e2 ♗f5 10 ♗f4 ♘f6 11 ♘d2 0-0 12 0-0 ♕e7 13 f3 exf3 14 ♘dxf3± Mestel – Plaskett, Brighton 1984.

Sharp gambit play also follows on 4 ... ♘f6, the main alternative to the Cordel, as the illustrative game shows.

Beliavsky – Ivanchuk
Linares 1989

1	e4	e5
2	♘f3	♘c6
3	♗b5	♗c5
4	c3	♘f6
5	d4	♗b6

The correct move now may be 6 ♕e2 e.g. 6 ... exd4 7 e5 0-0 8 cxd4! ♖e8 (White was not threatening exf6, prior to this, on account of ... ♖e8) 9 ♗e3 ♘d5 10 ♘c3 ♘xe3 11 fxe3 d5 12 0-0 ♗g4 13 ♕f2 with advantage to White. Ivanchuk may well have had an improvement in mind in this line, but what follows looks less good for White.

6	♘xe5	♘xe5
7	dxe5	♘xe4
8	♕g4	♗xf2+

Black may already have a satisfactory position. In the game Ree – Zuidema, Holland 1962, for example, the continuation was now 9 ♔d1 ♕h4 10 ♕xg7 ♖f8 11 b4 ♕h5+ 12 ♔c2 ♗h4 13 ♗h6

♕e7 14 ♖f1 b6 15 e6 ♘d6 16 exd7+ ♗xd7 17 ♖e1 0-0-0 18 ♗a6+ ♔b8 19 ♖xe7 ♗a4+.

9	♔e2	♕h4
10	♕xg7	♖f8

If now 11 b4 f6! or 11 ♗h6 ♗c5 12 ♖f1 c6 13 ♖f4 ♕h5+ 14 ♔e1 cxb5 15 ♖xe4 b6 which was much better for Black in the game Florian – Forintos, Budapest 1961.

11	♘d2	♗c5

Later in the tournament Short – Gulko followed the game up to this point, where Gulko deviated by capturing the knight with 11 ... ♘xd2. This suggests that Beliavsky's errors came later in the game.

12	♘f3	♕f2+
13	♔d1	♗e7!

A brilliant retreat whch also permits the Black queen to mobilise backwards.

14	♖e1	♕b6
15	♖xe4	♕xb5
16	c4	♕c6
17	♕xh7	d5

With two bishops in a

wide open position and with White's king seriously exposed in the centre of the battlefield, Black's advantage is clear.

18	exd6	♕xd6+
19	♖d4	♕b6
20	♕e4	♖g8
21	♗e3	♕xb2
22	♖b1	♕xg2
23	♖b5	♗g4

White's next move is pure desperation.

24	♖f5	♕f1+
25	♔c2	♕e2+
	0-1	

Verdict ✳ ✳ ✳

Corkscrew
(Latvian Gambit)

1 e4 e5 2 ♘f3 f5 3 ♘xe5 ♘f6 4 ♗c4 fxe4 5 ♘f7 ♕e7 6 ♘xh8 d5

An utterly weird variant of the Greco-Latvian. Black is temporarily a rook in arrears, but will capture the errant white knight on h8. In compensation, Black has a big pawn centre. My head says dubious, but my heart says it could be tried, once ... so ...

Verdict ✳ ✳ ✳ (if you are feeling very brave).

Cunningham
(King's Gambit)

1 e4 e5 2 f4 exf4 3 ♘f3 ♗e7

Possible is 4 ♘c3 ♗h4+ 5 ♔e2 d5 6 ♘xd5 ♘f6 7 ♘xf6+ ♕xf6 8 d4 when White's king is exposed, but his centre pawns are powerful. Perhaps dangerous for White is 5 ... c6 6 d4 d5 7 e5 ♗g4 8 ♗xf4 f6! So ...

Verdict ✳ ✳ ✳ on 4 ♘c3 though Black must be prepared to meet 4 ♗c4 as well – see Bertin.

D

Dada

1 g3 e5 2 ♗g2 d5 3 b4

After 3 ... ♗xb4 4 c4 ♗e6 5 ♗b2?? ♘c6 6 f4 ♘ge7 7 ♘f3 d4∓, Larsen–Olafsson, Beverwijk 1959. Best is 5 ♕b3 ♘c6 6 a3! and White regains the pawn. "It is probably my only qualification as a dada artist" – Larsen.

Verdict ✳✳✳

Danish

1 e4 e5 2 d4 exd4 3 c3 dxc3

4 ♗c4

This is completely out of fashion. A reliable line for Black is 4 ... cxb2 5 ♗xb2 d5! 6 ♗xd5 ♘f6 7 ♗xf7+ ♔xf7 8 ♕xd8 ♗b4+ 9 ♕d2, which leads to an endgame which is completely equal.

Verdict ✳✳✳

Dilworth
(Open Ruy Lopez)

1 e4 e5 2 ♘f3 ♘c6 3 ♗b5 a6 4 ♗a4 ♘f6 5 0-0 ♘xe4 6 d4 b5 7 ♗b3 d5 8 dxe5 ♗e6 9 c3 ♗c5 10 ♘bd2 0-0 11 ♗c2 ♘xf2

Ljubojevic – Yusupov
Tilburg 1987

1	e4	e5
2	♘f3	♘c6
3	♗b5	a6
4	♗a4	♘f6
5	0-0	♘xe4

An active defence, a great favourite with Tarrasch and Korchnoi.

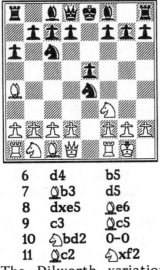

6	d4	b5
7	♗b3	d5
8	dxe5	♗e6
9	c3	♗c5
10	♘bd2	0-0
11	♗c2	♘xf2

The Dilworth variation. Theory frowns upon it, but in practice Black has fared well with it.

12	♖xf2	f6
13	exf6	♗xf2+
14	♔xf2	♕xf6
15	♔g1	♖ae8
16	♕f1	♗f5

Improving on 16 ...♔h8 17 h3 ♗f7 18 ♘b3 ♗h5 as played in the game Kozlov – Estrin, USSR 1973.

17	♗xf5	

White should consider 17 ♘b3.

17	...	♕xf5
18	b3	d4!
19	cxd4	♘xd4
20	♘xd4	♕c5

If now 21 ♕d3 ♖e1+ or 21 ♘2f3 ♖xf3!.

21	♗b2	♖xf1+
22	♖xf1	♖e2
23	♖f2	♖xf2
24	♔xf2	♕d6
25	♔e3?	♕e5+
	0-1	

26 ... c5 will win easily; White had to try 25 ♘d2-f3.

Verdict ✳✳✳

Dutch Defence

The main gambits in the Dutch are the Korchnoi (1 d4 f5 2 h3), the Krejcik (1 d4 f5 2 g4) and the Staunton (1 d4 f5 2 e4). These can be found elsewhere in the book.

E

1 e4 e5 2 ♘f3 d5

An old variation which some players have tried, but in vain, to rehabilitate.

Boleslavsky – Lilienthal
Moscow 1941

1	e4	e5
2	♘f3	d5
3	♘xe5	

According to theory, the strongest continuation is 3 exd5. It is apparent that Boleslavsky wants to avoid any possible surprises.

| 3 | ... | ♕e7 |

Modern Chess Openings gives 3 ... dxe4! as leading to an approximately equal game. 3 ... ♗d6, as recommended by Blumenfeld, is also more promising than the text move, e.g. 4 d4 dxe4 5 ♗c4 ♗xe5 6 ♕h5±.

| 4 | d4 | f6 |
| 5 | ♘d3! | |

Much stronger than the older continuation, 5 ♘f3 dxe4 6 ♘fd2, which leads to unclear variations.

| 5 | ... | dxe4 |

After 5 ... ♕xe4+ 6 ♗e3.
Now White easily gets a good square for the knight.

| 6 | ♘f4 | ♕f7? |

Clear loss of time. Correct was 6 ... f5, followed by ... ♘f6.

| 7 | ♘d2! | ♗f5 |

After 7 ... f5 8 ♗c4, too. White would have had a positional advantage which would doubtless be decisive.

8	g4	♗g6
9	♗c4	♕d7
10	♕e2	♕xd4

Despite White's advantage in development Black accepts the pawn sacrifice, and so hastens the catastrophe.

11	♘e6	♛b6
12	♘xe4	♘d7
13	♗f4	♘e5
14	0-0-0	♗f7
15	♘4g5!	

An elegant combination, which finishes the game off quickly.

15	...	fxg5
16	♗xe5	♗xe6
17	♗xc7!	1-0

After the reply 17 ... ♛xc7, White mates by 18 ♛xe6+ etc. A clear setback for the gambiteer, who allowed his opponent to sacrifice material for the initiative.

Cochrane – Staunton
London 1843

1	e4	e5
2	♘f3	d5
3	♘xe5	♛e7
4	d4	f6
5	♘c3	fxe5

6	♘xd5	♛f7
7	♗c4	♗e6
8	0-0	c6
9	f4	

9	...	cxd5
10	fxe5	♛d7
11	exd5	♗xd5
12	e6!	♛c6
13	♛h5+	g6
14	♛xd5	♘e7
15	♛e5	♛xc4
16	♛xh8	♘f5
17	♗h6	♛b4
18	♛xf8+	♛xf8
19	♗xf8	♔xf8
20	g4	1-0

Verdict ✶✶

English Defence

---

1 d4 e6 2 c4 b6 3 e4 ♗b7

This defence has had a huge amount of attention devoted to it in recent games. It is a double-edged system and has spawned several gambits for both

White and Black.

**Rodriguez - Keene
Alicante 1977**

1	d4	e6
2	c4	b6
3	♘c3	♗b7
4	e4	♗b4
5	♗d3	f5
6	♕h5+	

White avails himself of the opportunity to give this check, but on the evidence so far it is not clear that it helps him.

6	...	g6
7	♕e2	♘f6
8	♗g5	

8 f3 is a gambit offer which Black unwisely accepted in Botvinnik-Wallis, Simultaneous Game, Leicester 1967. After 8 ... fxe4 9 fxe4 ♗xc3+ 10 bxc3 ♘xe4 11 ♘f3! he was in difficulties. Play continued: 11 ... ♘f6 12 ♗g5 ♕e7 13 0-0 d6 14 ♘e5! 0-0 15 ♘g4 ♘bd7 16 ♖f2 and White was winning.

This gambit is remini-

scent of the line in Larsen's Opening (considered later): 1 b3 e5 2 ♗b2 ♘c6 3 e3 d5 4 ♗b5 ♗d6 5 f4 ♕h4+ 6 g3 ♕e7 7 ♘f3 f6 6 fxe5 fxe5 9 ♗xc6+ bxc6 10 ♘xe5 ♘f6!, where Black has tremendous play for the gambit pawn.

8 f3 ♘c6!?, however, is worth consideration and has scored 100% so far. In Adorjan - Spassky, Toluca Interzonal 1982, White played 9 e5?? and was rudely surprised by 9 ... ♘xd4 10 ♕f2 ♘h5. White has no compensation whatsoever for the pawn and he now threw in his queen as well: 11 ♕xd4? ♗c5 and duly lost (0-1, 23).

| 8 | ... | fxe4 |
| 9 | ♗c2 | |

A dubious gambit,

9	...	♕e7
10	0-0-0	♗xc3
11	bxc3	♘c6
12	f3	♕a3+!?

Vigorous but risky. The sober counter-sacrifice 12 ... e3! would have taken all the fire out of White's game. This is a typical anti-gambit theme where White plays f3.

13	♔b1	0-0
14	♗c1!	

The only way to gain counter-chances is to sacrifice a second pawn.

14	...	♛xc3
15	♗b2	♛a5

Threatening ... ♘b4.

16	a3	e5
17	d5	♘d4
18	♖xd4	

Again the only chance. White has to sacrifice the exchange to stay in the game.

18	...	exd4
19	fxe4	b5?!

After the game this was criticised (rightly) as over-sharp. The sensible procedure would have been 19 ... c5!.

20	♘f3	♗a6
21	c5	b4
22	♛d2	♖ab8

Black's violent effort to blast open the queenside

files against White's king could have led to some confusion if Rodriguez had now found the subtle 23 ♖c1!. Pressed for time he made the obvious capture and his game soon collapsed.

23	♘xd4	♛xc5
24	♘b3	♛c4
25	a4	♘xe4
26	♗xe4	♛xe4+
27	♔a1	♛d3
28	♛h6	♖f7
29	♘c1	♛e4
30	♖d1	♖e8
31	♖d4	♛e3
32	♛h4	♖f1
	0-1	

Verdict ✳ ✳

Brondum - Plaskett
Copenhagen 1981

1	d4	e6
2	c4	b6
3	e4	♗b7
4	♗d3	f5
5	exf5	♗b4+
6	♔f1	♘f6

The gambit moment. It is fascinating, even in the queenside openings, how often the move ... f5 crops up as the key gambit move.

7	♗g5	0-0
8	a3	♗d6
9	♘c3	exf5
10	d5	h6
11	♗d2	♘a6
12	b4	c6

13	dxc6	dxc6
14	♕b1	♗xb4!

Black, having had his pawn spurned, invests a piece.

15	axb4	♘xb4
16	♕xb4	

16 ♗xf5 ♕xd2 17 ♕xb4 ♘e4! wins.

16	...	♕xd3+
17	♘ce2	♘e4
18	♗e1	c5
19	♕b1	

Upon 19 ♕a4 ♘d6 gives Black real compensation. White seeks to ease his development problems with an exchange of queens but Black gets three healthy passed pawns and an initiative for his piece.

19	...	♕xc4
20	♕a2	♕xa2
21	♖xa2	a5
22	f3	a4!
23	♘f4	♘d6
24	♔f2	b5
25	♘ge2	b4
26	♖a1	♖fc8
27	♖d1	♘b5
28	♖d7	♗c6

29	♖e7	♖e8
30	♖xe8+	♗xe8
31	♘d3	a3
32	♘xc5	a2
33	♗xb4	a1♕
34	♖xa1	♖xa1
35	g4	♖a2
36	♔e3	♘d6
37	h4	♘c4+
38	♔d4	♖xe2
39	♔xc4	♖f2
	0-1	

An entertaining game but there are many questions to be asked. For instance, does Black have enough compensation after 6 ... ♘f6 7 c5 bxc5 8 a3 c4 9 ♗xc4 and 10 fxe6 ? I rather doubt it.

Verdict ✱✱

Ree – Miles
Wijk aan Zee 1979

1	c4	b6
2	d4	e6
3	e4	♗b7
4	f3	f5
5	exf5	♘h6!?

Also possible is the solid 5 ... exf5, but Miles's gambit choice is the most ambitious.

6   fxe6

As ever, 6 ♗xh6?! ♕h4+! 7 g3 ♕xh6 gives Black a lot for his gambit – the bishop pair, activity and development.

6   ...   ♘f5!

Asking White to accelerate Black's development even further in the name of materialism and setting up immediate kingside threats with ... ♕h4+. White must tread very carefully to avoid being swept away in the face of this early aggression.

7   ♘e2

To protect d4 and defuse ... ♕h4+.

7   ...   ♗d6!

Black's bishop takes up this threatening post in one move and this suggests that Ree must be under even more pressure here. His solution is drastic.

8   h4!?

Trying to lure Black's knight from its influential post.

8   ...   0-0

8 ... ♘xh4 is certainly playable but it allows White to shore up his defences with ♗e3-f2. 8 ... ♘g3 (or 8 ... ♗g3+ 9 ♘xg3 ♘xg3 10 ♖h3) 9 ♖h3 is not convincing, so Miles pursues the attack with all speed.

9   ♘bc3

More solid than 9 ♗g5 ♕e8 when Black is still coming and the bishop is not securely developed.

9   ...   ♕f6?!

Too much of a good thing. Miles hopes to force the line opening exd7 but Ree has a nasty trick up his sleeve. 9 ... dxe6 or 9 ... ♕e7!? are possible improvements.

10 c5!   ♗e7

A difficult decision but 10 ... ♗g3+ 11 ♘xg3 ♘xg3 12 ♖h3 ♕xe6+ 13 ♔f2 leaves White relatively unscathed. 10 ... bxc5? 11 e7! clears the way for the knockout 12 ♕b3+. Miles elects to play for an exchange of queens, relying on White's insecure king to provide counterchances.

11 exd7   ♕f7!?

11 ... ♘xd7 was also possible, but Miles's threat of ... ♗xh4+ makes Ree's next a sensible measure in view of his backward development.

12 ♕b3   ♕xb3

12 ... ♘xd7! gives Black good chances of recouping his sacrifices - c5 and h4 would be under attack with White still needing to unravel. The text allows Ree

to fortify his queenside pawn wedge and develops the rook on a1.

13 axb3   ♘xd7

Not 13 ... ♗xh4+?? 14 ♖xh4! ♘xh4 15 ♗g5.

14 b4   ♗xh4+
15 ♔d1

At first glance Black appears to have good compensation - the weak d-pawn keeping White congested and tied down - but on closer inspection it becomes clear that all Ree needs to do is develop his king's bishop and the tables turn completely. Thus the logical 15 ... ♗f6 meets with 16 ♘f4! and the d-pawn cannot be captured because of the horrific threat of ♗c4+.

Trying to tie down the knight of e2 with 15 ... ♖fe8 leaves Black awkwardly placed after 16 ♘b5, so Miles is reduced to:

15 ...   ♖fd8
16 ♔c2?

16 ♖xh4! ♘xh4 17 ♗g5

♘f5 18 ♗xd8 ♘e3+ 19 ♔d2 ♘xf1+ 20 ♖xf1 ♖xd8 21 ♔c2 leaves White safe a pawn up.

16 ...   ♗f6
17 ♘b5   ♘f8!

Prevents knights from intruding into e6 or g6 and bringing d4 under fire.

18 ♘xc7?!

Opening a Pandora's box of complications. More sensible was 18 ♖xa7.

18 ...   ♖ac8
19 ♘b5   a6
20 ♘a7   ♖a8!

20 ... ♖c7 21 ♗f4!.

21 c6

21 cxb6? leaves White's knight stranded after 21 ♘d7!.

21 ...   ♖xa7
22 cxb7   ♖xb7
23 ♖xa6

23 g4!? to force Black to capture on d4 immediately looks better as then the dormant bishop on f1 can come out to c4 or a6. The second wave of chaos has ended and Black can now hardly be worse. White's c-pawn is doomed and his extra b-pawn virtually meaningless. Black must only take care that the bishop on f1 does not achieve a dominating post and his ongoing initiative should guarantee him excellent chances.

23 ...   ♘e6!

24	♔b1	h6!
25	g4	

25 d5 ♖xd5 26 ♘c3 ♖d4! keeps White bottled up.

25	...	♘fxd4
26	♘xd4	♖xd4!
27	♖a8+	♔f7
28	♖c8	b5!
29	♖h5	♗g5
30	♖h2	♗xc1
31	♖xc1	♖xb4
32	♗d3	♖d4
33	♗e4	♖e7
34	♗c2?	♔f6
35	♗b3	♖d3
36	♗xe6	♖xe6
37	♖f2	b4!

Suddenly life is very unpleasant for White. The advancing b-pawn threatens to plague White's forces with distracting mate threats and allows Black to bring further pressure to bear on the sensitive f- and g-pawns.

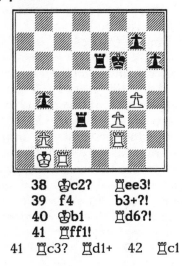

38	♔c2?	♖ee3!
39	f4	b3+?!
40	♔b1	♖d6?!
41	♖ff1!	

41 ♖c3? ♖d1+ 42 ♖c1 ♖xc1+ 43 ♔xc1 ♖g3 and 41 ♖g1? ♖g3! 42 ♖ff1 ♖xg1 43 ♖xg1 ♖d4! 44 ♖f1 ♖d3 both lose for White.

41	...	♖g3
42	♖c3	♖xc3?

42 ... ♖dd3! 43 ♖c6+ ♔e7 (43 ... ♔f7? 44 g5! =) 44 ♖g6 ♔f7 45 f5 ♖g2! or 44 ♖e1+ ♔f7! wins the g-pawn.

43	bxc3	♖d2
44	c4	♖g2
45	g5+!	hxg5
46	fxg5+	♔xg5
47	♖c1	♔f6
48	♖c3	b2
49	♖e3!	g5
50	c5	♖h2
51	c6	g4
52	♖c3	♖h8
53	♔xb2	♔e6
54	♔c2	♖g8
55	c7	♖c8
	½–½	

Verdict ✳✳✳✳

English Opening

All of the gambits which follow, 1 c4 c5 2 ♘f3 ♘f6 3 d4 cxd4 4 ♘xd4 e5 5 ♘b5 d5!?; 1 c4 c5 2 ♘f3 ♘c6 ♘c3 d5 4 cxd5 ♘xd5 5 e4 followed by d4 (similar to the previous gambit, but with colours reversed); and 1 c4 ♘f6 2 ♘c3 e6 3 e4 c5 4 e5 ♘g8 5 ♘f3 ♘c6 6 d4, have been pioneered by World

Champion Gary Kasparov.

I Ivanov – Kumaran
London 1991

1	c4	c5
2	♘f3	♘f6
3	d4	

Strange to say, I suspect that this move is already a mistake and should be replaced with the developing move 3 ♘c3. The reasons for this will soon become apparent.

3	...	cxd4
4	♘xd4	e5

In the strategic sense this central advance appears naive and misguided since Black is left with a backward pawn on the open d-file. However, the concept is bound up with a powerful gambit which has become increasingly popular in recent years.

5	♘b5	d5
6	cxd5	

Black cannot now regain his pawn for 6 ... ♘xd5 fails miserably to the trick 7 ♕xd5 ♕xd5 8 ♘c7+ ultimately emerging a piece ahead. Nevertheless, having sacrificed the d5-pawn Black swiftly obtains a remarkably free development and in attempting to cling on the the extra pawn in the d-file White often finds himself in severe difficulties.

6	...	♗b4+

The mere fact that Black has a choice of two good moves here suggests that his opening has already been a success. In the game Komljenovic – Macaya, Olot 1991, the continuation was 6 ... ♗c5 7 ♘5c3 0-0 8 g3 ♕b6 9 e3 ♗g4 10 f3 ♗xe3 11 fxg4 ♗f2+ 12 ♔d2 ♘c6 13 ♘a3 ♘e4+ 14 ♔c2 ♘d4+ 15 ♔d3 ♘c5+ 16 ♔d2 ♕h6+ 0-1. An illustration of the horrors which lie in wait for any player who sacrifices king safety and development for an extra pawn.

7	♘1c3	0-0
8	♕b3	♘a6
9	♗d2	♗f5
10	g3	♘e4
11	♖d1	♖c8
12	♘xe4	♗xe4
13	♗xb4	

White had doubtless now been expecting Black to play 13 ... ♘xb4 14 ♕xb4 ♗xh1 when 15 f3 traps the bishop and threatens some such maneouvre as ♗h3 followed by ♘c3 and ♔f2 to trap Black's stranded piece. Instead Kumaran strikes from an entirely different direction.

13	...	♗c2
14	♕a3	♘xb4
15	♕xb4	♗xd1
16	♗g2	

The ghastly truth now

dawns on White that 16 ♔xd1 loses outright to 16 ... ♕xd5+.

| 16 | ... | ♕b6 |

Threatening ... a6 winning White's pinned knight.

17	a3	a5
18	♕d2	♕xb5
19	♕xd1	♕xb2
20	0-0	♕xa3

Black's material advantage is now overwhelming.

21	♗h3	♖cd8
22	e4	b5
23	♕h5	♕d6
24	♘f5	g6
25	♕g5	h6
26	♕g4	♔h7
27	♖c1	gxf5
28	♕xf5+	♕g6
29	♕h3	a4
30	♖c6	♖d6
	0-1	

Verdict ✳✳✳✳

Kasparov - Korchnoi
Skelleftea 1989

1	c4	♘f6
2	♘c3	c5
3	♘f3	d5
4	cxd5	♘xd5
5	e4	♘b4
6	♗b5+	♘8c6
7	d4	

The gambit moment!

7	...	cxd4
8	a3	dxc3
9	♕xd8+	♔xd8
10	axb4	cxb2
11	♗xb2	f6

Black has won a pawn, but even in the position without queens, his king remains exposed to attack. 11 ... e6 looks better than 11 ... f6, since Black is never given the chance to play ... e5.

12	e5!	♗g4
13	♗xc6	bxc6
14	♘d4	fxe5
15	♘xc6+	♔c7
16	♘xe5	♗h5
17	0-0	♗e8
18	♖fc1+	♔b7
19	♘c4	e5
20	♗xe5	h5
21	♘a5+	♔b6
22	♗c7+	♔a6
23	♘c6+	1-0

After 23 ... ♔b7 24 ♘d8+ ♔c8 25 ♗a5+ ♔d7 26 ♖c7+ is humiliating.

Verdict ✳✳✳✳✳

Kasparov - A Sokolov
Belfort 1988

| 1 | c4 | ♘f6 |
| 2 | ♘c3 | e6 |

3	e4	c5
4	e5	♞g8
5	♞f3	♞c6
6	d4	cxd4
7	♞xd4	♞xe5

This extremely dangerous gambit line had obviously been prepared by Kasparov to play against Karpov in their Seville world title match in 1987. This partly explains why Kasparov persisted in opening with 1 c4. That Karpov smelled a chessboard rat can be deduced from the fact that he determinedly replied with the move order 1 c4 e6 2 ♞c3 d5 which sidesteps the entire variation.

8	♞db5	a6
9	♞d6+	♝xd6
10	♛xd6	f6
11	♝e3	♞e7

White has gambitted a pawn but in compensation has more space, two bishops and dark-square control.

12	♝b6	♞f5
13	♛c5	d6
14	♛a5	♛e7
15	0-0-0	0-0
16	f4	♞c6
17	♛a3	e5
18	g4	♞fd4
19	♞d5	♛f7

Amazingly, all this is theory. Up to, and including, White's next move everything is charted and given as advantageous for White by the Cuban Grandmaster Amador Rodriguez, annotating a game he played with Black against Hernandez at Havana in 1980. Rodriguez suggests in his notes that 18 ...♞h6! is a superior defence.

20	f5	g6
21	♜g1	gxf5
22	g5	♚h8
23	gxf6	♝e6
24	♛xd6	♝xd5
25	cxd5	♛xf6
26	♛xf6+	♜xf6

Sokolov has defended cleverly in that 27 dxc6 now fails to 27 ... ♜xc6+ regaining the piece. However, Black cannot eradicate the long-term problem of the hemmed-in nature of his king, nor can he contain the fierce activity of Kasparov's bishops.

27	♚b1	♞d8
28	♝c5	♜c8
29	♝e7	♜f7
30	♝d6	♞f3
31	♜g3	e4

32	♗e2	♖f6
33	♗f4	♖g6
34	♗xf3	♖xg3
35	♗xe4	

A very fine intermediate move which leaves Black's attacked rook no constructive escape square.

35	...	fxe4
36	hxg3	♔g7
37	♖d4	♘f7
38	♖xe4	♖d8
39	♖e7	♖xd5
40	♖xb7	h5
41	♖a7	a5
42	a4	1-0

Kasparov seems to revel in gambits where queens are exchanged!

Verdict ✳✳✳✳✳

Englund-Charlick

---

1 d4 e5

See Charlick-Englund.

Evans
(Giuoco Piano)

**1 e5 e5 2 ♘f3 ♘c6 3 ♗c4 ♗c5
4 b4**

The Evans Gambit is one of the oldest Open Gambits and is extremely dangerous for the unwary as the fol-lowing games illustrate.

**Staunton - Cochrane
London 1842**

1	e4	e5
2	♘f3	♘c6
3	♗c4	♗c5
4	b4	

The characteristic move of the Evans Gambit, which was at the time probably the most popular of all openings, at least in English chess circles. For the pawn, White obtains open lines and time for developing an attack.

| 4 | ... | ♗xb4 |
| 5 | c3 | |

The modern way is 5 c3 ♗e7 6 d4 ♘a5 7 ♘xe5 ♘xc4 8 ♘xc4 d5 9 exd5 ♕xd5 10 ♘e3 ♕d7 11 0-0 ♘f6 12 c4 b5!=.

| 5 | ... | ♗a5 |
| 6 | 0-0!? | |

An inaccurate move, but one often played by Tchigorin. Anderssen, Morphy and most 20th Century ex-

ponents of the Evans pre-
ferred 6 d4, which reduces
Black's defensive options.

    6   **...**   **♗b6!**

Black anticipates the
discovery of Lasker's De-
fence by 50 years. Now if
7 d4 d6 8 dxe5 dxe5! and
White can regain his pawn
after 9 ♛xd8+ (Tchigorin -
Pillsbury, London 1899), or
9 ♛b3 ♛f6 10 ♗g5 ♛g6 11
♗d5 ♘ge7 but either way an
ending results where
Black's two bishops can
take advantage or White's
queenside pawn weaknes-
ses.

    7   **♗a3!?**

White should none the
less play 7 d4, since with
care he can maintain the
balance. The move played
commits him prematurely.

    7   **...**   **d6**
    8   **d4**   **exd4!?**

A sound line for Black is
8 ... ♛f6! since White has
denied himself the thematic reply ♗g5. Then 9 ♗b5
♗d7 10 ♘bd2 ♘ge7 leaves
him with no compensation
for his pawn.

    9   **cxd4**   **♘f6?**
    10   **e5!**   **dxe5?**

A further mistake after
which Black is doomed.
Only 10 ... ♘g4 offered
chances, although White
stands well with 11 h3 ♘h6
12 exd6 cxd6 13 ♖e1+ ♘e7 14
♘c3.

    11   **♛b3**   **♛d7**

The only conceivable de-
fence, but it is attractively
refuted.

    12   **dxe5**   **♘a5**

White now ignores this
demonstration and pursues
his attacking theme with
single-minded vigour.

    13   **exf6!**   **♘xb3**
    14   **♖e1+**   **♔d8**
    15   **♗e7+**   **♔e8**
    16   **fxg7**

    16   **...**   **♖g8**
    17   **♗f6+**   **♛e6**
    18   **♗xe6**   **♗xe6**
    19   **axb3**

Staunton's beautiful
queen sacrifice secured the
gain of a piece in every variation.

    1-0

Staunton & Owen - Lowenthal & Barnes Consultation Game, London 1856

    1   **e4**   **e5**
    2   **♘f3**   **♘c6**
    3   **♗c4**   **♗c5**

4	b4	♗xb4
5	c3	♗a5
6	d4	exd4
7	0-0	d6

Black's best move is probably 7 ... ♘ge7 to meet 8 cxd4 with 8 ... d5 and then 8 ♘g5 also with 8 ... d5! 9 exd5 ♘e5. This line was known from a few of Anderssen's games of this period but never became popular, probably because of a general 19th Century fear of the open e-file and because it involves returning the pawn. The "Compromised" Defence 7 ... dxc3 is not as bad as it sounds or as it was thought to be when it was so named, but a century of analysis still tends to find in favour of White after 8 ♕b3 ♕f6 9 e5 ♕g6 10 ♘xc3.

8 ♕b3!

This could well have been played on the previous move, to forestall the defence mentioned in the previous note, and is one of the current critical lines of the Evans Gambit. The objection to 8 ♕b3 has always been that it is decentralising and permits the resource ... ♘a5 to Black in many cases; analysis on the other hand supports the move quite strongly.

The text move was originally proposed by the Irishman, George Waller, in the *Chess Player's Chronicle* in 1848 and was further analysed in the *Deutsche Schachzeitung* and the *Chess Player's Companion* in the following year.

8 ... ♕f6

Black can also try 8 ... ♕d7?! or 8 ... ♕e7 but White will always get good attacking chances.

9 cxd4?

It is now regarded as correct to play 9 e5! dxe5 10 ♖e1!, the last move being introduced by Morphy in a casual game at Birmingham in 1858, and was therefore not known at the time when the present game was played. The variation has since been analysed practically to mate for White.

9	...	♗b6
10	♗b5	♗d7
11	e5	dxe5
12	♖e1	♘ge7
13	dxe5	♕g6
14	♗d3	

In contrast to Thompson, the white players retire their bishop to embarrass the black queen.

14 ... ♕h5?

Here Black could have moved into the lead with the coup 14 ... ♗f5! 15 ♘h4 ♘d4! 16 ♕a4+ (better than 16 ♗xf5 ♘xb3 17 ♘xg6 hxg6) 16 ... ♕c6 17 ♕xc6+ bxc6 18 ♘xf5 ♘exf5 19 ♘c3, but a pawn is a pawn in such positions. Now the game becomes very complicated.

15	♖e4	♘g6
16	♘bd2	♗e6
17	♕a4	♗d5
18	♖g4	h6?

By adding a weakness on g6 to the already precarious situation of their queen, the black partners unwittingly provide the motif for a beautiful combinative onslaught.

19 ♖xg6!! ♗xf3

Not 19 ... fxg6 20 g4 ♕h3 21 ♗f1.

20	♘xf3	fxg6
21	g4	♕h3
22	♗xg6+	♔d8
23	♕f4	

The incarceration of Black's queen makes his defeat certain.

23	...	♘e7
24	♗f7	♔c8
25	♗a3	♘c6
26	♗f8!	

A most attractive blow. With Black's queen already *in angustis*, White goes hunting for Black's cornered rook.

26	...	♘d8
27	♗xg7	♘xf7
28	♗xh8	♘xh8
29	♕f5+	♔d8
30	♕f6+	♔e8
31	♕xh8+	1-0

Anderssen – Dufresne
Berlin 1853

1	e4	e5
2	♘f3	♘c6
3	♗c4	♗c5
4	b4	♗xb4
5	c3	♗a5
6	d4	exd4
7	0-0	d3
8	♕b3	♕f6
9	e5	♕g6
10	♖e1	♘ge7
11	♗a3	b5?!

A characteristically violent bid for counterplay, which has certain affinities with Bryan's Counter-Gambit (qv).

12	♕xb5	♖b8
13	♕a4	♗b6
14	♘bd2	♗b7
15	♘e4	♕f5
16	♗xd3	♕h5

White's positional advantage is vast, for instance 17 ♘g3 ♕h6 18 ♗c1 ♕e6 19 ♗c4, and Black's days are numbered, but in that case this game would not have become memorable.

17 ♘f6+!?

Investing a piece to keep Black's king in the centre, and envisaging a fantastic mating combination to come. In fact this brilliant move makes the winning process more complex, but given the choice between a simple victory and a combinational adventure, Anderssen tended to prefer the latter.

	17	...	gxf6
	18	exf6	♖g8
	19	♖ad1	♕xf3

19 ... ♖g4 has variously been suggested as a saving line, but then Ivkov gives: 20 c4 ♖f4 21 ♗g6!! ♗xf2+ 22 ♔f1! ♕g4 23 ♖xe7+ ♘xe7 24 ♗xf7+ ♔xf7 25 ♘e5+ and wins.

| | 20 | ♖xe7+ | ♘xe7 |

The conclusive error. Necessary was 20 ... ♔d8! 21 ♖xd7+ ♔c8 22 ♖d8+! ♔xd8 (22 ... ♘xd8 23 ♕d7+ ♔xd7 24 ♗f5+ ♔e8 and 25 ♗d7+) 23 ♗f5+ ♕xd1+ 24 ♕xd1+ ♘d4 25 g3! ♗d5 26 cxd4 although White already

enjoys a material advantage and will soon begin to prey on Black's kingside pawns.

| | 21 | ♕xd7+ | |

The coup Black had overlooked. The whole combination is a wondeful testimony to Anderssen's depth of vision.

	21	...	♔xd7
	22	♗f5+	♔e8
	23	♘d7+	♔f8
	24	♗xe7 mate	

Kolisch - Anderssen
Paris 1860

1	e4	e5
2	♘f3	♘c6
3	♗c4	♗c5
4	b4	♗xb4
5	c3	♗a5
6	d4	exd4
7	0-0	dxc3

The so-called "Compromised Defence." To my mind the Evans Gambit forms a sort of nineteenth century parallel with the modern Najdorf variation of the Sicilian: both (in their time) heavily analysed and extremely popular, both leading to ultra-sharp clashes in which the antagonists seek to emphasize the strengths of their own positions (e.g. material vs. development or flexibility plus queenside expansion vs. development). And in both cases Black often

risks a prolonged sojourn
of his king in the centre
while he concentrates on
the exploitation of his own
particular advantages.

8	♕b3	♕f6
9	e5	♕g6
10	♘xc3	b5

Quite in Anderssen's
counter-attacking style,
but 10 ... ♘ge7 is more
trustworthy.

11	♘xb5	♖b8
12	♕e3	♘ge7
13	♕e2	♕h5
14	♗a3	♗b7
15	♖ad1	♘f5

Overlooking the combination which follows.

16 ♖xd7!

16	...	♔xd7
17	e6+	♔c8

Or 17 ... fxe6 18 ♕xe6+
♔d8 19 ♖d1+ ♘cd4 20
♘bxd4.

18	exf7	♗a8

19 ♘xa7+!?

Exuberance is beauty,
so the combination continues. Clearly White could
also have won in more
cold-blooded fashion, as
also on move 22.

19	...	♘xa7
20	♕e6+	♔d8
21	♖d1+	♘d6
22	♖xd6+	

More exuberance, but
the quiet 22 ♗xd6 wins
more quickly.

22	...	cxd6
23	♕xd6+	♔c8
24	♗e6+	♔b7
25	♗d5+	

Inadequate is 25 ... ♔c8 26
f8♕+ ♖xf8 27 ♕xf8+ ♔c7 28
♕e7+. In view of this Anderssen has to sacrifice his
queen in most unfavourable
circumstances. The concluding moves were:

25	...	♕xd5
26	♕xd5+	♔a6
27	♕c4+	♔b7
28	♕e4+	♘c6
29	♘e5	♔a6
30	♕c4+	♔a7
31	♗c5+	♖b6
32	♗xb6+	♗xb6
33	♘xc6+	♗xc6
34	♕xc6	1-0

Verdict ✳ ✳ ✳

Fajarowicz (Budapest)	Falkbeer (King's Gambit)

1 d4 ♘f6 2 c4 e5 3 dxe5 ♘e4

1 e4 e5 2 f4 d5

This version of the Budapest has a poor reputation, but it is almost playable. Black only has to sidestep the disastrous line 4 ♘f3 ♘c6 5 a3 d6 6 ♕c2 ♗f5 (6 ... d5!) 7 ♘c3! ♘xf2 8 ♕xf5 ♘xh1 9 e6±. A simpler plan for White, in any case, is 6 exd6 ♗xd6 7 ♘bd2 ♗f5 8 e3 ♕f6 10 ♗d3±/± Dlugy - Aristizabal, Montpellier 1985.

The original Falkbeer Counter-Gambit was based on 3 ... e4 but nowadays White has a solid way of obtaining an advantage after this move. Attention has therefore switched to 3 ... c6, in which Black aims for swift development.

Deep Thought - Valvo
Played by Computer Mail
1988/89

Verdict ✳✳

1   e4   e5

2	f4	d5
3	exd5	c6

Slightly unusual. 3 ... e4 is more common, e.g. 4 d3 ♘f6 5 dxe4 ♘xe4 6 ♘f3 ♗c5 7 ♕e2 ♗f5 8 ♘c3 ♕e7 9 ♗e3 ♗xe3 10 ♕xe3 ♘xc3 11 ♕xe7+ ♔xe7 12 bxc3± Bronstein - Vaisman, Sandomir 1976.

4	♘c3	exf4
5	♘f3	♗d6
6	d4	♘e7
7	dxc6	♘bxc6
8	d5	♘b4
9	♗c4	0-0
10	a3	b5!
11	♗b3	

Up to here the position is known to theory, but at this point Deep Thought tries an improvement on 11 ♗xb5 on account of 11 ... ♘bxd5 12 ♗xd5 ♘xd5 13 c4 ♖e8+ 14 ♔f1 ♗c5 15 ♕xd5 ♗f5 with a murderous attack.

11	...	♘a6
12	♘xb5	♕a5+
13	♘c3	♘c5
14	♗a2	

An ambitious move which seeks to cling to the extra pawn on d5 while simultaneously threatening b4 to fork Black's queen and knight. Safer would have been 14 0-0 ♘xb3 15 cxb3 even though 15 ... ♗b7 regains the pawn.

| 14 | ... | ♗a6 |

Giving up a piece to prevent White from castl-

ing.

15	b4	♕c7
16	bxc5	

If instead 16 b5 ♗xb5 17 ♘xb5 ♕a5+. At this point, Deep Thought looked 19 single moves deep into Black's sacrifice but could not refute it. However, Deep Thought was also unable to find anything better than taking the piece.

16	...	♖fe8
17	♘e2	♕xc5
18	c4	♘xd5
19	♕d4	

If 19 ♕xd5 ♖xe2+ 20 ♔d1 ♕xd5+ 21 cxd5 ♖xg2 with the plan of ... g5 - g4.

19	...	♕xd4
20	♘fxd4	♗c5
21	♔d2	

White has several alternatives here to break the pins but most fail to ... ♖e4.

21	...	♘e3
22	♔c3	♖ac8
23	♗b2	♘xg2
24	♖af1	♖cd8
25	♖hg1	♖e3+
26	♔d2	f3
27	♖xf3	

If 27 ♖xg2? either 27 ... ♖xe2+ or 27 ... fxe2.

27	...	♖xf3
28	♖xg2	♖h3

Not 28 ... ♗xa3? 29 ♔c2.

| 29 | ♔c1 | g6 |

Preventing any ♖xg7+ tricks.

| 30 | a4 | ♗b7 |

31 ♖f2   ♗a8

White is in virtual zugzwang. If instead 31 ... ♗e4 32 ♘b1 ♗xb1 33 ♔xb1 ♖d3 34 ♔c2 ♖3xd4 35 ♘xd4 ♗xd4 36 ♗xd4 ♖xd4 37 ♔c3 and White has chances with the passed c-pawn.

32 ♗b1   ♖b8
33 ♗a2   ♖d3
34 ♖f4   ♖d2!!

This brilliant move breaks the back of White's resistance.

35 ♔xd2   ♖xb2+
36 ♘c2   ♖xa2
37 ♘c3   ♖b2
38 ♖f6   ♔g7
39 ♖f1

If 39 ♖a6 ♗b6 40 a5 ♗g1 and Black wins.

39 ...   f5
40 ♘d5   ♗xd5
41 cxd5   ♖b3
42 h4   ♔f6
43 ♖e1   ♖h3
44 ♖e6+   ♔f7
45 a5   ♖xh4
46 ♖c6   ♗b4+
47 ♘xb4   ♖xb4
48 ♖c7+   ♔f6

0-1

If 49 ♖xh7 ♖d4+ 50 ♔e3 ♖xd5 51 ♖xa7 ♔g5 and Black's pawns promote, while the black rook will station itself on the a-file behind White's passed pawn to terminate its progress.

Verdict ✳✳✳

Fegatello
(Two Knights)

1 e4 e5 2 ♘f3 ♘c6 3 ♗c4 ♘f6 4 ♘g5 d5 5 exd5 ♘xd5 6 ♘xf7

A most promising method - which hovers in an uncertain radius between combination and positional sacrifice - of drawing Black's king into the centre.

von der Lasa - Mayet
Berlin 1839

1   e4   e5

2	♘f3	♘c6
3	♗c4	♘f6
4	♘g5	d5
5	exd5	♘xd5
6	♘xf7	♔xf7
7	♕f3+	♔e6
8	♘c3	♘ce7

A better defence is afforded by 8 ... ♘cb4 9 ♕e4 c6 10 a3 ♘a6 11 d4 ♘ac7 12 ♗f4 ♔f7 13 ♗xe5 ♗e6 14 0-0 ♗e7 and the outcome is not yet clear.

9	d4	b5

The theoretical scheme of the sacrificial concept employed in this game begins to emerge, for the text move actually represents a divergence from a previously played game which had reached the identical position. Polerio - Domenico, Rome 1600, had gone instead: 9 ... c6 10 ♗g5 h6 11 ♗xe7 ♗xe7 12 0-0-0 ♖f8 13 ♕e4 ♖xf2 14 dxe5 ♗g5+ 15 ♔b1 ♖d2 16 h4 ♖xd1+ 17 ♖xd1 ♗xh4 18 ♘xd5 cxd5 19 ♖xd5 winning.

10	♘xb5	

Another method of maintaining his momentum consists of 10 ♗xd5+ ♘xd5 11 ♗g5 ♕d7 12 0-0-0 but von der Lasa's choice is also excellent in that it grants White a virtually material equivalent for his piece, in addition to his attacking chances.

10	...	c6

11	♘c3	♕b6
12	dxe5	♗b7
13	♘e4	♕b4+
14	♗d2	♕xc4
15	♕g4+	♔xe5
16	f4+	♔d4

Defence by acceptance, again, but even without this Black's game is doubtless indefensible.

17	c3+	

Also deserving of attention was the quiet 17 0-0-0 (17 ... ♕xa2 18 ♗c3+ ♔c4 19 ♕e2 mate).

17	...	♘xc3
18	♗xc3+	♔xe4
19	f5+	♔d5
20	0-0-0+	♔c5
21	b4+	♔b5
22	a4+	1-0

Verdict ✳ ✳ ✳

Fischer's Defence
(King's Gambit)

---

1 e4 e5 2 f4 exf4 3 ♘f3 d6

As one might expect, from so illustrious a source, this is a perfectly solid defence to the King's Gambit. The main line is 4 d4 g5 5 h4 g4 6 ♘g1 ♗h6 7 ♘e2 ♕f6 8 ♘bc3 ♘e7 9 ♕d2 ♘bc6 10 g3 ♗d7=; or 6 ... f3!? 7 gxf3 ♗e7 8 ♗e3 ♗xh4+ 9 ♔d2 c5 10 ♔c1 cxd4 11 ♕xd4 ♘f6∞ Gallagher – Conquest, British Ch. 1988.

Fischer's Gambit
(English Opening)

1 c4 e5 2 ♘c3 ♘c6 3 g3 f5
4 ♗g2 ♘f6 5 d3 ♗c5 6 e3 f4

This gambit is aimed, amongst other line-opening motifs, at uncovering the approaches to White's f-pawn. It should qualify under Spielmann's definition of a real sacrifice, which requires the consequences to be incalculable and the compensation not abso-

lutely tangible.

Saidy – Fischer
New York 1969

1	c4	e5
2	♘c3	♘c6
3	g3	f5
4	♗g2	♘f6

This is one of the more active systems with which to engage to English.

5	d3	♗c5
6	e3	f4!?
7	exf4	0–0
8	♘ge2?	

Best is 8 fxe5.

8	...	♕e8
9	0–0	

If 9 fxe5 ♘g4.

9	...	d6

The activity of the black pieces, domination of d4, and White's weak d-pawn all add up to more than full compensation for the pawn sacrificed.

10	♘a4	♗d4!
11	♘xd4	exd4!

Leaving White badly placed and fixing White's d-pawn as a target.

12	h3	h5
13	a3	a5!
14	b3	♕g6
15	♘b2	♗f5
16	♕c2	♘d7!
17	♖e1	♘c5
18	♗f1	

(*see following diagram*)

18	...	♖a6!

Fischer is trying to use

every piece to exert pressure against White's position. This move seems to carry it to extremes as it requires great judgement to see that the rook is not being put out of play.

19	♗d2	♖b6
20	♗xa5	♖xb3
21	♗d2	♖a8
22	a4	♖a6
23	a5	♔h7
24	♖ed1	b6
25	♗e1	bxa5
26	♘a4	♖xd3
27	♗xd3	♗xd3
28	♕a2	♘b4
29	♕a3	♘c2
30	♕b2	♘xa1
31	♖xa1	♘xa4
32	♖xa4	♕e4
33	♗xa5??	

Better would be 33 ♗d2 though 33 ... ♖b6 should win. If 33 ♖a1 then 33 ... ♗xc4 or 33 ♕d2 ♖b6 34 ♖a1 ♗xc4.

33	...	♖xa5
34	♖xa5	♕e1+
35	♔h2	♕xa5
	0-1	

Compare with the game Hodgson - Nunn in the Sicilian section, later in this volume.

Verdict ✳✳✳

Four Knights Game

Two gambit systems of the Four Knights are dealt with in this book; see the respective sections on the Belgrade Gambit: 1 e4 e5 2 ♘f3 ♘c6 3 ♘c3 ♘f6 4 d4 exd4 5 ♘d5 and Rubinstein's Gambit: 1 e4 e5 2 ♘f3 ♘c6 3 ♘c3 ♘f6 4 ♗b5 ♘d4.

Frankenstein–Dracula
(Vienna)

1 e4 e5 2 ♘c3 ♘f6 3 ♗c4 ♘xe4 4 ♕h5 ♘d6 5 ♗b3 ♘c6 6 ♘b5 g6 7 ♕f3 f5 8 ♕d5 ♕e7 9 ♘xc7+ ♔d8 10 ♘xa8

An unfathomable position. Black has good compensation, e.g. 10 ... b6 11 d3 ♗b7 12 h4 f5 13 ♕f3 ♗h6 Wibe - Bryson, corr. 1985, when 14 ♘d5! is now best. For obvious reasons, most of the theory in this line has been developed in postal tournaments!

Verdict ✻✻✻

French Defence

The French Defence provides gambit opportunities for both sides in nearly every major variation. The following selection has been chosen to reflect important gambit themes.

Nimzowitsch - Haakanson Kristianstad 1922

1	e4	e6
2	d4	d5
3	e5	c5
4	♕g4	

Nimzowitsch's speciality. The idea is to gambit a pawn in order to exert a cramping effect against the whole black position.

4	...	cxd4
5	♘f3	♘c6
6	♗d3	f5

This line is still playable, as demonstrated in the recent game Hector - King, London 1991, which continued 6 ... g6 7 0-0 f5 8 ♕g3 ♕b6 9 a3 and White won.

7	♕g3	♘ge7
8	0-0	♘g6
9	h4	♕c7
10	♖e1	♗d7
11	a3	0-0-0
12	b4	a6
13	h5	♘ge7
14	♗d2	h6
15	a4	g5
16	b5	f4
17	♕g4	♘b8
18	c3	

Obtaining further attacking chances by opening the c-file.

18	...	♖e8
19	cxd4	♔d8
20	♖c1	♕b6
21	a5	♕a7
22	b6	♕a8
23	♖c7	♘f5
24	♘c3	♗e7

After this move, White forces the win in brilliant manner.

25	♘xd5	♘xd4

| 26 | ♘xd4 | exd5 |
| 27 | ♕xd7+ | 1-0 |

Verdict ✳✳✳✳

Keres - Alexandrescu
Munich Olympiad 1936

1	e4	e6
2	d4	d5
3	e5	c5
4	dxc5	♘c6
5	♘f3	♗xc5
6	♗d3	♘ge7

Instead 6 ... f6 is better, now or on the previous move. Black riskily plays to win the irrelevant b2-pawn.

7	♗f4	♕b6
8	0-0	♕xb2
9	♘bd2	♕b6
10	c4	h6

If 10 ... 0-0? 11 ♗xh7+! is a winning sacrifice. Keres's next prepares ♘b3 and ♗xh6 so keeping the black king in the centre of the board.

11	♕c1!	♘b4
12	♗e2	♗d7
13	a3	♘a6
14	♖b1	♕c6
15	♗g3	♘f5?

Trying to eliminate the bishop, Black encourages a decisive attack. this was the last chance to castle.

| 16 | cxd5 | exd5 |
| 17 | e6! | fxe6 |

Both 17 ... ♗xe6 18 ♗b5 and 17 ... ♕xe6 18 ♗xa6 lose at once.

18	♘e5	♘xg3
19	hxg3	♕c7
20	♘xd7	♔xd7
21	♕b2	♗b6

If 21 ... ♖hg8 22 ♖fc1 threatens to win a piece by 23 ♗xa6 bxa6 24 ♘b3.

22	♕xg7+	♔d6
23	♘e4+!	dxe4
24	♖fd1+	1-0

Verdict ✳✳✳✳✳

Alekhine - Nimzowitsch
Bled 1931

1	e4	e6
2	d4	d5
3	♘c3	♗b4
4	♘ge2	dxe4

An interesting Russian idea is 4 ... ♘e7 5 a3 ♗a5 6 b4 ♗b6 7 e5 a5! with good counterplay.

| 5 | a3 | ♗xc3+ |

5 ... ♗e7 is more circumspect.

| 6 | ♘xc3 | f5 |

Heroic defence but most perilous in this case; 6 ... ♘c6 is much better.

7 f3

A game Thomas - Nimzowitsch, Marienbad 1925 went 7 ♗f4 ♘f6 8 f3 0-0 9 fxe4 ♘xe4 10 ♘xe4 fxe4 11 ♕d2 ♘d7 12 ♗e2 c5 and Black maintained his extra material into the endgame and this eventually brought him victory, in spite of White's bishops and the precarious nature of Black's booty.

| 7 | ... | exf3 |
| 8 | ♕xf3 | ♕xd4 |

Absolutely consistent with heroic defence.

| 9 | ♕g3 | ♘f6 |
| 10 | ♕xg7 | ♕e5+? |

10 ... ♖g8! 11 ♕xc7 ♘c6 - Alekhine - and Black can fight on.

11	♗e2	♖g8
12	♕h6	♖g6
13	♕h4	♗d7
14	♗g5	♗c6
15	0-0-0	♗xg2
16	♖he1	♗e4
17	♗h5	♘xh5
18	♖d8+	♔f7
19	♕xh5	

Nimzowitsch quite rightly resigned here, as there are no more decent moves for Black - even 19 ... ♔g7 would lose the queen after 20 ♘xe4 fxe4 21 ♗h6+! This was, I believe, the shortest defeat ever in his career (Alekhine).

1-0

Verdict ✳ ✳ ✳ ✳ ✳

Chandler - Vaganian
London 1986

1	e4	e6
2	d4	d5
3	♘c3	♗b4
4	e5	c5
5	a3	♗a5

An unusual variation which Vaganian tries to revive from time to time.

6 b4!

A gambit suggested by the fertile brain of the great Alekhine.

6 ... cxd4

The main point is 6 ... cxb4 7 ♘b5! bxa3+ 8 c3 followed by ♗xa3 with a fierce attack.

7	♘b5	♗c7
8	f4	♗d7
9	♘f3	♗xb5
10	♗xb5+	♘c6
11	0-0	♘ge7
12	♗d3	a6
13	♔h1	h6
14	♕e2	

Vaganian had done well

from an almost identical position against Nigel Short in their game from the Biel Interzonal in 1985. Short's plan had been to place his queen on d2 and then advance with a4. True to his aggressive style Chandler throws everything into an all-out assault against the black king.

14	...	♕d7
15	♗b2	♘b6
16	♖ae1	♖c8

A move which commits Black's king to an unsafe residence in the centre of the board. 16 ... 0-0-0 would have bee preferable.

17	g4	g6
18	♘h4	h5
19	f5	

The intention is to sacrifice a piece in order to come to grips with the black king.

19	...	hxg4
20	fxg6	♖xh4
21	gxf7+	♔f8
22	♗c1!	

A deep move with the hidden threat of sacrificing the queen to give mate by means of a subsequent ♕d2 followed by ♕h6+.

| 22 | ... | ♘f5 |
| 23 | ♗xf5 | d3 |

(*see following diagram*)

If 23 ... exf5 24 e6 ♕d6 25 ♗f4 ♕e7 26 ♕d2 wins.

| 24 | ♗xd3 | g3 |
| 25 | ♕g2!! | |

A brilliant queen sacrifice which enables the remainder of White's forces to close the ring around Black's hapless king.

25	...	♖xh2+
26	♕xh2	gxh2
27	♗h6+	♔e7
28	♗g5+	♔f8
29	♗h6+	♔e7
30	♗g6	♗c7
31	♗g5+	♔f8
32	♗h6+	♔e7
33	f8♕+	♖xf8
34	♗xf8+	♔d8
35	♖f7	♕e8
36	♗g7	♘xe5
37	♗f6+	1-0

Verdict ✻✻✻✻✻

**Lewitzky - Marshall
Breslau 1991**

1	d4	e6
2	e4	d5
3	♘c3	c5

This was Marshall's favourite move, but modern theory frowns on it because of 4 exd5 exd5 5 dxc5 d4 6 ♗b5+ ♘c6 7 ♗xc6+ bxc6 8 ♘ce2 when Black may well not get enough for the gambit pawn.

4	♘f3	♘c6
5	exd5	exd5
6	♗e2	♘f6
7	0-0	♗e7
8	♗g5	0-0
9	dxc5	♗e6
10	♘d4	♗xc5
11	♘xe6	fxe6
12	♗g4	♕d6
13	♗h3	♖ae8
14	♕d2	♗b4
15	♗xf6	♖xf6
16	♖ad1	♕c5
17	♕e2	

White is under uncomfortable pressure and this is the start of a deep defensive combination which, however, has a hidden flaw which leads to his downfall.

17	...	♗xc3
18	bxc3	♕xc3
19	♖xd5	♘d4
20	♕h5	

If 20 ♕e5 ♘f3+ 21 gxf3 ♖g6+ wins.

20	...	♖ef8
21	♖e5	

Not 21 ♖c5 on account of 21 ... ♖xf2 when Black's attack triumphs.

21	...	♖h6
22	♕g5	

If 22 ♕g4 then 22 ... ♘f3+ wins.

22	...	♖xh3
23	♖c5	♕g3

0-1

Verdict ✳✳✳

See also the Chatard-Alekhine Attack and the Poisoned Pawn (French Winawer).

Fritz
(Two Knights)

---

1 e4 e5 2 ♘f3 ♘c6 3 ♗c4 ♘f6 4 ♘g5 d5 5 exd5 ♘d4

According to the brilliant US postal player and former postal World Champion Hans Berliner, this line is razor-sharp, but playable, e.g. 6 c3 b5 7 ♗f1 ♘xd5 8 ♘e4 ♕h4!! 9 ♘g3 ♗g4 10 f3 e4 11 cxd4 ♗d6 12 ♗xb5+ ♔d8 13 0-0 exf3 14 ♖xf3 ♖b8 15 a4 a6 16 ♗xa6 ♖e8 17 ♘c3 ♘b4 18 ♗f1∞. Nevertheless, analysis by Estrin suggests that 14 ♕b3!! may refute the entire line.

Verdict ✳ ✳

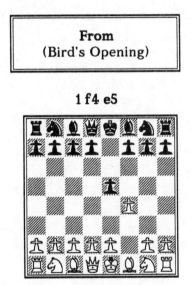

From
(Bird's Opening)

1 f4 e5

This gambit is certainly

worth a try for Black. The main line is 2 fxe5 d6 3 exd6 ♗xd6 4 ♘f3 ♘f6 (4 ... g5 leads to very sharp play) 5 g3 ♘c6 6 ♗g2 ♗g4 7 d3 ♗c5 8 ♘c3 a6 9 ♗g5 h6 10 ♗xf6 ♕xf6 11 ♕d2∞/±.

Verdict ✳ ✳ ✳

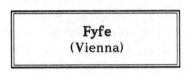

Fyfe
(Vienna)

1 e4 e5 2 ♘c3 ♘c6 3 d4

The best White can hope for after either 3 ... exd4 or 3 ... ♘xd4 is somehow to regain the pawn.

Verdict ✳ ✳

Ghulam Khassim
(King's Gambit)

**1 e4 e5 2 f4 exf4 3 ♘f3 g5
4 ♗c4 g4 5 d4**

After 5 ... gxf3 6 ♕xf3 d5!
7 ♗xd5 ♘f6 8 0-0 c6 White's
compensation is not really
adequate, though in the
Muzio-related King's Gam-
bits there are always ways
to continue. These might
be 9 ♗xf4 cxd5 10 ♗e5 or
even 9 ♗xf7+ ♔xf7 10 ♗xf4,
throwing caution to the
winds. However, objectively
it must be assessed as ...

Verdict ✳✳

Giuoco Piano

The next gambit used to be
popular but is now more or
less burnt out, leading to
perpetual check.

Anon - Anon
Italy c. 1932

1	e4	e5
2	♘f3	♘c6
3	♗c4	♗c5
4	c3	♘f6
5	d4	exd4
6	cxd4	♗b4+
7	♘c3	

Introducing the sharp
Moller Attack of the so-
called Giuoco Piano. If
White really does want to
play *pianissimo*, rather than
offer a sharp gambit, he
can choose 7 ♗d2 which
leads to total equality.

7	...	♘xe4
8	0-0	♗xc3
9	d5	

This is the only way for
White to proceed if he wishes to infuse some life

into his position. The immediate recapture suffered a dreadful buffeting in one game from the second Steinitz - Lasker match, from which its reputation never recovered viz. 9 bxc3 d5 10 ♗a3 dxc4 11 ♖e1 ♗e6 12 ♖xe4 ♕d5 13 ♕e2 0-0-0 and Black has an excellent position, Steinitz - Lasker, Match 1896/97.

9	...	♗f6
10	♖e1	♘e7
11	♖xe4	d6
12	♗g5	

12	...	0-0

This allows his king's position to be broken up. A continuation which has been thoroughly analysed is 12 ... ♗xg5 13 ♘xg5 0-0 14 ♘xh7 ♔xh7 15 ♕h5+ ♔g8 16 ♖h4 f5 17 ♕h7+ ♔f7 18 ♖h6 ♖g8 19 ♖e1 ♕f8 20 ♗b5 ♖h8 21 ♕xh8 gxh6 22 ♕h7+ ♔f6 23 ♖xe7 ♕xe7 24 ♕xh6+ and the game ends in a draw by perpetual check. Also possible is 12 ... ♗xg5 13 ♘xg5 h6 14 ♕h5 0-0 15 ♖ae1 ♘f5

16 ♘e6 fxe6 17 dxe6 ♕e7 18 ♖f4 Bateman - Boisvert, corr. 1984 with a large advantage to White but Black should in fact play 17 ... ♘e7. Perhaps modern players, taking Nigel Short's lead in the Four Knight's Game, could improve on this analysis somewhere and resurrect the line for White.

13	♗xf6	gxf6
14	♘h4	

The value of this move lies in the fact that the queen can now reach the critical sector with the utmost rapidity.

14	...	♘g6
15	♕h5	♔h8
16	♖ae1	♗d7
17	♗d3	♖g8

Hoping to consolidate his position with ... ♖g7.

18	♖e7	

This move, an elegant unmasking sacrifice, banishes any illusions Black may have harboured as to the rescue of his shattered king's flank. Black cannot play 18 ... ♘xe7 on account of 19 ♕xh7 mate.

18	...	♖g7
19	♗xg6	fxg6
20	♘xg6+	♔g8
21	♖xg7+	1-0

Notes to these games are partially based on those by Tartakower and Du Mont in their book *500 Master*

Games, where, incidentally, this game is erroneously given as Spielmann - Duras, Carlsbad 1907! The above attribution, although vague, is more accurate.

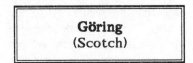

Göring
(Scotch)

1 e4 e5 2 ♘f3 ♘c6 3 d4 exd4
4 c3

The Göring Gambit is another line which, due to its potentially mind-boggling complexity, is more often tested out in correspondence chess than over the board.

Kronberg - Liubmirov
World corr. Ch.
Semi-Final 1985

1	e4	e5
2	♘f3	♘c6
3	d4	exd4
4	c3	dxc3

5 ♘xc3

On 5 ♗c4, *ECO* gives the acceptance of the second pawn a categoric ±, however 5 ... cxb2 6 ♗xb2 d6 7 0-0 ♗e6 8 ♗xe6 (8 ♗d5 ♘f6 9 ♘g5 ♗xd5 10 exd5 ♘e5! Christensen - From, Danish corr. Ch. 1984) 8 ... fxe6 9 ♕b3 ♕d7 10 ♘g5 ♘d8 11 f4 ♘f6 12 e5! is critical. After 12 ... dxe5 13 fxe5 ♘d5 14 ♘d2 ♗e7! 15 ♘de4 h6!? (15 ... ♗xg5 16 ♘xg5 ♕e7 Smit) 16 ♕h3 ♕c6! 17 ♗d4 ♖f8 18 ♖xf8+ ♗xf8 19 ♕h5+ ♔d7 20 ♘h7 ♗e7 21 ♕g6! ♕c4! Nun - Dunhaupt, 8th World corr. Ch. went Black's way (0-1 38 moves). In the 1985 Danish corr. Ch., Pedersen - Tronhjem saw 7 ♘c3 instead of 7 0-0 with the continuation 7 ... ♗e6 8 ♘d5 ♘a5 9 ♗e2 c6 10 ♘f4 ♘f6? (10 ... ♗c4 is correct) 11 ♘xe6 fxe6 12 ♘g5! d5 13 ♗c3! ♘c4 14 e5! and a quick win for White.

5	...	♗b4
6	♗c4	d6
7	♕b3	

7 0-0 ♗xc3 8 bxc3 ♘f6 9 e5 gives only equality.

7	...	♗xc3+
8	♕xc3	

Fresher than the old book 8 bxc3 and after 8 ... ♕d7 9 ♕c2 ♘f6 10 0-0 0-0∓.

8	...	♕f6
9	♕b3	♘ge7
10	0-0	h6

| 11 | ♗d2 | 0-0 |
| 12 | ♖ae1 | |

Already with a clear idea of his attack.

12	...	♗e6
13	♗d5	♘d8
14	♗c3	♕g6

15	♖e3	c6
16	♘h4!	♕h5
17	♖g3	g6
18	♗xe6	fxe6
19	♘xg6!	♘xg6
20	♕d1!	

The sort of retro-move easily missed in an analysis but seen by White at move 12!

20	...	♕xd1
21	♖xg6+	♔f7
22	♖g7+	♔e8
23	♖xd1	♘f7
24	♖g6	♔e7
25	e5!	♖g8
26	exd6+	♔d7
27	♖f6	♖af8
28	f4	h5
29	g3	c5
30	♔g2	b5
31	b3	

Black finds just a little bit of play ... not enough

31	...	♘d8
32	♔f3	♘c6
33	♖h6	e5
34	♖xh5	exf4
35	♖h7+	♔e6
36	gxf4	b4
37	♗a1	♖f5
38	d7	♘d8

The third time this goes down on the scoresheet ... but there's no luck in that!

39	♖e1+	♔d6
40	♖e8	♖ff8
41	♗e5+	♔c6
42	♖he7	♘b7
43	♖xf8	1-0

Notes from the *British Chess Magazine*.

Verdict ✳✳✳✳

Greco
(King's Gambit)

---

1 e4 e5 2 f4 exf4 3 ♘f3 g5 4 ♗c4 ♗g7 5 h4 h6 6 d4 d6 7 ♘c3 c6 8 hxg5 hxg5 9 ♖xh8 ♗xh8

Black's position is solid, so White must sacrifice a piece with 10 g3! g4 11 ♗xf4 gxf3 12 ♕xf3. As Grandmaster Nick de Firmian notes: "This type of position is what King's Gambit players strive for!".

Verdict ✳✳✳

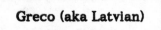

Greco (aka Latvian)

1 e4 e5 2 ♘f3 f5

The Greco (or Latvian) Counter-Gambit is one of the most risky choices for Black, but is still popular at club level with attack-minded players. However, Black must be well prepared or he may slip instantly into a lost position.

Spielmann - Nimzowitsch Semmering 1926

First prize in the tournament depended upon the result of this game.

1	e4	e5
2	♘f3	f5!?
3	♘xe5	

Of late 3 ♗c4 has grown in popularity, but this book is no place for such an exhaustive analysis of the modern refinements of confused and confusing tactical lines. Suffice it to mention that the text is a sensible method of maintaining such a small plus for White.

| 3 | ... | ♕f6 |

3 ... ♘c6?! is considered in the next game.

| 4 | d4 | |

4 ♘c4 fxe4 5 ♘c3 ♕f7 6 d4 ♘f6 7 ♗g5 ♗b4 8 ♘e5 ♕e6 9 ♗c4 ♕f5 10 ♗xf6 gxf6 11 ♘g4 ♕g6 12 ♘e3± Dubinsky - Chebotarev, USSR 1968.

4	...	d6
5	♘c4	fxe4
6	♘c3	

As one might expect, Spielmann opts for a developing move rather than the hyper-subtle 6 ♘e3, which was Nimzowitsch's own recommendation in this position, introduced in his brilliancy versus Behting, played at Riga in 1919, which continued: 6 ♘e3 (the blockading knight - Nimzowitsch wrote of this move: "Even if all the rest of the world play here 6 ♘c3, I yet hold my move ♘e3 to be more correct, and this for reasons based on 'the system'"). 6 ... c6 (or 6 ... ♘c6 7 d5 ♘e5 8 ♘c3 ♕g6 9 ♕d4 ♘f6 10 ♘b5) 7 ♗c4 d5 8 ♗b3 ♗e6 9 c4 ♕f7 10 ♕e2 ♘f6 11 0-0 ♗b4 12 ♗d2 ♗xd2 13 ♘xd2 0-0 14 f4 dxc4 15 ♘dxc4 ♕e7 16 f5 ♗d5 17 ♘xd5 cxd5 18 ♘e3 ♕d7 19 ♘xd5! ♘xd5 20 ♕xe4 ♖d8 21 f6! gxf6 (21 ... ♘c6 22 f7+ ♔f8 23 ♕xh7) 22 ♖f5 ♔h8 23 ♖xd5 ♖e8 24 ♖xd7 ♖xe4 25 ♖d8+ ♔g7 26 ♖g8+ ♔h6 27 ♖f1 1-0.

We can only speculate concerning the line Nimzowitsch would have adopted had Spielmann chosen to play 6 ♘e3 against its inventor.

6 ... ♕g6
7 d5?!

White decides to surround Black's e-pawn but, as a result, Black streaks past him in the matter of mobilisation. 7 f3 is more dynamic.

7 ... ♘f6
8 ♗e3 ♗e7
9 ♕d4 0-0
10 ♘d2

Perhaps White had anticipated a black defence of the e-pawn by 10 ... ♗f5 when 11 h3 h5 12 0-0-0 followed by ♗e2 and g4 would leave White on top. Instead

Nimzowitsch willingly sacrifices the pawn in the interests of seizing the initiative.

10 ... c5!
11 dxc6 ♘xc6
12 ♕c4+ ♔h8
13 0-0-0

White cannot capture the e-pawn as yet in view of the defence ... d5.

13 ... ♗g4
14 f3 d5!

The feeble 14 ... exf3 15 gxf3 ♗f5 would react in White's favour after 16 ♖g1.

15 ♘xd5

White has no choice.

15 ... ♘xd5
16 ♕xd5 exf3
17 gxf3

17 ... ♖ac8?

One mistake and the whole of Black's good work is spoiled. The text, threatening as it does ... ♘b4, looks most fearsome, but it grants White a vital tempo which he turns to account by launching a counter-offensive in the g-file.

Two superior possibilities, suggested by Tartakower, are:

(a) The alarming: 17 ... ♛xc2+ 18 ♔xc2 ♞b4+ 19 ♔b1 ♞xd5 with a good position for Black; and

(b) The cunning: 17 ... ♞b4 18 ♕b3 a5! with the threat of ... a4.

18 ♗d3

A sure way to lose was 18 fxg4? ♞b4 19 ♕e4 ♜xc2+ 20 ♔b1 ♜xd2 with evil intentions against both members of the white "royal family".

18	...	♗f5
19	♗xf5	♜xf5
20	♕c4	

The defence just holds, since White can co-ordinate his forces with continual gains of tempo. Here White pins Black's knight, while the white queen's flight on the following turn obliges the retreat of her sable counterparts.

20	...	b5
21	♕g4	♕f7
22	♜hg1	♞b4
23	c3	♞xa2+
24	♔b1	b4

The concentration of hostile force in the vicinity of White's king suggests that Black will arrive first, but with his next move White heralds his own attack, and this packs the greater punch.

25	♗d4	♗g5
26	c4	b3
27	♞e4	♕g6
28	♕xg5!	♜xg5
29	♜xg5	♕f7
30	♞d6	♕xf3
31	♗xg7+	♔g8
32	♗e5+	♔f8
33	♜f5+	1-0

Nimzowitsch's decision in this game to abandon the style of gradually unfolding aggression we normally associate with his post-war strategic formulations represents a throw-back to his youth, when his tactical flair predominated over any nascent awareness of strategic principles. Whatever the explanation, Nimzowitsch never again grappled with Spielmann on the latter's home ground (i.e. gambit territory). In their subsequent clashes Nimzowitsch preferred to involve Spielmann in protracted wars of attrition stemming from closed openings.

Verdict ✳✳✳

Hindle - J Littlewood
Hastings 1963

1	e4	e5
2	♞f3	f5
3	♞xe5	♞c6

A poor alternative to the usual 3 ... ♕f6.

4	♕h5+	

4 ♘xc6 dxc6 5 ♘c3 ♛e7 6 d3 ♘f6 7 ♗g5 ♗d7 8 f3 0-0-0 9 ♗e2 h6 10 ♗d2 g5 11 exf5 ♗xf5± is a safe way to a slight advantage for White.

4 ... g6
5 ♘xg6 ♘f6
6 ♛h4 hxg6

6 ... ♖g8 seems a little better.

7 ♛xh8 fxe4
8 d4!

Based on the conviction that his bishops are going to be horribly effective.

8 ... ♔f7

This move will be forced, in any event, after for instance 8 ... d5 9 ♗g5. Nor is 8 ... exd3 9 ♗xd3 any more attractive.

9 ♘c3 ♘xd4

9 ... ♗g7 or 9 ... ♗b4 would be natural and good consolidating moves, e.g. 10 ♗c4+ d5 ... if only Black were not the exchange and a pawn down!

10 ♗g5

Hindle plays the whole game superbly. He is in his element in this kind of situation.

10 ... ♘xc2+
11 ♔d1 ♘xa1

White is now a piece down, but it is a trapped piece and he is at least four moves ahead in development, and has a boa constrictor grip on Black's king's knight.

12 ♗c4+ d5
13 ♘xd5

Though White's knight is pinned, it sets up an effective third attack on Black's king's knight.

13 ... b5

13 ... ♗e7 would be no good because of 14 ♛xd8 (destroying the pin on the white knight) 14 ... ♗xd8 15 ♘xf6+.

14 ♗xf6 ♛d6
15 ♛h7+ ♔e6

If 15 ... ♔e8 16 ♛xg6+ ♔d7 17 ♗xb5+ c6 18 ♛f7+ leads to situations akin to the game; but 16 ♗xb5+ c6 17 ♗xc6+ ♛xc6 18 ♘c7+, though it wins Black's queen, is not quite so clear.

16 ♛g8+ ♔d7

Not 16 ... ♔f5 17 g4+! ♔xg4 18 ♛xg6+.

17 ♗xb5+

The black king must not be allowed to escape via c6.

17 ... c6
18 ♛f7+ ♗e7

19	♗xe7	♛e6
20	♛xe6+	1-0

Verdict ✳✳

Grob

I have never been quite sure whether this is the worst opening move or whether that dubious title belongs to 1 f3. At least after 1 f3 d5 White can play 2 f4 or after 1 f3 e5 2 e4 ♗c5 3 f4, but 1 g4 gives no such options.

One of the best ways to manhandle this miserable move is to play a sharp gambit against it.

Basman – Keene
Manchester 1981

1	g4	d5
2	h3	e5
3	♗g2	c6
4	d4	e4
5	c4	♗d6
6	♘c3	♘e7!

A powerful gambit, which casts doubt on White's whole opening.

7   g5

In his book, *The Killer Grob*, Basman recommends instead accepting the gambit with 7 ♛b3 0-0 8 ♗g5 f6 9 cxd5 cxd5 10 ♘xd5 ♗e6 11 ♘xe7+ ♛xe7 12 d5 but then

12 ... ♗f7 13 ♗e3 ♘a6 or 13 ... ♘d7 leaves White virtually lost since he will automatically lose the pawn on d5 and he cannot meanwhile develop his kingside.

7	...	♗e6
8	h4	♘f5
9	♗h3	

Not 9 e3 ♘xh4 10 ♖xh4 ♛xg5 winning.

9	...	0-0
10	cxd5	cxd5
11	♘xd5	

Or 11 ♗xf5 ♗xf5 12 ♘xd5 ♛a5+ 13 ♘c3 ♘c6 with a decisive lead in development.

| 11 | ... | ♘g3 |

Basman completely overlooked this. If 12 fxg3 ♗xg3+ and 13 ... ♗xd5 or 12 ♗xe6 ♘xh1 13 ♗h3 ♗h2! stabbing White's knights in the back. The rest is a slaughter.

12	♘f6+	gxf6
13	fxg3	♗xg3+
14	♔f1	♘c6
15	♗e3	♘b4
16	♔g2	♘d5
17	♔xg3	♘xe3

18	♕d2	♕d6+
19	♔f2	♕f4+
20	♘f3	exf3
	0-1	

21 ♕xe3 ♕xh4+ is hopeless for White.

Verdict ✳✳✳✳✳

Grünfeld Defence

A medley of gambits in the Grünfeld, both accepted and declined.

Zsu Polgar - Wolff
San Francisco 1991

1	d4	♘f6
2	c4	g6
3	♘c3	d5
4	cxd5	♘xd5
5	e4	♘xc3
6	bxc3	♗g7
7	♗c4	c5
8	♘e2	♘c6
9	♗e3	0-0
10	0-0	♗g4
11	f3	♘a5
12	♗xf7+	

The Seville Gambit. It has now been established that Black has plenty of counterplay.

| 12 | ... | ♖xf7 |

(*see following diagram*)

13	fxg4	♖xf1+
14	♔xf1	♕d6
15	e5	

15 ♔g1 ♕e6 16 ♕d3 ♕c4! 17

♕xc4+ ♘xc4 18 ♗f2 cxd4 19 cxd4 e5 20 d5± was Karpov - Kasparov, World Ch. (11), Seville 1987.

15	...	♕d5
16	♗f2	♖d8
17	♕c2	♕c4
18	♕b2	♖f8
19	♔g1	♕d3
20	♘g3	♗h6
21	♕e2	♕xc3
22	♖d1	cxd4
23	♗xd4	♕c4
24	♗xa7	♕xe2
25	♘xe2	♘c6
26	♗c5	♖a8
27	♘c3	♖a5
28	♗b6	♖a3
29	♘d5	♖xa2
30	♖e1	♗g7
31	e6	♖d2
32	♘c7	♗e5
33	♖e4	♖d1+
34	♔f2	♖b1
35	♘a8	♗xh2
36	♗c7	♗g1+
37	♔e2	♖b2+
38	♔f1	♗d4
39	♗f4	♖f2+
40	♔e1	♖xg2
41	♗h6	♖h2

42	♗g5	♖a2
43	♘c7	♖a5
44	♗h6	♗e5
45	♗f4	♗xf4
46	♖xf4	♖c5
47	♔f2	♘e5
	0-1	

Verdict ✳✳✳

Shirov - Ernst
Gausdal 1991

1	d4	♘f6
2	c4	g6
3	♘c3	d5
4	♘f3	♗g7
5	♗g5	♘e4
6	cxd5	♘xg5
7	♘xg5	c6!?

Black offers a promising gambit.

8	e3	cxd5
9	♕f3	f6
10	♘h3	♗xh3
11	♕xh3	f5
12	g4	

This move heralds a powerful attack on the g-file.

| 12 | ... | 0-0 |

13	gxf5	gxf5
14	♖g1	e6
15	♘e2	♖f6
16	♘f4	♘c6
17	♗d3	♕e7
18	♔e2	♖af8
19	♖g5	♖8f7
20	♖ag1	♕c7
21	♖h5	♘xd4+
22	exd4	♕xf4
23	♖xh7	1-0

Verdict ✳✳✳

Keene - Eales
Cambridge 1971

1	d4	♘f6
2	c4	g6
3	♘c3	d5
4	♗g5	♘e4
5	♗h4	c5
6	e3	♘c6
7	cxd5	♘xc3
8	bxc3	♕xd5
9	♘f3	

The original Taimanov idea here was 9 ♕f3 aiming to win the ending after 9 ... ♕xf3 10 ♘xf3. White has a different idea in mind.

9	...	cxd4
10	exd4!?	♗g7
11	♗e2	♕a5?!

A risky move. If 11 ... 0-0 12 0-0 White will continue with ♕b3, again angling for a favourable ending.

12	0-0	♕xc3
13	♖c1	♕b4
14	♖b1	

Not 14 d5? ♘e5!.

BUSINESS REPLY MAIL

FIRST-CLASS MAIL   PERMIT NO. 32   NEWBURGH, N.Y.

POSTAGE WILL BE PAID BY ADDRESSEE

US CHESS FEDERATION, DEPT 69
186 ROUTE 9W
NEW WINDSOR NY 12553-9919

NO POSTAGE
NECESSARY
IF MAILED
IN THE
UNITED STATES

14	...	♛d6
15	♗g3	♛d5

15 ... ♛d8 16 d5 ♞b8 17 d6 0-0 18 dxe7 ♛xe7 19 ♗d6 winning material prosaically.

16	♖b5	♛xa2
17	d5	♞b8
18	d6	0-0

Neither 18 ... ♞c6 19 dxe7 or 18 ... e6 19 ♞e5 holds out much hope.

19	dxe7	♖e8
20	♞e5!	

Clearer than 20 ♛d8 ♗d7.

20	...	♗xe5
21	♗xe5	♞c6
22	♗a1	♛e6

If 22 ... ♖xe7 23 ♛c1! threatening both 24 ♗c4 and 24 ♛h6.

23	♛d2	f6
24	♖d5	

24	...	♛xe7
25	♗c4	♗e6
26	♖d7	♛c5

26 ... ♛f8 27 ♛a2 ♗xc4 28 ♛xc4+ ♔h8 29 ♖f7 winning,

27	♛h6	1-0

Verdict ✳✳✳✳

1 e4 e5 2 ♘c3 ♘c6 3 f4 exf4
4 ♘f3 g5 5 h4 g4 6 ♘g5

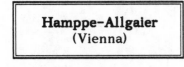

This gambit was pioneered by Carl Hamppe, (1814-76) of Swiss origin, who became a senior government official in Vienna, and Johann Baptist Allgaier (1763-1823), chess tutor to the Vienna Imperial family.

However, if Black takes the immediate sacrifice White's compensation is inadequate, thus 6 ... h6! 7 ♘xf7 ♔xf7 8 d4 d5 9 ♗xf4 ♗b4 10 ♗e2 ♗xc3+∓; or 8 ♗c4+ d5 9 ♗xd5+ ♔g7 10 d4 f3∓.

Verdict ✳

1 e4 e5 2 ♘c3 ♘c6 3 f4 exf4
4 ♘f3 g5 5 ♗c4 g4 6 0-0

After 6 ... gxf3 White cannot play 7 ♕xf3 on account of the fork 7 ... ♘e5. Therefore he is committed to 7 d4!. If now 7 ... ♘xd4 8 ♗xf4! (not 8 ♕xd4? ♕g5! threatening checkmate, ... ♗c5 and holding ... ♕c5+ in reserve) 8 ... ♕f6 9 ♘d5 ♕g7

10 ♘xc7+ ♚d8 11 g3!± (Keres).

So, 7 d4 d5 8 exd5 ♗g4 9 ♕d2 ♘ce7 10 ♕xf4 ♕d7 is the time-honoured line. Some sources give this as '∓' but Glaskov, the Russian analyst, continues with 11 d6! ♘g6 12 ♕e4+ ♚d8 13 h3! with advantage to White. Fascinating.

Verdict ✳✳✳

Hanstein
(King's Gambit)

1 e4 e5 2 f4 exf4 3 ♘f3 g5 4 ♗c4 ♗g7 5 0-0

A gambit cited by the 18th Century Italian aristocrat Carlo Francisco Cozio, this position is complicated and balanced, e.g. in the main line 5 ... h6 6 d4 d6 7 c3 ♘c6 8 h4 (8 g3 g4 or even 8 ... ♗h3 9 gxf4 ♕d7! 10 f5 ♗xf1 tend to give

White inadequate compensation) 8 ... ♗g4 9 ♕b3 ♘a5 10 ♗xf7+ ♚f8 11 ♕a4 ♚xf7 12 ♕xa5 ♗xf3 13 ♖xf3 c5= according to the Danish master Hoi. This is one of those positions where, it seems to me, both sides stand badly!

Verdict ✳✳✳

Harksen
(Open Ruy Lopez)

1 e4 e5 2 ♘f3 ♘c6 3 ♗b5 a6 4 ♗a4 ♘f6 5 0-0 ♘xe4 6 d4 b5 7 ♗b3 d5 8 c4

A forgotten idea of the Swede Alfred Harksen. White's idea is to disrupt Black's development either after 8 ... dxc4 9 ♗c2 or 8 ... bxc4 9 ♗a4.

Instead, 8 ... ♗g4 9 cxd5 ♘xd4 10 ♖e1 f5 11 h3 ♘xf3+ 12 gxf3 ♕h4! is considered '=' by theory. Geller - Lubensky, 1947 Ukraine Ch continued 13 ♖xe4 fxe4 14 fxg4 ♗c5 15 ♕c2 ♕g3+ with perpetual check.

Verdict ✳✳✳

> **Hennig-Schara**
> (Queen's Gambit
> Declined - Tarrasch)

1 d4 d5 2 c4 e6 3 ♘c3 c5 4 cxd5 cxd4

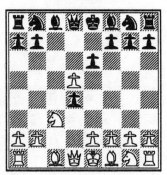

The Hennig-Schara is another gambit which, while not theoretically sound, has resulted in good practical results for club players since it gives Black chances for rapid development and a kingside attack.

**Polugayevsky - Zaitsev
USSR Ch 1969**

1	d4	d5
2	c4	e6
3	♘c3	c5

4	cxd5	cxd4
5	♕xd4	♘c6
6	♕d1	exd5
7	♕xd5	♗d7

In this position Black has many methods of developing his pieces and can gain time by attacking the white queen, but White has an extra pawn. This gambit can be effective against an inexperienced opponent but is likely to come unstuck against accurate defence.

| 8 | ♘f3 | ♘f6 |
| 9 | ♕d1 | |

9 ♕b3 ♗c5 10 e3 ♕e7 (10 ... 0-0 left Black with insufficient compensation in Karpov - Hector, Haninge 1990) 11 ♗e2 0-0-0 12 ♗d2 ♗f5 13 0-0 g5 14 ♖fd1 g4 15 ♘d4 ♖xd4 16 exd4 ♘xd4 17 ♕c4 b5 18 ♘xb5 ♘xe2+ 19 ♔f1 g3 20 ♗f4 ♘xf4 21 ♘d6+ ♔b8 (Black had a fantastic draw with 21 ... ♕xd6!! 22 ♖xd6 gxh2 23 ♕xc5+ ♔b8 24 ♕b5+ ♔a8 25 ♕c6+ ♔b8 and if White tries to win with 26 g3? then 26 ... ♗e4!) 22 ♘xf5 ♕e4 23 ♕xe4 ♘xe4 24 hxg3 ♘e6 25 f3 ♘f6 26 b4 ♗b6 27 ♖ac1 h5 28 a4 a6 29 a5 ♗a7 30 ♘e7 1-0 Aagard - I Andersen, Copenhagen 1991.

| 9 | ... | ♗c5 |
| 10 | e3 | ♕e7 |

Intending to castle on the opposite side to White

and then launch a pawn
storm against White's king.

| 11 | ♗e2 | 0-0-0 |
| 12 | 0-0 | g5 |

It would naturally be a
dangerous waste of time
for White to accept this
pawn sacrifice, so he prefers to centralise.

| 13 | ♘d4 | g4 |

| 14 | b4 | ♗xb4 |

Even worse is the retreat
14 ... ♗b6 15 b5 ♘e5 16 ♕b3
Hartston - Messa, Berlin
1980.

15	♗b2	h5
16	♘cb5	♔b8
17	♕a4	a6
18	♘xc6+	♗xc6
19	♗xf6	♕xf6
20	♕xb4	axb5
21	♗xb5	♕d6
22	♖ab1	

White still has an extra
pawn and Black's king is
more exposed. So, nat-
urally, White went on to
win.

1-0

Verdict   ✳ ✳ ✳

Icelandic

1 e4 d5 2 exd5 ♘f6 3 c4 e6

See Centre Counter Defence.

Irish
(aka Chicago or Schulze-Muller Gambit)

1 e4 e5 2 ♘f3 ♘c6 3 ♘xe5 ♘xe5 4 d4

This gambit is quite obviously unsound!

Verdict ✳

J

Jaenisch-Schliemann
(Ruy Lopez)

1 e4 e5 2 ♘f3 ♘c6 3 ♗b5 f5

Once again, the move ... f5 proves the linchpin of a Black counter-attacking gambit. In spite of many efforts at refutation, this gambit has held up and is a favourite of many aggressive players.

Timman - Speelman
Candidates Semi-final 1989

1	e4	e5
2	♘f3	♘c6
3	♗b5	f5

A wild move, hovering on the frontiers of soundness. Nevertheless, Jon Speelman had thoroughly prepared this variation, and it turned out to be a most valuable shock weapon, since Timman could not possibly have expected it.

4	♘c3	fxe4
5	♘xe4	d5
6	♘xe5	dxe4
7	♘xc6	♛g5

Black must counter-attack against the bishop on b5 and the pawn on g2. The simple recapture 7 ... bxc6 fails to a combination of ♛h5+ and ♗xc6+.

8	♛e2	♘f6
9	f4	♛xf4
10	♘e5+	c6
11	d4	♛h4+
12	g3	♛h3
13	♗c4	♗e6
14	♗g5	0-0-0
15	0-0-0	♗d6

It may seem remarkable, but all this represents well-known theory. Speelman, though, had been swotting it up the night before, while Timman, in sharp contrast, more or less had to dredge up the variations from his sub-conscious. The best move now is 16 ♕f1 which stems, ironically, from a game by Sax, one of Timman's seconds in London.

16	♘f7	♗xf7
17	♗xf7	♖hf8
18	♗c4	♖de8

Timman's next move is a strategical blunder which reduces the scope of his own bishop on c4. By now, faced with this arcane opening, Timman was running severely short of time.

19	d5	c5
20	♖hf1	♔b8
21	♗f4	♖d8

Speelman's position, with the aggressively posted black queen, and the passed pawn on e4, is excellent. Timman now tries to repeat moves, but to no avail.

22	♗g5	a6

White has to play 23 a4 to restrict the expansion of Black's queenside pawns.

What occurs leads to alarmingly swift disaster.

23	♗xf6	gxf6
24	♕xe4	♕xh2
25	♖h1	♕xg3
26	♖xh7	♖fe8

Suddenly Black's forces are active. White's back rank is exposed and the bishop on e4 is beginning to look like a fat pawn rather than a mobile piece. If now 27 ♕h4 ♕f4+ 28 ♔xf4 ♗xf4+ 29 ♔b1 b5 30 ♗f1 ♖xd5!! 21 ♖b7+ ♔a8! and Black wins, in view of White's inability to protect his back rank. This could have occurred on move 28.

27	♕f5	b5
28	♗f1	♖e1

White's next loses at once, but 29 c3 is hopeless after 29 ... ♗f4+.

29	♕h5	♕f4+
30	♔b1	♕xf1
	0–1	

Verdict ✳✳✳✳

Jerome
(Giuoco Piano)

---

1 e4 e5 2 ♘f3 ♘c6 3 ♗c4 ♗c5 4 ♗xf7+ ♔xf7 5 ♘xe5+

This is totally unsound and should never be tried!

Verdict ✳

K

1 e4 e5 2 f4 ♛h4+ 3 g3 ♛e7
4 fxe5 d6

Bilguer in the 19th Century mentioned 4 ... ♛xe5, which is horrible for Black. My idea was 4 ... d6 5 exd6 ♛xe4+ 6 ♛e2 ♛xe2+ and 7 ... ♗xd6=. I managed to test the viability of the idea in the following game:

Milner-Barry – Keene
Cambridge 1969

1	e4	e5
2	f4	♛h4+
3	g3	♛e7
4	♘c3	d6
5	♘f3	♗g4
6	h3	♗xf3
7	♛xf3	♘f6
8	fxe5	dxe5
9	♗c4	♘c6
10	d3	♘d4
11	♛f2	c6
12	♗e3	♛d7
13	♗xd4	♛xd4
14	♛xd4	exd4
15	♘e2	♗c5
16	0-0	♖f8
17	♖f5	♘d7
18	♖af1	f6
19	♖5f2	♘e5
20	♗b3	♔d7
21	♘f4	♖fe8
22	♘h5	♖e7
23	g4	a5
24	a4	♔c7
25	♘g3	♖ae8
26	♔g2	♖d7
27	♘f5	h6
28	♔g3	♗f8

Black has equalised and the position is drawish, but White now tries too hard to win.

(see following diagram)

29	♔g2	♗c5
30	♘g3	♖de7

31	♘e2	♘g6
32	♔g1	♖d8
33	♖f5	b6
34	♘f4	♘xf4
35	♖5xf4	♗d6
36	♖f5	♗e5
37	♔g2	♖b8
38	h4	♔d6
39	g5	hxg5
40	hxg5	♖h8
41	♖h1	♖xh1
42	♔xh1	g6
43	♖f1	♖h7+
44	♔g1	fxg5
45	♖f8	g4
46	♖g8	♖g7
47	♖xg7	♗xg7
48	♔g2	♗e5
49	♗f7	b5
50	axb5	cxb5
51	♗xg6	0-1

51 ... a4!-+.

Verdict ✳✳✳

This is the kind of weird adventure that many postal players seem to relish, e.g. 3 ... ♕h4+ 4 ♔e2 d5 5 ♘xd5 ♗g4+ 6 ♘f3 ♘c6 7 ♘xc7+ ♔d8 8 ♘xa8 ♘e5 9 h3 ♗xf3+ 10 gxf3 ♕g3 11 d3 ♕xf3+ 12 ♔e1 ♕xh1 13 ♗xf4 ♘f3+ 14 ♔e2 ♗c5 15 c3 '∞' (Estrin). Or 6 ... ♗d6 7 d4 ♘c6 8 c3 0-0-0 9 ♔d3 ♕h6 10 ♔c2± (Sveshnikov). There are obvious affinities with the Steinitz Gambit of the Vienna (qv). However, why not just play 4 ... d6 with the idea of ... ♗g4+, without immediately renouncing the extra material? This may be a stiffer test.

Verdict ✳✳✳

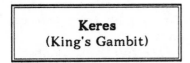

Keres
(King's Gambit)

1 e4 e5 2 f4 exf4 3 ♘c3

Kieseritzky
(King's Gambit)

1 e4 e5 2 f4 exf4 3 ♘f3 g5
4 h4 g4 5 ♘e5

The Kieseritzky, which is regarded by modern masters as the strongest continuation.

**Bronstein - Dubinin
Leningrad 1947**

1	e4	e5
2	f4	exf4
3	♘f3	g5
4	h4	g4
5	♘e5	h5

An old defence. The main line is 5 ♘e5 ♘f6 6 d4 d6 7 ♘d3 ♘xe4 8 ♕e2 ♕e7 9 ♗xf4 ♘c6=.

6	♗c4	♖h7
7	d4	♗h6

Allows White the opportunity of making a familiar combination; but other moves also lead to an advantage for White, according to theory.

8	♘c3	♘c6

(*see following diagram*)

9	♘xf7!	♖xf7
10	♗xf7+	♔xf7
11	♗xf4	♗xf4
12	0-0	♕xh4

13	♖xf4+	♔g7
14	♕d2	d6
15	♖af1	♘d8

Black must try artificial methods in order to develop his queenside or he will be unable to resist.

16	♘d5	♗d7
17	e5	

White embarks on the decisive attack.

17	...	dxe5
18	dxe5	♗c6
19	e6	

Now Black's defensive position falls to pieces.

19	...	♗xd5
20	♖f7+	♘xf7
21	♖xf7+	♔h8

After 21 ... ♔g6 22 ♕d3+ leads to mate.

22	♕c3+	♘f6
23	♖xf6	♕xf6
24	♕xf6+	♔h7
25	♕f5+	1-0

A convincing victory by grandmaster David Bronstein, a great specialist in the open games.

Verdict ✳✳

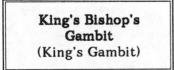

King's Bishop's Gambit
(King's Gambit)

1 e4 e5 2 f4 exf4 3 ♗c4

The King's Bishop Gambit, condemned by Emanuel Lasker, but revived by Bobby Fischer.

J Polgar - G Flear
Hastings 1988/89

1	e4	e5
2	f4	exf4
3	♗c4	♘f6
4	d3	

4 ♕e2 and 4 ♘c3 are more common, although there is scarcely a wealth of material in this variation.

After 4 ♘c3 play can continue 4 ... c6 5 ♗b3 d5 6 exd5 cxd5 7 d4 ♗d6 8 ♘ge2 0-0 9 ♗xf4 ♗xf4 10 ♘xf4 ♖e8+ 11 ♘fe2=.

| | 4 | ... | d5 |

Gives Black a good game

(*Play the King's Gambit* by Estrin and Glaskov) but the authors cite no analysis. Chigorin played 4 ... ♘c6 5 ♗xf4 d5 6 exd5 ♘xd5 in two games, against Alapin, St Petersburg 1881, and against Spielmann, Nuremburg 1906. You see, there is a certain dearth of modern material in this opening.

5	exd5	♘xd5
6	♘f3	♘b6
7	♗b3	♗d6
8	♕e2+!	

Trading queens is the best way to retrieve the f4-pawn.

8	...	♕e7
9	♘c3	♗g4
10	♕xe7+	♔xe7
11	♘e4	

In the long run Black could not avoid White playing ♘e4 or ♘b5 attacking the bishop which defends f4.

11	...	♗xf3
12	gxf3	♘c6
13	♘xd6	cxd6
14	♗xf4	

White has emerged from the opening with a very comfortable position. The split kingside pawns are not important, but the bishop is threatening to become dangerous. Flear hastens to trade one bishop.

14	...	♘d4
15	♔f2	♘xb3
16	axb3	a6
17	♖a5	

Judit has had to part company with one bishop but now she makes imaginative use of the half-open a-file she has gained in compensation. The plan is b4-b5 putting the Black queen's wing under pressure.

17	...	♗d7
18	b4	♖he8
19	c4	♖e6
20	b5	axb5
21	♖xb5	♔c6
22	♖c1	♖a2

Black has defended tenaciously and it is not obvious that he stands much worse. Indeed, he could also have considered doubling rooks by 22 ... ♖ae8. The text, however, looks like a reasonable way to counter-attack against White's queenside. So how should White proceed?

23 ♖b3!!

An incredibly difficult move to find. The point is, White has to play d4 without permitting ... ♘xc4. After the text, due to the threat of d4 - d5, Black's king suddenly finds itself in the firing line. As usual, Judit plays with immense technical sharpness. It is notable that White's possession of a bishop versus Black's knight permits her to mask her weaknesses (split kingside pawns) while highlighting those of her opponent.

23	...	♘d7

Perhaps 23 ... ♘a4!?.

24	d4	♖f6
25	♗g3	b6

To stop d5+ plus c5.

26	♖e1	

Seizing an open file.

26	...	d5
27	cxd5+	♔xd5
28	♖e7	♔c4
29	♖c3+	♔b4
30	♖c2	

Not 30 ♖xd7? ♖xb2+.

30	...	♔b3
31	♖d2	♖a7
32	d5	

Judit now queens her pawn with consummate ease. She has already seen a way to break the blockade of the passed d-pawn. Also good, though less clear, is 32 ♖e3+ ♔b4 33 ♗h4.

	32	...	b5
	33	d6	♖f5
	34	♖d3+	♔c2
	35	♖c3+	

The key. The rook penetrates to c7, when resistance crumbles.

	35	...	♔xb2
	36	♖c7	1-0

This elegant victory deservedly won the best game prize in the Challengers.

Stean - Corden
National Club
Championship 1974

1	e4	e5
2	f4	exf4
3	♗c4	d5
4	♗xd5	♘f6
5	♘c3	♗b4
6	♘f3	0-0
7	0-0	♗xc3
8	dxc3	c6
9	♗b3	♕b6+?

Black must trade queens, though White is still better.

10	♔h1	♘xe4
11	♕e1	♗f5

Loses. 11 ... ♘c5 12 ♗xf4 is much better for White but still a game.

12	♘h4	♖e8
13	♗xf4	

Even the blunder 13 ♘xf5 ♘f2+! is probably good for White after 14 ♕xf2 ♕xf2 15 ♗xf4.

13	...	♘f6
14	♕g3	♗g6
15	♘xg6	hxg6
16	♗xb8!	

16 ♕xg6? ♕xb3!

16	...	♖axb8
17	♖xf6!	gxf6
18	♕xg6+	♔h8
19	♗xf7	♕e3
20	♕xf6+	♔h7
21	♗g6+	1-0

Verdict ✳ ✳ ✳

King Knight's Gambit
(King's Gambit)

---

1 e4 e5 2 f4 exf4 ♘f3

This, the King's Knight's Gambit appears regularly throughout this book. Here we deal with the 'Modern' variation, for other systems consult the index at the back.

**Spassky - Bronstein
Soviet Ch 1960**

1	e4	e5
2	f4	exf4
3	♘f3	d5
4	exd5	♗d6
5	♘c3	♘e7
6	d4	0-0
7	♗d3	♘d7
8	0-0	h6
9	♘e4	♘xd5
10	c4	♘e3
11	♗xe3	fxe3
12	c5	♗e7
13	♗c2	♖e8
14	♕d3	e2

Bronstein could defend conventionally with 14 ... ♘f8 but prefers to throw a spanner into the works of White's attack. The only difficulty is that Spassky ignores him.

15 ♘d6!!

A truly extraordinary concept. Not only does he ignore the attack on his rook, he also hurls a further piece onto the sacrificial bonfire.

15 ... ♘f8

Black has one chance and only one chance to defend. He has to play 15 ... ♗xd6 so as to give his king a flight square at e7. Then comes 16 ♕h7+ ♔f8 17 cxd6 exf1♕+ 18 ♖xf1 cxd6 19 ♕h8+ ♔e7 20 ♖e1+ ♘e5 21 ♕xg7 ♖g8 22 ♕xh6 ♕b6 23 ♔h1 ♗e6 24 dxe5 d5 when White has compensation for his sacrificial material, but no forced win.

16 ♘xf7 exf1♕+

One of the most amazing positions in modern chess. Temporarily Black has a huge material advantage but he must soon give back a bishop in order to be able to defend by ... ♕d7 with gain of time.

17 ♖xf1 ♗f5

The aforementioned propriatory sacrifice of a bishop. If instead 17 ... ♔xf7

18 ♘e5+ ♔g8 19 ♕h7+ ♞xh7
20 ♗b3+ ♔h8 21 ♘g6 mate.

18	♕xf5	♕d7
19	♕f4	♗f6
20	♘3e5	♕e7
21	♗b3	♗xe5
22	♘xe5+	♔h7
23	♕e4+	1-0

As Cafferty points out, the fine finish of this game was adapted for use in the opening scene of the James Bond film *From Russia with Love*.

Verdict ✳ ✳ ✳ ✳

Hartston - Spassky
Hastings 1965

1	e4	e5
2	f4	exf4
3	♘f3	d5

Spassky has probably contributed more than anyone else in the world to the modern theory of the King's Gambit. Leonard Barden suggested that Hartston tackle Spassky with his own weapon. However, I feel that Hartston contributed to the debacle which followed rather more than Barden! Spassky said afterwards that he had seriously considered 3 ... g5 or Fischer's 3 ... d6 .

4	exd5	♘f6
5	♗b5+	

Spassky smashes this. The old line 5 c4 c6 6 d4

cxd5 7 ♗xf4 may revert to favour. A further alternative is 5 ♘c3 ♘xd5 6 ♘xd5 ♕xd5 7 d4 ♗e7! 8 ♗d3 g5 9 ♕e2 ♗f5 10 0-0! Hund - Sternberg, Lucerne Ol 1982.

5	...	c6
6	dxc6	♘xc6

Spassky's opponents in the 'simuls' had done so well with this against him that he had decided to try it for himself. 6 ... bxc6 is usual.

7	d4	

Better than 7 ♘c3.

7	...	♗d6
8	♕e2+	♗e6
9	♘e5	

Not 9 c4 0-0 10 d5 ♗g4!

9	...	0-0

The gambit moment.

10	♗xc6	bxc6
11	♗xf4	

A curious reversal of normal King's Gambit trends. White has the pawn, Black the development.

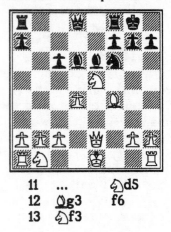

11	...	♘d5
12	♗g3	f6
13	♘f3	

Not 13 ♘xc6 ♗xg3+ 14 hxg3 ♕d6 followed by ... ♖ae8.

13	...	♗xg3+
14	hxg3	♖e8
15	♔f2	♗f5
16	♕c4	♔h8
17	♘c3	♘e3
18	♕c5	♘g4+

Preventing White from getting his second rook on to the h-file.

19	♔g1	♕d7
20	♖f1	

Pointless 20 ♖c1! Spassky shows that even potential World Champions will not refuse a gift pawn or two.

20	...	♗xc2
21	♖h4	♗e3
22	♖c1	g5
23	♖h6	♗g6
24	♘a4	♘g4
25	♖h3	♕e6
26	♕c3	♕xa2
27	♘c5	♖e3
28	♕d2	♖ae8
	0-1	

Verdict ✳✳✳✳✳

King's Gambit Declined
(King's Gambit)

Rubinstein - Hromadka
Mahrich-Ostrau 1923

1	e4	e5
2	f4	

Rubinstein, one of the world's leading experts in the Queen's Gambit, widened his opening repertoire after the First World War so as to include the ancient and stately King's Gambit, with which he obtained many a beautiful win.

2	...	♗c5
3	♘f3	d6
4	♘c3	

Many experts still regard 4 c3 as a stronger continuation that renders the correctness of the defence dubious, e.g. 4 ... ♘f6 5 fxe5 dxe5 6 ♘xe5 ♕e7 7 d4 ♗d6 8 ♘f3 ♘xe4 9 ♗e2 0-0 10 0-0.

4	...	♘f6

Usually 4 ... ♘c6 is played, whereupon Rubinstein, instead of 5 ♗c4 has often played 5 ♗b5 with success. The text move implies a pawn sacrifice which White does best to decline - 5 fxe5 dxe5 6 ♘xe5 0-0! 7 ♘f3 ♘c6 8 d3 ♗g4 9 ♗e2 ♖e8.

5	♗c4	♘c6
6	d3	♗g4

An old continuation which is reckoned inferior.

7	h3	

The most aggressive. A more solid continuation is 7 ♘a4.

7	...	♗xf3
8	♕xf3	♘d4

Svenonius recommends 8 ... exf4, which should indeed be better than the text move.

9 ♕g3

A well-known sacrificial line into which Black cannot venture without disadvantage.

9 ... ♕e7
10 fxe5 dxe5
11 ♔d1

White gives up the right to castle of his own accord, for he has full compensation in the two bishops and the open f-file.

11 ... c6
12 a4! ♖g8?

After this too passive move White obtains a clear advantage - better was 12 ... ♘h5.

13 ♖f1 h6
14 ♘e2 0-0-0
15 ♘xd4 ♗xd4
16 c3 ♗b6
17 a5 ♗c7
18 ♗e3 ♔b8
19 ♔c2 ♔a8

Better chances were offered by 19 ... a6.

20 ♖f3 ♘d5

Black tries to obtain counterplay. In fact, 21 exd5 would be very bad because of 21 ... cxd5 22 ♗a2 e4 23 ♗f4 exf3 24 ♗xc7 ♖c8 with a won position for Black.

21 ♗g1 ♘f4
22 ♕f2 ♗b8
23 g3!

Preparing the following brilliant combination.

23 ... ♘xh3
24 ♖xf7 ♕d6

After 24 ... ♘xf2 25 ♖xe7 ♖gf8 26 ♖f1 White wins easily.

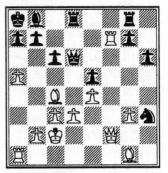

25 ♕b6!

This pretty line, which Rubinstein had planned long beforehand, is the most incisive way of concluding the struggle.

25 ... ♖d7

If Black accepts the queen sacrifice, there follows 25 ... axb6 26 axb6+ ♗a7 27 ♖xa7+ ♔b8 28 ♖fxb7+ ♔c8 29 ♗a6 and wins.

26 ♗c5!

The point of the combination. The black queen cannot move without loss in material.

26 ... ♖xf7
27 ♗xd6 ♖f2+
28 ♕xf2! ♘xf2
29 ♗c5 1-0

Still stronger than 29 ♗xg8 as now White wins a whole piece. Black therefore at once gave up the fight.

A game which, in a most agreeable way, shows the power of combination and the logical method of play of the Polish grandmaster.

Verdict ✳✳✳✳

```
┌─────────────────────────┐
│   King's Indian Attack  │
└─────────────────────────┘
```

Club players and home enthusiasts often ask me to recommend an openings system for White which is safe, yet aggressive and does not require a superb memory and months of intense learning. In such cases I invariably recommend the King's Indian Attack. In this system White's first four or five moves are fixed (1 ♘f3, 2 g3, 3 ♗g2, 4 0-0, 5 d3) and White can develop in isolation without devoting any attention at all to how Black is proceeding. In the middlegame White has plenty of opportunity to unleash an attack based on either c4 or e4, advancing in the centre.

I well remember that one of the first games I saw with this opening (and the game which forms the topic of this analysis) was an impressive struggle between the two Soviet champions Vassily Smyslov and Mikhail Botvinnik, played during the period when they were at the height of their battle for the world chess title, one which dominated the 1950s. I was particularly attracted by the way in which Smyslov whipped up an attack against the black king, commencing with a gambit on the other extremity of the board.

Smyslov – Botvinnik
USSR Championship 1955

1	♘f3	♘f6
2	g3	g6
3	♗g2	♗g7
4	0-0	0-0
5	d3	c5
6	e4	♘c6
7	♘bd2	d6
8	a4	♘e8

Botvinnik prepares a vigorous counter-attack in the f-file, but the safest and best treatment is ... ♖b8 followed by ... a6, shifting the weight of the struggle to the queenside.

9	♘c4	e5
10	c3	f5

Rather too enterprising. Sounder is 10 ... h6 followed by 11 ... ♗e6.

| 11 | b4! |

A well founded sacrifice: the b-file is opened and White diminishes Black's influence in centre by attacking the pawn on c5.

| 11 | ... | cxb4 |
| 12 | cxb4 | fxe4 |

If 12 ... ♘xb4 13 ♕b3! with fierce diagonal pressure towards the black king. The text plans to accept White's offer at a later stage, but 12 ... h6 would still have been a safer alternative.

13	dxe4	♗e6
14	♘e3	♘xb4
15	♖b1	a5
16	♗a3	♘c7
17	♗xb4	axb4
18	♖xb4	♗h6

Botvinnik relies on active defence. He hopes to meet 19 ♖xb7 with 19 ... ♗xe3 20 fxe3 ♘a6 followed by ... ♘c5.

19 ♖b6!

Establishing pressure against Black's d-pawn is more important than capturing the pawn on b7.

19	...	♗xe3
20	fxe3	♗c4
21	♖xd6	♕e8
22	♖e1	

White's material advantage is of little importance, since Black can easily regain his pawn. The chief defect of Black's position is the exposed situation of his king and the lack of coordination between his other pieces. If after 22 ♖e1 ♖xa4 then 23 ♘xe5! ♕xe5 24 ♕xa4 ♕xd6 25 ♕xc4+ and Black is clearly losing. The best chance, in fact, would have been 22 ... ♕xa4 23 ♕xa4 ♖xa4 24 ♘xe5 and although Black is a pawn down he has chances of survival since White's pawns are doubled.

22	...	♖f7
23	♘g5	♖e7
24	♗f1!	♗xf1
25	♖xf1	

Threatening ♕b3+ followed by ♖df6.

| 25 | ... | ♕xa4 |

If 25 ... h6 then 26 ♖ff6! hxg5 27 ♖xg6+ with a winning attack

| 26 | ♖d8+ | ♖e8 |
| 27 | ♕f3! | |

Suddenly, after such a sophisticated and ultra-modern opening, Smyslov has generated a brutal attack along the f-file which might just as well have arisen from a good old King's Gambit.

27 ...   ♛c4
28 ♜d7   1-0

After 28 ... ♜f8 White wins beautifully with 29 ♜xc7 ♛xc7 30 ♛xf8+ ♜xf8 31 ♜xf8+ ♚xf8 32 ♘e6+ leaving White a pawn ahead in the endgame.

In student tournaments I found the King's Indian Attack a most welcome stand-by against opponents who were armed to the teeth with the latest recondite analysis. The nature of the King's Indian Attack is that it throws the players very much on their own intellectual resources, as in the following game.

Keene - Hartston
London 1964

1 e4   c5
2 ♘f3   e6
3 d3

A prime virtue of the King's Indian Attack is its flexibility. One can commence with ♘f3, e4, d3 or even g3 on the first move. Here, for example, the normal Sicilian move is 3

d4 and my opponent seemed much surprised when my d-pawn only travelled one square.

3 ...   ♘c6
4 g3   g6
5 ♗g2   ♗g7
6 0-0   ♘ge7
7 ♘bd2   d6
8 a4   0-0
9 c3   e5
10 ♘c4   f5
11 b4

This gambit is known from and was indeed inspired by the very similar gambit played by Smyslov against Botvinnik in 1955.

11 ...   cxb4
12 cxb4   d5

Inaugurating a fierce counter-action in the centre. Of course, Black cannot play 12 ... ♘xb4 on account of 13 ♛b3 with veiled threats against the black king and direct threats against Black's knight. This sort of resource tends to render White's b-pawn immune from capture in the subsequent course of the game.

13 ♘cd2   fxe4
14 dxe4   dxe4
15 ♘g5   ♘d4

Black concentrates his forces in the central zone, but his position has already been undermined by excessive commitments from his pawns. If instead 15 ...

♘xb4 16 ♕b3+ ♘bd5 17 ♗a3 ♔h8 18 ♗xe4 with decisive pressure.

16	♘gxe4	♘d5
17	b5	♗f5
18	♗a3	♖e8
19	♖c1	♗f8
20	♘d6	

The decisive tactical stroke which nevertheless serves positional ends. White eliminates Black's aggressively posted central pieces and at the same time opens up the vulnerable diagonals towards the black king.

20	...	♗xd6
21	♗xd5+	♗e6
22	♗xe6+	♖xe6
23	♗b2	♖c8

In a desperate situation Black loses material to the pin which now arises in the a2 - g8 diagonal.

24	♗xd4	♖xc1
25	♕xc1	exd4
26	♕c4	♕f6
27	♘e4	1-0

Verdict ✳ ✳ ✳

King's Indian Defence

Black's gambit play in the King's Indian Defence often revolves around a release of energy based on ... b5 or sacrificing a pawn by leaving a knight on d4 to its fate. The following games show these themes in action.

Thorbergsson - Tal
Reykjavik 1964

1	d4	♘f6
2	c4	g6
3	♘c3	♗g7
4	e4	d6
5	f4	0-0
6	♘f3	c5
7	d5	e6
8	♗e2	exd5
9	exd5	

The very sharp 9 e5!? is adequately countered by 9 ... dxe5 10 fxe5 ♘e4 11 cxd5 ♘xc3 12 bxc3 ♗g4!=.

9 ... b5!?

The Benko Gambit idea. After 9 ... b5 10 cxb5 a6 Black will obtain good compensation by combining pressure in the open a- and b-files with the activity of his king's bishop. The move f4 is not very helpful to White in such situations.

Also possible is 9 ... ♖e8

10 0-0!? ♘xe4 11 ♘xe4 ♖xe4 12 ♗d3 ♖e8 13 f5 ♘d7 14 ♘g5 ♕f6 15 fxg6 ♕d4+ 16 ♔h1∞ Kouatly - Arnason, Innsbruck 1977.

10	♘xb5	♘e4
11	0-0	a6
12	♘a3?!	

Feeble. White should return the pawn with 12 ♘c3! ♘xc3 13 bxc3 ♗xc3 14 ♖b1.

12	...	♖a7
13	♗d3	♖e7
14	♘c2	♖fe8
15	♖e1	♘d7
16	♘e3	♘df6
17	♕c2	♘h5
18	g3	♗d4!

An original idea! Black is prepared to exchange his king's bishop in order to increase his control of e3.

19	♘xd4	cxd4
20	♘g2	♘g5!

Une petite combinaison.

21	♖xe7	♘h3+
22	♔f1	♖xe7!

Most players would have recaptured with the queen, but see Tal's 25th.

23	♗d2	♘f6
24	♘h4	♘g4
25	♘f3	♖e3!
26	♔g2	♕e7
27	♖e1	♘xf4+!

(*see following diagram*)

28	gxf4	♖xe1
29	♘xe1	♕h4
30	♗c1	

He has to defend f2.

30	...	♕xe1
31	h3	♘h6

32	f5	♘xf5
33	♗f4	♘h4+
34	♔h2	♘f3+
35	♔g2	♗xh3+!
36	♔xf3	♕g1
37	♗xg6	♕g4+
38	♔f2	♕xf4+
39	♔g1	hxg6
	0-1	

Verdict ✱✱✱

Szabo - Timman
Amsterdam 1975

1	c4	g6
2	♘c3	♗g7
3	d4	d6
4	e4	♘f6
5	f4	c5
6	d5	0-0
7	♘f3	e6
8	♗e2	exd5
9	cxd5	♖e8
10	e5	

A very sharp line. White tries to swamp Black with his centre pawns.

10	...	dxe5
11	fxe5	♘g4
12	♗g5	f6

13	exf6	♗xf6
14	♕d2	♗f5!

The games Forintos - Ghitescu and Forintos - Enklaar, Wijk aan Zee 1974, had continued respectively with 14 ... ♗xg5 and 14 ... ♘e5. In neither case did Black equalise.

15	0-0	♗xg5
16	♕xg5	♘d7

In Peev - Janosevic, Nis 1972, Black lost a tempo by playing at once 16 ... ♘e3 which was met by 17 ♕h6! Now White has to waste a move with his h-pawn to force the desired attacking formation.

17	h3	♘e3
18	♕h6	

White prepares to give up material to get to grips with Black's king.

18	...	♘xf1
19	♘g5	♕e7
20	d6	

After a wild opening Black decides to play for a win. He could instead have drawn with 20 ... ♕g7 21 ♗c4+ ♔h8 22 ♘f7+ etc. That is the drawback of such lines as the Four Pawns Attack. They look hyper-aggressive but can fizzle out to equality against accurate defence.

20	...	♕e3+

The battle flares up again.

21	♔xf1	♘f8
22	♖d1	♖e5
23	d7	♖d8
24	♗c4+	♗e6

All seems well, but Szabo springs a horrid surprise.

25	♘xe6!!	

If now 25 ... ♕xh6 26 ♘xd8+ ♔g7 27 ♘e6+ ♘xe6 28 ♗xe6 and the d-pawn queens. Alternatively 25 ... ♘xe6 26 ♕xe3 ♖xe3 27 ♘d5.

25	...	♖f5+
26	♘f4+	♔h8
27	♘cd5	♕e4
28	♗e2	♘e6
29	♗f3	♕c4+
30	♔g1	♘xf4
31	♘e3	

The end of a remarkable combination. Black cannot protect all of his pieces. Meanwhile, White's d-pawn remains as a terrible threat.

31	...	♕e6
32	♘xf5	♕xf5
33	♖e1	♘e6
34	♗g4	1-0

Verdict ✳ ✳ ✳ ✳

Gheorghiu – Watson
Lloyds Bank Masters 1980

1	d4	♘f6
2	c4	g6
3	♘c3	♗g7
4	e4	0-0
5	♗e3	♘c6

A provocation which White ignores. The conventional move here is 5 ... d6.

6 f3

There is possibly more to be gained from 6 d5 or 6 e5 ♘e8 7 f4 gaining space in the centre.

6	...	e5
7	d5	♘d4
8	♘ge2	

Of course, White sensibly avoids the trap 8 ♗xd4 exd4 9 ♕xd4 ♘xe4! 10 ♕xe4 ♖e8 winning the queen.

8 ... c5

8 ... ♘xe2 would be miserably tame. The text, which entails a gambit, proves that Black is in adventurous mood, the best psychology when a young player is faced with an experienced grandmaster.

9	dxc6	dxc6
10	♘xd4	exd4
11	♗xd4	

11 ♕xd4 ♘d5 is horrible for White, but the move chosen permits Black to develop a fierce initiative at the cost of a piece.

11	...	♘xe4!!
12	♗xg7	

If 12 ♘xe4 ♗xd4 is crushing.

12	...	♕h4+
13	g3	

If 13 ♔e2 ♕f2+ 14 ♔d3 ♘c5+.

13	...	♘xg3
14	♗f6	

A neat trick to deflect the black queen from her menacing post and probably the resource upon which Gheorghiu had relied when he accepted Black's pawn offer. If 14 ♗xf8 ♘xh1+ while 14 hxg3 ♕xg3+ 15 ♔d2 ♖d8+ 16 ♗d3 ♗f5 17 ♘e4 ♗xe4 18 fxe4 ♖xd3+ is a disaster for White.

14 ... ♖e8+

But Black has seen further. Naturally, he is not content with the feeble 14 ... ♕xf6 15 hxg3 when White has survived the attack and will win with his extra piece.

15 ♘e4

Better would be 15 ♗e2 although after 15 ... ♕xf6 16 hxg3 ♕xf3 17 ♖g1 ♕e3 18 ♖g2 ♗h3 Black's attack should still be sufficient to win.

15	...	♖xe4+!
16	fxe4	♕xe4+
17	♔f2	♗g4

(*see following diagram*)
Mobilising his final reserves.

18	♕d3	♘xh1+
19	♔g1	

It looks as if Black's knight is stranded, but Watson has one more surprise for his grandmaster opponent.

19	...	♘f2!
20	♕g3	

If 20 ♕xe4 ♘xe4 wins, while 20 ♔xf2 allows 20 ... ♕f4+ picking up the bishop on f6.

20	...	♘d1
21	h3	♗h5
22	b3	♖e8
23	♖c1	♕e3+
24	♕xe3	♘xe3
25	♗d3	♖e6
26	♗g5	f6
27	♗f4	♔f7
28	b4	a6
29	b5	g5
30	♗b8	♗g6

Two pawns ahead, Black should not experience any difficulty in winning.

31	bxa6	bxa6
32	♗e2	♘c2
33	♔f2	♘d4
34	♗f1	♗h5
35	♖c3	c5
36	♗a7	♖e5
37	♖a3	♗e2
38	♖xa6?	

A blunder which loses a piece. After this White should have resigned.

38	...	♖f5+
39	♔e3	♗xf1
40	♖a5	♘e6
41	♗b8	♗xh3
42	a4	♗g4
	0-1	

A splendidly energetic game by Watson.

Verdict ✳✳✳

Petursson – Gufeld
Hastings 1986

1	d4	♘f6
2	c4	g6
3	♘c3	♗g7
4	e4	d6
5	f3	0-0
6	♗e3	♘c6
7	♕d2	a6
8	0-0-0	

8 ♘ge2 is more usual and flexible. Black's reply 8 ... b5!, a new move, offers a new gambit. If accepted, Black can complete his mobilization speedily and enter a kind of Benko Gambit where White's king is the target.

8	...	b5!

(*see following diagram*)

The gambit moment.

9	cxb5	axb5
10	♗xb5	♘a5
11	♔b1	♗a6

12	♗xa6	♖xa6
13	♕d3	♕a8
14	♘ge2	♖b8
15	♗c1	e6

A logical continuation of the attack. Black prepares to conquer and occupy the c4 square with his knight.

16	h4	d5
17	h5	♘c4
18	hxg6	hxg6
19	b3	c5
20	dxc5	

Now Black could draw with 20 ... ♖xb3+ 21 axb3 ♖a1+ 22 ♔c2 ♖a2+ etc ... but he prefers to gambit a third pawn to prosecute his offensive.

20	...	♘d7
21	exd5	exd5
22	♕xd5	

Not 22 ♘xd5? ♘xc5 23 ♕xc4 ♖xb3+ 24 axb3 ♖a1+ and ♕a2.

22	...	♖xb3+
23	axb3	

White avoids 23 ♔c2? ♖b2+ 24 ♗xb2 ♘e3+ or 23 ♔c2 ♖b2+ 24 ♔d3 ♕xd5+ 25 ♘xd5 ♘de5+ and Black

wins.

23	...	♖a1+
24	♔c2	♖xc1+

The dramatic climax of Black's attack. If now 25 ♔d3 ♕xd5+ 26 ♘xd5 ♘xc5+ and White's king is slaughtered in mid-board. Also if 24 ... ♖xc1+ 25 ♔xc1 ♕a3+. Petursson finds the best defence.

25	♘xc1	♘e3+
26	♔b1	♘xd5
27	♖xd5	♗xc3
28	♖xd7	♕a3
29	♔c2	♕xc5
30	♖hd1	♗f6+
31	♔b1	♕c3
32	♖7d2	♕a1+
33	♔c2	♕c3+
34	♔b1	♕a1+
35	♔c2	♔g7
36	f4	

White is passive but has a fortress set up. Petursson felt that 36 f4 was his best chance. In any case, he is short of other moves and shedding the f-pawn decoys Black's queen from its threats against the white king.

36	...	♛b2+
37	♔d3	♛d4+
38	♔c2	♛b2+
39	♔d3	♛d4+
40	♔c2	♛xf4
41	♔b1	♛g4
42	♖f1	♛e4+
43	♖c2	g5
44	♖f3	g4
45	♖d3	♛e5
46	♖a2	♝g5
47	♖c2	♝f6
48	♖a2	♝g5
49	♖c2	♛f5

Black only has practical chances to win this ending. In what follows he is blocked by resourceful defence at every stage.

50	♖dc3	♛f1
51	g3	♝f6
52	♖c4	♛f3
53	♖f4	♛xg3
54	♖cc4	♛h2
55	♖xg4+	♔h6
56	♖c2	♛e5
57	♖a4	♝g5
58	♖ac4	½-½

Black can no longer make progress.

Verdict ✳✳✳

Gheorghiu – Kavalek
Amsterdam 1969

1	d4	♞f6
2	c4	g6
3	♞c3	♝g7
4	e4	d6
5	f3	0-0

6	♝e3	♞c6
7	♞ge2	♖b8
8	♛d2	♖e8
9	♖d1	a6
10	♞c1	e5
11	dxe5	♞xe5
12	♝e2	

After this game 12 b3 came into fashion!

| 12 | ... | b5! |

This gambit thrust releases all of the energy stored in the Black position.

13	cxb5	axb5
14	♝xb5	

Or 14 ♞xb5 ♞xf3+ 15 gxf3 ♞xe4 16 fxe4 ♛h4+ 17 ♝f2 ♛xe4 with a powerful attack.

| 14 | ... | ♞xe4! |

15	fxe4	♖xb5
16	♞xb5	♞c4
17	♛f2	

17 ♛d3! was White's last chance to make a fight of it.

17	...	♖xe4
18	0-0	♞xe3
19	♛xf7+	♔h8
20	♛xc7	♛xc7

21	♘xc7	♘xd1
22	♖xd1	♗d4+
23	♔f1	♗g4
24	♖d2	♗e3
25	♖c2	♖d4
	0-1	

The three games, Gheorghiu - Watson, Petursson - Gufeld and Gheorghiu - Kavalek form a thematic unity. There are valuable lessons to be drawn from all three games.

Verdict ✳✳✳✳✳

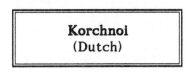

Korchnoi
(Dutch)

1 d4 f5 2 h3

An idea once tried by Viktor Korchnoi, the point being 2 ... ♘f6 3 g4 fxg4 4 hxg4 ♘xg4 5 e4 with fantastic compensation.

Verdict ✳✳✳

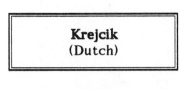

Kotrc-Mieses
(Scandinavian)

1 e4 d5 2 exd5 ♕xd5 3 ♘c3 ♕a5 4 b4

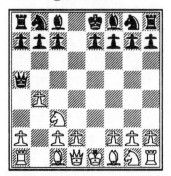

White's intention is 4 ... ♕xb4 5 ♖b1 ♕d6 6 ♘f3 ♘f6 7 d4 a6 8 ♗c4 but after 8 ... e6 Black's position is solid.

Verdict ✳✳

Krejcik
(Dutch)

1 d4 f5 2 g4

Cognate with Korchnoi's Gambit (qv). 2 ... fxg4 3 e4 d6 4 h3 ♘f6 5 ♘c3 e5 6 d5 ♗e7 7 hxg4 ♗xg4 8 f3 ♗c8 9 ♗e3 ♘bd7 10 ♕d2 c5 11 dxc6 bxc6 12 ♗c4 gives White plenty of open lines for the gambit pawn, Piket - Weemaes, Amsterdam 1986. Worth a try.

Verdict ✳ ✳ ✳

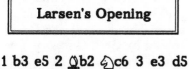

Larsen's Opening

1 b3 e5 2 ♗b2 ♘c6 3 e3 d5
4 ♗b5 ♗d6 5 f4 ♕h4+ 6 g3
♕e7 7 ♘f3 f6 8 ♗xc6+ bxc6
9 fxe5 fxe5 10 ♘xe5 ♘f6

White's plan is to meet
10 ... ♗xe5 with 11 ♕h5+±
but the gambit 10 ... ♘f6
gives Black active play and
superb development, es-
pecially after the further
capture 11 ♘xc6 ♕e4. I
would prefer 8 ♘c3 to the
capture of the gambit
pawn(s). This may prove a
better test.

Verdict ✳✳✳

Latvian

1 e4 e5 2 ♘f3 f5

See Greco.

Lesser Bishop's Gambit
(King's Gambit)

1 e4 e5 2 f4 exf4 3 ♗e2

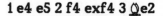

The limited or lesser Bi-
shop's Gambit was intro-
duced by Jaenisch more
than a hundred years ago
and reintroduced by Tartakower at the New York 1924

tournament. It should not give Black much trouble and lacks the vigour of the King's Knight's Gambit.

N Littlewood – Lengyel
Hastings 1963

1	e4	e5
2	f4	exf4
3	♗e2	d5

This is the best reply; there is little point for Black to compromise his kingside position here by ... g5. Also good is 3 ... ♘e7, as Alekhine played against Tartakower in the 1924 Tournament, with the continuation of 4 d4 d5 5 exd5 ♘xd5 6 ♘f3 ♗b4+ 7 c3 ♗e7 8 0-0 0-0 9 c4 ♘e3 with the better game for Black.

4	exd5	♘e7
5	♘f3	

5 d4 would transpose to the Tartakower – Alekhine game, whilst it is Black who has the initiative after 5 c4 c6.

5	...	♘xd5

Black could still have played 5 ... c6! with advantage.

6	♘e2	♗e7
7	0-0	0-0
8	c4	♘f6
9	d4	g5?

Giving White just the chance he is looking for. Instead of weakening his kingside pawn structure in this way he should play 9 ... ♘c6 and if 10 ♗xf4 ♗g4 or if 10 d5 ♘e5 or finally, if 10 ♗xc6 bxc6 11 ♗xf4 ♗g4, in all cases with an excellent game for Black.

10	♘bc3	♔h8
11	b4	♘bd7

Acceptance of the second pawn puts White very much ahead in development after ♗b2 or even ♕b3, followed by ♗b2. One wonders what White would have played after 11 ... g4: would he have played the quiet ♗e4 or would he have gone in for a sort of Muzio by 12 ♘ (or ♗)xf4? Knowing Littlewood, one imagines the second course the more likely.

12	♗b2	♖e8
13	d5	♘e5?

Plausible but nevertheless a mistake as White brilliantly demonstrates. There were two courses that opened up prospects of a better defence: one was by 13 ... ♘f8 and the other with 13 ... h6 14 ♘e4 ♔g7 though admittedly White already had a strong attack.

14	♘e4	♘xe4
15	♗xe4	♗f6

(*see following diagram*)

16	♘xf4!!	

The point of this sacrifice really appears with the further sacrifice on his 18th

move.

16	...	gxf4
17	♕h5	♘g6
18	♖xf4!	♗xb2
19	♖xf7	♗d4+
20	♔h1	♗g7
21	♗xg6	h6
22	♖xg7	♔xg7
23	♗xe8	

White has recovered all his sacrificial material with two pawns as interest.

23	...	♕f6
24	♖e1	♗f5
25	♖f1	♗g6
26	♕d1	♕c3
27	♗xg6	1-0

A true gambit game, by an heroic gambiteer.

Verdict ✻✻

Sadly, in spite of the beautiful game.

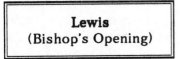

Lewis
(Bishop's Opening)

1 e4 e5 2 ♗c4 ♗c5 3 c3 d5

A good gambit response to 3 c3. After 4 exd5 ♘f6 5 ♗b5+ ♗d7 6 ♗xd7+ ♕xd7 7 c4 c6! Black gets good play; similarly 4 ♗xd5 ♘f6 5 ♕f3 0-0. Here White should consider giving back the pawn with 6 d4 exd4 7 ♗g5 ♗e7 to escape from his constriction.

Verdict ✻✻✻✻

Lisitsin

1 ♘f3 f5 2 e4

A very sharp means of avoiding the Dutch Defence with similarities to From's Gambit against the Bird's Opening.

Rohde – Palatnik
Philadelphia 1990

1	♘f3	f5
2	e4	fxe4
3	♘g5	♘f6

The most commonly played move. Black has a very important alternative in 3 ... d5 which both *ECO* and Botvinnik in his *Modern Chess Theory* article fail to consider.

The point is to meet 4 d3 with 4 ... ♛d6! 5 dxe4 h6. Now after Black has a clear advantage and White has to fight very hard to get the pawn back. Even if he does, Black's development will be much superior.

This evaluation was supported by the game Leski – Akesson, Groningen 1980, which continued: 6 ♘h3 dxe4 7 ♘f4 (7 ♕e2 ♘f6 8 ♘c3 ♘c6 9 ♘xe4 ♛b4+ 10 ♘c3 ♘d4 and Black is better; or 7 ♗f4 ♛xd1+ 8 ♔xd1 c6 with an edge to Black) 7 ... ♛xd1+ 8 ♔xd1 ♗f5 9 ♘d5 ♘a6 10 ♘e3 0-0-0+ 11 ♘d2 e6 12 ♗xa6 bxa6 13 ♔e2 ♘f6 with a slight advantage to Black.

Botvinnik, in his notes to his game with Lisitsin, in the first volume (1923 – 1941) of his best games trilogy published in 1984, gives a similar variation with the same assessment: 4 d3 ♛d6 5 dxe4 h6 6 ♘f3 dxe4 7 ♘fd2 ♘f6 8 ♘c3 ♗f5 9 ♘b5 ♛d7 10 ♘c4 ♛xd1+ 11 ♔xd1 ♘a6. But he also gives the line 3 ... d5 4 d3 ♛d6 5 dxe4 h6 6 ♕h5+ g6 7 ♕h4 ♗g7 8 ♘h3 ♗f6 9 ♕g3 ♛xg3 10 hxg3 dxe4 11 ♘f4 with compensation for the pawn.

Although this looks quite playable for White, he has better in 5 ♘c3! a move that grandmaster Larry Christiansen analysed in the early 1980s in the now defunct *Players Chess News*.

After 5 ♘c3 Christiansen gave:

a) 5 ... h6 6 ♘b5 ♛b4+ 7 c3 ♛xb5 8 ♕h5+ ♔d7 9 ♕g4+ ♔d8 10 ♘f7+ ♔e8 11 ♕g6 or 5 ♘c3 h6 6 ♘b5 ♛g6 7 ♘xe4 dxe4 8 ♘xc7+ ♔d8 9 ♘xa8 with a winning advantage for White in both cases.

b) 5 ... ♘f6 6 dxe4 h6 7 ♘b5 ♛d8 8 e5! hxg5 9 exf6 exf6 10 ♕xd5 with a clear edge to White.

With the "refutation" answered we can now return to the game.

4	d3	e5

Accepting the gambit is foolhardy - 4 ... exd3 5

♗xd3 (The position is exactly the same as From's Gambit: 1 f4 e5 2 fxe5 d6 3 exd6 ♗xd6 4 ♘f3 ♘f6 with the exception that White's knight is already on g5, which spells a quick end for Black) 5 ... g6 (5 ... d5? 6 ♗xh7) 6 h4 (Botvinnik gives 6 ♘xh7 ♖xh7 7 ♗xg6+ ♖f7 8 g4! d5 9 g5 ♘e4 10 ♕h5 ♘d6 [10 ... ♗e6 11 ♗xf7+ ♗xf7 12 g6] 11 ♗xf7+ ♘xf7 12 g6 winning) 6 ... d5 (6 ... e6 7 h5 ♖g8 8 ♘xh7 with a winning game Dorfman – Villareal, Mexico 1977) 7 h5 ♗g4 8 f3 ♗xh5 9 g4 ♕d6 10 gxh5 ♘xh5 11 ♖xh5! ♕g3+ (11 ... gxh5 12 f4 ♕f6 13 ♕xh5+ ♔d7 14 ♘f7 ♖g8 15 ♕xd5+) 12 ♔f1 gxh5 13 f4 ♕h4 14 ♕f3 c6 15 ♘e6 ♔d7 16 ♗f5 ♘h6 17 ♗e3 ♘a6 18 ♘c3 ♘c7 19 ♘c5+ ♔e8 20 ♗f2 ♕f6 21 ♕xh5+ ♕f7 22 ♗d7+) analysis by *King's Pawn* in a 1956 issue of *Chess*.

Besides 4 ... e5 Black has two important alternatives in 4 ... e3 and 4 ... d5. The former is considered in the next game whilst after the latter White gets the edge via 4 ... d5 5 dxe4 h6 6 ♘f3 dxe4 7 ♕xd8+ ♔xd8 8 ♘e5 ♔e8 (8 ... ♗e6 9 ♘c3 ♘bd7 10 ♗f4 c6 11 0-0-0 ♔e8 12 ♘xd7 ♗xd7 13 ♗c4 ♗f5 14 h3 g5 15 ♗e5 ♗g7 16 g4 ♗g6 17 ♖he1 and White is better

in Sergievyky – Chistyakov USSR 1964) 9 ♗c4 e6 10 ♘g6 ♖g8 11 ♘xf8 ♖xf8 12 ♘c3 as in Podzielny – Castro, Dortmund 1977.

5   dxe4   ♗c5

On 5 ... c6, intending to meet 6 ♗c4 with 6 ... d5, White has the choice between 6 ♘c3 and 6 f4!?.

6   ♗c4   ♕e7

7   ♗f7+!

The inaugural game in this variation Lisitsin – Botvinnik, saw 7 ♘c3 ♗xf2+ 8 ♔xf2 ♕c5+ 9 ♔g3 ♕xc4 10 ♖f1 0-0 11 ♖xf6! gxf6 12 ♕h5 ♖f7 13 ♘xf7 ♕xf7 14 ♕g4+ ♔h8 15 ♘d5 ♘a6 16 ♕h4 d6 17 ♗h6 ♗e6 18 ♕xf6+ with equal success.

7   ...   ♔f8
8   ♗b3   h6
9   ♘f3   d6

On 9 ... ♘xe4 Botvinnik gives 10 ♕e2! ♗xf2+ (10 ... ♘xf2 11 ♘xe5!) 11 ♔f1 d5 12 ♗xd5 ♘f6 13 ♘xe5! winning.

10   ♘c3   g5?!

The first move out of theory, but this novelty by

the grandmaster from Odessa doesn't look like it was the product of home analysis. Previously 10 ... g6 was seen when 11 0-0 ♔g7 12 ♔h1?! ♘c6 gave Black good play in Pithart - Alster, Marianske Lazne 1956. More logical is Botvinnik's 10 ... g6 11 ♕e2 ♔g7 12 ♗e3 preserving the possibility of castling queenside.

11	h4!	g4
12	♘h2	♗b4?!

Losing more critical time. The rest can pass without comment.

13	f3	♗xc3+
14	bxc3	♕g7
15	fxg4	♔e8
16	0-0	♘c6
17	g5	hxg5
18	♗xg5	♘xe4
19	♗f7+	1-0

Gligoric - Kostic
Yugoslav Ch. 1951

1	♘f3	f5
2	e4	fxe4
3	♘g5	♘f6
4	d3	e3
5	♗xe3	e5
6	d4	e4

Gligoric points out in his notes to this game that the correct answer to 6 ... exd4 is not 7 ♗xd4 as Botvinnik claims, but 7♕xd4.

After 6 ... exd4 7 ♗xd4 ♘c6 8 ♗c4 d5 (8 ... ♗b4+ 9 ♘c3 d5 10 ♕e2+ ♕e7 11 ♗b5

♕xe2+ 12 ♔xe2 0-0 and Black is fine, from Lechtynsky - Knaak, Tallin 1979) 9 ♗xf6 ♕xf6 10 ♕xd5 ♘e5 11 ♘e4 ♕f4 12 ♘bd2 White is better. But 6 ... exd4 7 ♗xd4 ♘c6 8 ♗c4 d5 9 ♗xf6 ♕xf6 10 ♕xd5 ♘b4 11 ♕f7+ ♕xf7 12 ♗xf7+ ♔e7 13 ♗b3 ♗f5 gives the second player active play for the pawn.

Instead, 7 ♕xd4 ♗e7 (7 ... ♘c6 8 ♕h4 ♗e7 9 ♗d3) 8 ♘c3 ♘c6 9 ♕d2 followed by 0-0-0 with pressure down the queen's file gives White the edge (Gligoric).

7	f3	

Botvinnik quotes Voitsikh - Kopasovskaya, Moscow Women's Ch. 1969, which continued 7 ♘xe4 ♘xe4 8 ♕h5+ g6 9 ♕e5+ ♕e7 10 ♕xh8 ♘f6 11 ♗e2 and White has the edge. Gligoric rejected 7 ♘xe4 because of 7 ... ♘xe4 8 ♕h5+ g6 9 ♕e5+ ♕e7 10 ♕xh8 ♘f6 11 ♗d3 ♘c6 12 0-0 ♔f7 13 ♗g5 ♗g7 14 ♗xf6 ♕xf6 15 ♕xh7 d5 16 ♘c3 ♗e6 17 ♖ae1 ♘xd4. However, as David Levy points out in *Gligoric's Best Games 1945 - 1970*, Game 14, White has a simple answer with 18 ♖xe6.

7	...	exf3
8	♕xf3	d5
9	♗d3	♗g4
10	♕f2	♗d6
11	h3	♗h5

Better was 11 ... ♗d7 to

keep control of e6.

| 12 | 0-0 | ♕e7 |
| 13 | ♘c3 | c6? |

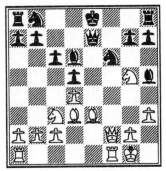

Essential was 13 ... ♘c6 followed by castling as soon as possible.

14	♖ae1	0-0
15	♗f4	♕d7
16	♗xd6	♕xd6
17	♘xh7!	♖f7
18	♘xf6+	♖xf6
19	♕h4	♖h6
20	♕xh5	1-0

Black never got going in this game, which was a powerful and thematic victory for the gambiteer.

Rohde - Castro
Philadelphia 1990

1	♘f3	f5
2	e4	fxe4
3	♘g5	e5

ECO (Romanishin) gives this as Black's best try.

| 4 | d4!? | |

The gambit moment; this is a new move which seeks to exploit White's lead in development. Previously 4 ♘xe4 and 4 d3 had been seen.

After 4 d3 Botvinnik gives 4 ... e3 5 ♗xe3 ♘c6 6 c4! ♘f6 7 ♘c3 ♗e7 8 ♗e2 0-0 9 0-0 d6 and now either 10 f4 or d4 with a slight advantage. Romanishin prefers 6 g3 ♘f6 7 ♗g2 d5 8 c4 dxc4 9 ♕a4 with unclear play.

4	...	exd4
5	♘xe4	♘c6
6	♗c4	♘f6

On 6 ... d5 White has 7 ♕h5+ g6 8 ♕xd5 ♕xd5 9 ♗xd5 ♘b4 10 ♗b3 with a clear advantage thanks to his better development and strongly placed bishop on b3.

7	♗g5	♗e7
8	♘xf6+	♗xf6
9	♕h5+	g6
10	♕e2+	♗e7
11	♗d5	♖f8
12	h4	♖f5
13	♗xc6	dxc6
14	♘d2	h6
15	g4	♖f7
16	h5	

| 16 | ... | ♛d5? |

Necessary was 16 ... gxh5 17 ♗xh6 ♗xg4 18 f3 ♛d5 and Black is okay.

17	♘e4	hxg5
18	hxg6	♖f4
19	♖h8+	♚d7
20	f3	b6
21	g7	♗b7
22	0-0-0	c5
23	♖e1	♛f7
24	♘g3	♛xg7??

Black had to try 24 ... ♗xf3 when 25 ♛xe7+ ♛xe7 26 ♖xe7+ ♚xe7 27 ♖xa8 ♗d5 28 g8♛ ♗xg8 29 ♖xg8 ♖xg4 leaves White a piece up for three pawns. Unquestionably White can do better but Black had to try this.

| 25 | ♛e6+ | 1-0 |

Verdict ✳ ✳ ✳ ✳ ✳

```
Lockock
(Philidor)
```

1 e4 e5 2 ♘f3 d6 3 d4 ♘f6 4 ♘g5 h6 5 ♘xf7

White definitely gets a promising attack after 5 ... ♚xf7 6 dxe5 but 4 ... ♗e7 or 4 ... exd4 5 ♗c4 d5! makes nonsense of this line.

Verdict ✳ ✳

```
Lolli
(Two Knights)
```

1 e4 e5 2 ♘f3 ♘c6 3 ♗c4 ♘f6 4 ♘g5 d5 5 exd5 ♘xd5 6 d4

The immediate recapture 5 ... ♘xd5 has always suffered from a poor reputation, because of all White's existing sacrificial tries, but things may not be so clear, e.g. 6 ... ♗b4+ (not 6 ... exd4 7 0-0 ♗e6 8 ♖e1± Euwe) 7 c3 ♗e7 8 ♘xf7 ♔xf7 9 ♕f3 ♗e6 10 ♕e4 b5 11 ♗xb5 ♗b7 12 f4 g6! 13 fxe5 ♖f8 14 ♕g4+ ♖f5 15 ♗d3 ♘xd4. Now best is 16 cxd4 ♘b4 17 ♗xf5+ gxf5∞. Instead 16 ♖f1 led to disaster after 16 ... ♘e3!! 17 ♗xe3 ♘f3+ 18 gxf3 ♕d3 19 ♕d4 ♗h4+ 20 ♕xh4 ♕xe3+ 0-1 Kalvach - Putina, corr. 1986.

An absolutely fascinating line, in which Black's succeeds in wrenching the gambit prerogative from White. This may well point the finger to future major developments in the Two Knights!

Verdict ✳✳✳✳

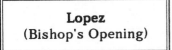

Lopez
(Bishop's Opening)

1 e4 e5 2 ♗c4 ♗c5 3 ♕e2
This is officially designated a 'gambit' by the sacred texts, but, as *The Oxford Companion* points out, 3 ♕e2 does not make a true gambit. "Lopez's idea, apart from the incidental threat of ♗xf7+ and ♕c4+,

is that White should soon continue with f4, instituting a kind of King's Gambit Declined."

The next game, a classic of its genre, shows these ideas in operation.

**De La Bourdonnais -
McDonnell
1st Match, London 1834**

1	e4	e5
2	♗c4	♗c5
3	♕e2	♘f6
4	d3	

4 ♗xf7+ ♔xf7 5 ♕c4+ d5 would be more than useless for White.

4	...	♘c6
5	c3	♘e7
6	f4	

Here is the Deferred King's Gambit, cited in the preamble.

6	...	exf4
7	d4	♗b6
8	♗xf4	

The Frenchman has constructed a powerful pawn

centre but over his next few moves he vacillates, losing time and thus enabling Black to set up severe counter-pressure, in particular in the semi-open e-file against White's pawn on e4.

8	...	d6
9	♗d3	♘g6
10	♗e3	0-0
11	h3	♖e8
12	♘d2	♛e7
13	0-0-0	c5
14	♔b1	cxd4
15	cxd4	a5

The ambitious career of this pawn should be watched. Ultimately it provides one of the main devices in encircling the white king.

16	♘gf3	♗d7
17	g4	

Faced with Black's attack on the queen's wing, White feels that he must undertake something himself. The text heralds an offensive in the g-file which, judged by White's concentration of forces in that sector after move 32, comes perilously close to success.

17	...	h6
18	♖dg1	a4
19	g5	hxg5
20	♗xg5	a3
21	b3	♗c6
22	♖g4	♗a5
23	h4	♗xd2
24	♘xd2	♖a5

25	h5	♖xg5

To quote Tartakower and Du Mont, this sacrifice, which completely alters the picture, is both compulsory and compelling. It proves, by the way, that Black's lateral development of his rook was both an offensive as well as a defensive measure.

26	♖xg5	♘f4
27	♛f3	♘xd3
28	d5	

If instead 28 ♛xd3 ♘xe4 wins.

28	...	♘xd5

If now 29 ♖xd5 ♗xd5 30 exd5 ♛e5 31 ♘c4 ♛c3-+.

29	♖hg1	♘c3+
30	♔a1	

Or 30 ♔c2 ♛xg5 31 ♖xg5 ♘e1+ winning.

30	...	♗xe4
31	♖xg7+	♔h8
32	♛g3	

White threatens mate in two either by 33 ♖g8+ or 33 ♖h7+.

32	...	♗g6
33	hxg6	♛e1+

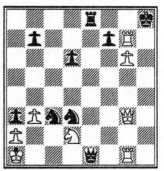

A queen sacrifice leading to a most original finish whereby White's entombed monarch cannot avoid a deadly knight check on c2. But White should refuse this offer.

34 ♖xe1

White misses a brilliant chance to justify his own attacking schemes, but to do this he must spurn Black's offer of the queen by means of 34 ♘b1 ♔xg7 35 gxf7+ ♕xg3 36 fxe8♘+ (a rare but effacious example of an underpromotion being necessary) followed by 37 ♖xg3 when White wins. Alternatively, 34 ♘b1 ♕xg3 35 ♖h7+ ♔g8 36 gxf7+ ♔xh7 37 ♖h1+ ♔g7 38 fxe8♕ and White wins.

34	...	♖xe1+
35	♕xe1	♘xe1
36	♖h7+	♔g8
37	gxf7+	♔xh7
38	f8♘+	♔h6
39	♘b1	♘c2+

Imaginative chess at its very best.

0–1

Verdict ✳✳✳✳

Lopez Counter-Gambit
(Philidor)

---

1 e4 e5 2 ♘f3 d6 3 ♗c4 f5

This is not a true gambit unless White plays 4 d4 transposing to Philidor's Counter-Gambit (qv). In other cases, Black obtains excellent play, e.g. 4 ♗xg8 ♖xg8 5 d3 ♘c6 6 ♗g5 ♗e7 or 4 d3 ♘f6 5 ♗g5 h6 6 ♗xf6 ♕xf6. Grandmaster Tony Kosten, the acknowledged expert on the Philidor, favours Black's chances in both cases.

Verdict ✳✳✳

Lopez-Gianutio Counter-Gambit
(King's Bishop's Gambit)

---

1 e4 e5 2 f4 exf4 3 ♗c4 f5

This gambit looks like total nonsense since it weakens the a2-g8 diagonal on which White is basing his attack. However, the move 3 ... f5 is quite well

founded in that after 4 exf5
♘f6 Black will play the
liberating move ... d5 with
gain of time against White's
king's bishop, and also opening up the possibility of
playing ... ♗f5 advantageo-
usly.

Verdict ✶✶✶

McDonnell
(King's Gambit)

**1 e4 e5 2 f4 exf4 3 ♘f3 g5
4 ♗c4 g4 5 ♘c3**

Here White's opening represents one of the most rudimentary attempts to assail the traditional weakness at f7.

McDonnell –
De la Bourdonnais
London 1834

1	e4	e5
2	f4	exf4
3	♘f3	g5
4	♗c4	g4

Black continues in chivalrous fashion as was the custom of the day.

5 ♘c3

McDonnell's speciality, in place of the normal 5 0-0, see the Muzio.

**5 ... gxf3
6 0-0**

McDonnell also favoured 6 ♕xf3, as in game 54 of his series with De la Bourdonnais: 6 ... ♗h6 7 d4 ♘c6 8 0-0 ♘xd4? 9 ♗xf7+ ♔xf7 10 ♕h5+ ♔g7 11 ♗xf4 ♗xf4 12 ♖xf4 ♘f6 13 ♕g5+ ♔f7 14 ♖af1. Black has devoured too much and now stands to lose.

6 ... c6?

Somewhat of an irrelevancy. He should have tried to consolidate with 6 ... d6 followed by ... ♗e6.

**7 ♕xf3 ♕f6
8 e5**

From now on it's sacrifice (and accept it!) all the way.

**8 ... ♕xe5
9 ♗xf7+**

The hallowed irruption.

9 ... ♔xf7

10 d4

Speedy mobilisation is essential with White two pieces in arrears (by move 10!).

	10	...	♛xd4+
	11	♗e3	♛g7
	12	♗xf4	♞f6
	13	♞e4	♗e7
	14	♗g5	♖g8
	15	♛h5+	♛g6
	16	♞d6+!	

16 ... ♚e6?

This rash advance is tantamount to suicide, but the lure of another sacrifice seems to exert magnetic power over the black king. It was, however, high time to reverse his previous policy of maximum risk and seek security with 16 ... ♚f8 17 ♗h6+ ♖g7 18 ♗xg7+ ♚xg7 19 ♛e5 ♗xd6 20 ♛xd6. Black has three minor pieces for a rook but the threat of ♖ae1 is painful. But it could not have been worse than the move chosen.

17 ♖ae1+! ♚xd6

Black's peripatetic mo-narch is doomed, e.g. 17 ... ♚d5 18 c4+ ♚c5 19 ♗e3+ ♚b4 20 ♛c5+ ♚a4 21 b3+.

18 ♗f4+ 1-0

Maroczy – Chigorin
Vienna 1903

	1	e4	e5
	2	f4	exf4
	3	♞f3	g5
	4	♗c4	g4
	5	♞c3	gxf3
	6	♛xf3	d6
	7	d4	♗e6
	8	♞d5	c6

Having already devoured one piece this looks too greedy. Black should now attend to the matter of his development.

	9	0-0	cxd5
	10	exd5	♗f5
	11	♗xf4	♗g6
	12	♗b5+	♞d7

In spite of being two pieces ahead Black has just one piece in action. Meanwhile, the white army is fully mobilised and ready to invade.

	13	♖ae1+	♗e7
	14	♗xd6	♚f8
	15	♖xe7	♞xe7
	16	♖e1	♚g7
	17	♗xe7	♛a5
	18	♛e2	♞f6

Maroczy's next move is the decisive blow. Black cannot capture, since he would be checkmated by ♛e5.

19	♗xf6+	♔g8
20	♕e5	h6
21	♗xh8	f6
22	♕e7	♔xh8
23	♕xf6+	♔g8
	1-0	

After the reply 24 ♖e7 Black is helpless. After this crushing defeat Chigorin, nevertheless, went on to emerge as victor of the tournament.

Verdict ✳✳✳

McDonnell Single and Double Gambits
(Bishop's Opening)

---

1 e4 e5 2 ♗c4 ♗c5 3 b4 ♗xb4

A combination of the Evans Gambit, with overtones of the King's Gambit, these gambits are really too ambitious. White's praiseworthy effort to introduce a new gambit in the subsequent game is

punished in horrific fashion. Note that the loser, Rev. G. A. McDonnell (1830-1899) is not to be confused with the inventor, Alexander McDonnell (1798-1835).

McDonnell - Boden
London 1865

1	e4	e5
2	♗c4	♗c5
3	b4	♗xb4
4	c3	

After 4 f4 (McDonnell's Double Gambit) Black ought to parry with 4 ... d5 5 exd5 e4 6 ♘e2 ♘f6. This was tried in 1834 and no-one has felt it necessary to repeat it since then!

4	...	♗c5
5	d4	exd4
6	cxd4	♗b4+
7	♔f1	♗a5
8	♕h5	

This looks alarming but is in fact inferior to 8 ♗xf7+ ♔xf7 9 ♕h5+ g6 10 ♕xa5 when Black's king has been dislodged.

8	...	d5
9	♗xd5	♕e7
10	♗a3	♘f6

Black's position had appeared critical but this counter-attack is a complete answer. Hereafter Black takes the lead in decisive fashion.

11	♗xf7+	♕xf7
12	♕xa5	♘c6
13	♕a4	♘xe4
14	♘f3	♗d7
15	♘bd2	♘xd2+
16	♘xd2	0-0-0
17	♖b1	♕d5

White's position is completely disorganised but the punishment meted out is more dramatic than one would normally expect.

18	♘f3	♗f5
19	♖d1	♖he8
20	♗c5	♕xf3

A break-up sacrifice of the queen.

| 21 | gxf3 | ♗h3+ |
| 22 | ♔g1 | ♖e6 |

Threatening a fatal check on g6.

23 ♕c2

Watching the fateful g6-square and preparing to sacrifice his queen there should Black play ... ♖g6+.

23 ... ♖xd4

(*see following diagram*)

But this diabolical machination puts an end to all White's vain resistance.

24 ♗xd4

If 24 ♖xd4 ♖e1+; or 24 ♖b1 ♘e5 25 ♖b3 ♖d1+ 26 ♕xd1 ♖g6+.

24 ... ♘xd4

0-1

White is unable to control all three key points at the same moment namely g6, f3 and e1. Thus if 25 ♖xd4 ♖e1+ or if 25 ♕d3 ♖g6+ 26 ♕xg6 ♘e2+. A brilliant denouement.

Verdict ✳✳

Marshall Attack
(Ruy Lopez)

---

1 e4 e5 2 ♘f3 ♘c6 3 ♗b5 a6 4 ♗a4 ♘f6 5 0-0 ♗e7 6 ♖e1 b5 7 ♗b3 0-0 8 c3 d5

Possibly the most famous of all gambits, it was introduced in a famous game by Frank Marshall against Capablanca no less. Although Marshall lost that game his invention has survived - probably more books and articles have been devoted to this than any other gambit.

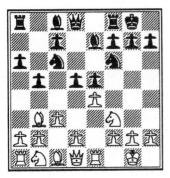

Ivanchuk – Adams
Terrassa 1991

1	e4	e5
2	♘f3	♘c6
3	♗b5	a6
4	♗a4	♘f6
5	0-0	♗e7
6	♖e1	b5
7	♗b3	0-0
8	c3	d5

Frank Marshall's famous gambit, designed to seize the initiative at an early stage. It is also a favourite of Ivanchuk and therefore required some courage on Michael's part to employ it. Alternatively it was very cunning psychology.

9	exd5	♘xd5
10	♘xe5	♘xe5
11	♖xe5	c6
12	d4	♗d6

An important branching of ways.

13 ♖e1

This is the usual move, but also possible is:

13 ♖e2 as used in Kamsky – Ivanchuk, Linares 1991. That game continued 13 ... ♗g4 14 f3 ♗h5 (14 ... ♗f5 was less successful in Georgiev – Nikolic, Wijk aan Zee 1988. After 15 ♗xd5 cxd5 16 ♘d2 ♕d3 17 ♖f2 ♕c7 18 g3 ♖ae8 19 ♘f1 ♗g6 20 ♘e3 White went on to win in 39 moves.) 15 ♗xd5 cxd5 16 ♘d2 f5 17 ♕b3 ♗f7 18 ♘f1 f4 (The point is to deprive White's minor pieces of egress squares on e3 or g3.) 19 ♗d2 ♕d7 20 ♖ae1 a5 21 a3 a4 (Having established his domination of the king's flank Ivanchuk now sets up a parallel grip on the opposite wing.) 22 ♕d1 ♗g6 23 ♗c1 ♖f7 24 h3 ♗f5 25 ♘h2 h5 26 ♖f2 ♖af8 27 ♘f1 ♖f6 28 ♘h2 ♔h8 29 b3 (Black's position looks impressive but the White set-up is also solid and he does have an extra pawn. It is quite

understandable that Kamsky is looking for some active counterplay but if he was to do nothing it is doubtful that Black could achieve more than a draw.) 29 ... ♖c8 30 ♗b2 ♔h7 31 ♘f1 ♖ff8 32 ♖fe2 ♖c7 33 ♘h2 ♖fc8 34 ♘f1 (An incautious move, played in the belief that Black can undertake nothing. But there is a surprise in store.) 34 ... b4!! (A remarkable breakthrough. White has two ways to capture but if 35 cxb4 ♗c2 followed by ... axb3 gives Black a giant passed pawn.) 35 axb4 a3 36 ♗xa3 (If 36 ♗a1 ♖xc3 37 ♗xc3 ♖xc3 with ... ♗xb4 to follow gives Black immense compensation for the sacrificed exchange. Now White is two pawns up but his position is a wreck.) 36 ... ♖xc3 37 ♔h2 ♖a8 38 ♗b2 ♖d3 39 ♕c1 (If White tries to alleviate the pressure by exchanges with 39 ♖d2 then 39 ... ♗xb4 40 ♖xd3 ♗xe1 traps White's rook on d3.) 39 ... ♖c8 40 ♖c2 ♖xc2 41 ♕xc2 ♗g6 42 ♕f2 ♗xb4 43 ♖e5 ♖d1 44 ♕e2 ♖b1 45 ♖g5 ♕c6 46 ♖e5 ♕c2 47 ♖xh5+ (With White's forces trapped behind their own lines Kamsky goes for a desperate perpetual check.) 47 ... ♔g8 48 ♕e6+ ♗f7 (The spectacular refutatation of White's last

ditch tactics. Every white piece is now under attack.) 49 ♖h8+ ♔xh8 50 ♕xf7 ♕c6 (By stopping any threat of a draw by perpetual check Ivanchuk forces an easy win.) 51 ♗c3 ♗xc3 52 ♕f8+ ♔h7 53 ♕f5+ ♕g6 0-1.

Now we return to the main game.

13	...	♕h4
14	g3	♕h3
15	♗e3	

Timman - Ivanchuk from Linares 1991 diverged with 15 ♖e4 and ended in a highly unclear draw after 15 ... g5 16 ♕f3 ♗f5 17 ♗xd5 cxd5 18 ♖e3 ♗e4 19 ♖xe4 dxe4 20 ♕f6 ♕g4 21 ♘d2 ♖ae8 22 ♘f1 ♗e7 23 ♕xa6 f5 24 ♕xb5 f4 ½-½. Michael himself recently suffered after 15 ♖e4, e.g. 15 ... ♕d7 16 ♘d2 f5 17 ♖e1 f4 18 ♘e4 ♕h3 19 ♕e2 ♗g4 20 ♕f1 ♕h5 21 ♗d1 ♗xd1 22 ♖xd1 fxg3 23 hxg3 ♖xf2 24 ♔xf2 ♖f8+ 25 ♔g2 ♖xf1 26 ♖xf1 ♕e2+ 27 ♘f2 ♗xg3 28 a4 b4 29 cxb4 ♗xf2 30 ♖xf2 ♕g4+ 31 ♔h2 ♕xd4 32 ♔g2 ♘xb4 33 ♗d2 ♘d3 34 ♖ff1 ♕g4+ 35 ♔h1 h5 36 ♗c3 h4 37 ♖ad1 ♘f2+ 38 ♖xf2 ♕xd1+ 39 ♔h2 ♕xa4 40 ♖g2 ♕f4+ 0-1 Adams - I Sokolov, Wijk aan Zee 1991. This reverse may have encouraged Michael to adopt the gambit himself.

| 15 | ... | ♗g4 |
| 16 | ♕d3 | |

To meet 16 ... ♘f3 with 17 ♕f1.

16	...	♖ae8
17	♘d2	♕h5

The latest try for Black. A recent example of the older attempt is: 17 ... f5 18 ♕f1 ♕h5 19 f4 ♔h8 20 ♗xd5 cxd5 21 ♕g2 g5 22 ♕xd5 ♖d8 23 ♕c6 gxf4 24 ♗xf4 ♗xf4 25 gxf4 ♗e2 26 ♔h1 ♖de8 27 ♖g1 ♕h4 28 ♕g2 ♖g8 29 ♕c6 ♖gf8 30 ♕g2 ♖g8 31 ♕c6 ½–½ A Sokolov - Nunn, Rotterdam 1989. The alternative 17 ... ♖e6 is considered in the next game.

18	♘f1	♖e6
19	♗d1	f5
20	♗xg4	♕xg4
21	♘d2	♖g6
22	♔g2	f4
23	f3	♕h5
24	g4	♕h4
25	♖e2?	

Walking directly into an ambush. His idea is clear, to prepare doubling rooks in the e-file by the manoeuvre ♗e1 - f2. This would have the effect of driving away the black queen and adding to the defences of the white king. However, Ivanchuk has overlooked an unpleasant shot. White would like to play 25 ♖e4 but this allows 25 ... ♖xg4+ 26 fxg4 f3+ 27 ♔h1 ♕h3 or 25 h3 but this allows ... ♖h6. Since White, in spite of his extra pawn, has no natural consolidating move available it must be concluded that his position is already rather difficult.

25	...	♖xg4+!

This temporary sacrifice has the effect of exposing White's king and makes it virtually impossible for him to survive in the practical struggle.

26	fxg4	f3+
27	♔h1	fxe2
28	♕xe2	♔h8
29	♔g1	h6
30	♕g2	♗f4
31	♗e1	♕g5
32	h3	♕g6
33	♖d1	♗b8

It is very impressive over the last few moves how Adams has played such a controlled waiting game. He cannot break through with a direct attack but it soon becomes clear that White's position evinces targets both on the queenside as well as the king's.

34	♖d2	♕b1

35 ♗f2   ♔g8

A very subtle move. White is so tied up that he is almost in *zugzwang*, i.e. any move that he makes will lead to a further deterioration of his position.

36 b3

Hoping for 36 ... ♘xc3 37 ♕xc6 but Adams arranges this capture with tempo.

36 ...   ♗f4
37 ♖e2   ♘xc3
38 ♖e6   ♕xa2
39 ♖xc6   ♕xb3
40 ♖xa6   ♘e2+
41 ♔h1   ♗b8
42 ♗e1   ♕d1
    0-1

The only way to drag on his somewhat hopeless resistance would be by 43 ♖a1 ♕xa1 44 ♕xe2 but even in that case 44 ... ♖xf1+ 45 ♕xf1 ♗g3 nets a clear piece. Alternatively 43 ♖a1 ♕xa1 44 ♕xe2 ♕xd4 is also quite sufficient to persuade White to resign.

Verdict ✳✳✳✳

**Short - Pinter
Rotterdam 1988**

1 e4   e5
2 ♘f3   ♘c6
3 ♗b5   a6
4 ♗a4   ♘f6
5 0-0   ♗e7
6 ♖e1   b5
7 ♗b3   0-0

8 c3   d5
9 exd5   ♘xd5
10 ♘xe5   ♘xe5
11 ♖xe5   c6
12 d4   ♗d6
13 ♖e1   ♕h4
14 g3   ♕h3
15 ♗e3   ♗g4
16 ♕d3   ♖ae8
17 ♘d2   ♖e6
18 a4   bxa4

An alternative is 18 ... ♕h5 19 axb5 axb5 20 ♗d1 ♗xd1 21 ♖axd1 f5 22 ♘f1 f4 23 ♗c1 ♖ef6 24 ♕e4 ♔h8 25 ♕d3 h6 26 b3 b4 27 cxb4 fxg3 28 fxg3 ♗xb4 29 ♘d2 ♖f2 30 h4 ♘c3 0-1 Hellers - I Sokolov, Haninge 1989.

19 ♖xa4   f5
20 ♕f1   ♕h5
21 f4

A well-known postion from the Marshall gambit. Black is happy to sacrifice pawns for an attack on the kingside. It is a variation which John Nunn has studied in depth, though mainly from Black's point of view.

21	...	♖b8
22	♗xd5	cxd5
23	♖xa6	♖be8
24	♕b5!	

The new move which casts doubt on Black's entire system, and an improvement on 24 ♕f2 g5 after which White went down to defeat in the game Prandstetter - Blatny from the 1986 Championship of Czechoslovakia.

24	...	♕f7
25	h3!	

A key move. If instead 25 ♕xd5 ♖xe3 26 ♕xf7+ ♔xf7 27 ♖xe3 ♖xe3 28 ♖xd6 ♖e1+ 29 ♔f2 ♖e2+ winning a piece. Alternatively, if 29 ♘f1 ♗h3. The point of White's 25th move is to deflect the black bishop either from its control of e2 or its ability to go to h3.

25	...	♗h5

If 25 ... ♗xh3 26 ♕xd5 ♖xe3 27 ♕xf7+ ♔xf7 28 ♖xe3 ♖xe3 29 ♖xd6 ♖e1+ 30 ♔f2 and Black is helpless since he cannot play ... ♖e2+. Pinter decides instead to retain control of e2 with his bishop.

26	♕xd5	♗xf4

This is absolute desperation, but if 26 ... ♖xe3 27 ♕xf7+ ♔xf7 28 ♖xe3 ♖xe3 29 ♖xd6 ♖e1+ 30 ♘f1 ♗e2 31 ♔f2 and White emerges on top.

27	♖xe6	♖xe6

28	♘f1	

Not of course 28 gxf4?? ♖g6+ winning the White's queen.

28	...	♗xg3

Quite hopeless, but any other move would simply leave him two pawns down for quite inadequate compensation.

29	♘xg3	f4
30	♕xh5	♖g6
31	♔h2	1-0

del Campo - Pein
Mexico City 1991

1	e4	e5
2	♘f3	♘c6
3	♗b5	a6
4	♗a4	♘f6
5	0-0	♗e7
6	♖e1	b5
7	♗b3	0-0
8	a4	

The Anti-Marshall; White discourages Black from sacrificing a pawn with ... d5.

8	...	b4

Now 9 d3 is the solid line.

9	c3	d5!?

Since a4 and play down the a-file is White's normal plan in the positions arising after 9 c3 d5, it occurred to Pein that the insertion of a4 b4 might help Black.

10	exd5	e4

The Herman Steiner Variation, discredited in the

normal position without a4 b4. Pein had suddenly realised a significant difference - see move 15.

11	dxc6	exf3
12	d4	fxg2
13	♗g5	

13 ♕f3 is the book refutation but now 13 ... ♗e6 hits the bishop. The answer to ... ♗e6 in the main line is simply ♗f4.

13	...	♘d5

13 ... ♗g4 and 14 ... ♖e8 are also possible.

14	♗xe7	♘xe7
15	♕f3	♗e6

Without a4 and ... b4 this is pointless but now it gains time.

16	♘d2	♖b8
17	♗xe6	

White wants to avoid this but if 17 ♖b1 ♖b6!

17	...	fxe6
18	♕g4	bxc3
19	bxc3	

19 ♕xe6+ ♔h8 20 ♕xe7 cxd2 is good for Black.

19	...	♘g6
20	♘c4	

If 20 ♕xg2 ♖b2 21 ♖ad1 ♘h4 22 ♕ moves exd2!? If here 21 ♘f3 ♘f4 and ... ♕f6.

20	...	♘f4
21	♖e4	h5
22	♕f3	

22 ♕g3 h4 and h3.

22	...	♕h4
23	♖ae1	g5

This wins.

24	♕e3	

24 ♕g3 ♘h3+ 25 ♔xg2 ♘xf2+ 26 ♔h1 ♕xe4 mate.

24	...	♘h3+
25	♔xg2	♖xf2+
26	♔h1	♖xh2+

Decisive.

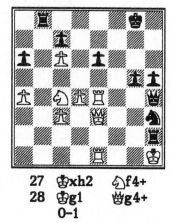

27	♔xh2	♘f4+
28	♔g1	♕g4+
0-1		

Verdict ✳✳✳

Mikenas
(Benoni - Modern)

---

1 d4 ♘f6 2 c4 c5 3 d5 e6 4 ♘c3 exd5 5 cxd5 d6 6 e4 g6 7 f4 ♗g7 8 e5

The Mikenas Gambit can be deadly if Black does not know how to respond, e.g. 8 ... dxe5 9 fxe5 ♘fd7 10 e6!±. However, in the main line White is exposed to the danger of overextending his centre.

Taylor – Donnelly
British Correspondence
Championship 1990

1	d4	♘f6
2	c4	c5
3	d5	e6
4	♘c3	exd5
5	cxd5	d6
6	e4	g6
7	f4	♗g7
8	e5	♘fd7
9	♘b5	dxe5
10	♘d6+	♔e7
11	♘b5!?	

This is a complex and as yet barely explored alternative to the more often seen 11 ♘xc8+.

After 11 ♘xc8+ ♛xc8 12 ♘f3 ♖e8 13 ♗c4 ♘b6!! 14 d6+ ♔f8 15 ♗b5 e4! 16 ♘g5 h6 17 ♗xe8 ♛xe8 18 ♘h3 e3! is ∓.

| 11 | ... | ♖e8! |

Although allowing the following knight fork, this seems to be the best solution towards a co-ordinated development of the black pieces.

| 12 | d6+ | ♔f8 |
| 13 | ♘c7 | |

| 13 | ... | exf4+ |
| 14 | ♗e2 | |

An intended improvement over 14 ♘xe8 ♛xe8+ 15 ♗e2 ♘e5 16 ♗xf4 ♘bc6 17 ♘f3 ♘xf3+ 18 gxf3 ♗xb2! (clearer than the known 18 ... ♗h3 19 d7!? ♗xd7 20 ♛d6+ and 21 0-0-0) 19 ♔f2 ♘d4+ 20 ♔g3 ♛e6! with advantage for Black, as in Taylor – Garside, BCCC Candidates 1989–90.

| 14 | ... | ♘c6 |
| 15 | ♘f3 | |

If 15 ♘xe8 ♛xe8 16 ♘f3 transposes back into the game continuation. In his book *The Benoni for the Tournament Player*, John Nunn points outs that 15 ♘xa8 is critical for an assessment of this line since it nets a whole rook and the knight can escape to c7 with a gain of tempo. The reply Black had prepared was 15 ... ♘d4 (intending to play ... ♛f6 and ... ♛xd6, eventually picking up the knight on a8) 16 ♘c7

♖e4 with ... ♘f6 and ... ♕xd6 to follow. Although Black has just three pawns for the rook, the white king remains stuck in the centre and open to attack, whilst both white rooks will remain as spectators for some time.

15 ... ♘d4
16 ♘xe8
If 16 ♘xd4 ♗xd4 17 ♗xf4 ♘e5 18 ♘xa8 ♕xd6 19 ♕d2 ♗f5 followed by ... ♖xa8.

16 ... ♕xe8
17 ♘xd4 ♗xd4
18 ♗xf4 ♘e5
19 a4?!
A clever effort to complicate the position further. After the orthodox developing move 19 ♕d2 ♗f5 (threat 20 ... ♘d3+) 20 0-0-0 ♖d8, Black equalises the material and has the better prospects.

19 ... ♗f5
Less clear is 19 ... ♗xb2 20 0-0! ♗d4+ 21 ♔h1 ♗f5 22 ♖a3 ♕e6 23 ♗h6+ ♔g8 24 ♖g3 with h4 to follow, generating some play.

20 ♗b5 ♕e6
Not 20 ... ♘f3+ 21 ♔f1 winning, nor 20 ... ♘d3+ 21 ♔f1 ♕e4 22 ♗h6+ ♔g8 23 ♗xd3 ♕xd3+ 24 ♕xd3 ♗xd3+ 25 ♔e1 ♗xb2 26 ♖d1 c4 27 ♗g5, which is unclear.

21 ♔f1
Now forced since 21 ♕e2 ♗g4 22 ♕e4 f5 23 ♕xb7 ♘d3+ leads to mate, or if 21 ♗xe5 ♕xe5+ 22 ♔e2 ♗xb2 or 22 ♕xd6 with advantage.

21 ... ♗xb2
Both 21 ... ♖d8 and 21 ... a6 were feasible here, but each lets White generate play, e.g. 21 ... ♖d8 22 ♗xe5 ♕xe5 23 ♕e2 ♗xb2 24 ♖d1 or 21 ... a6 22 ♗e2 ♗xb2 23 ♖b1! ♗xb1 24 ♕xb1 ♗d4 25 ♕xb7.

22 h3!
Another resourceful move in a difficult position. The text controls g4 and allows the king a flight a flight square on h2. Now 22 ... ♗xa1 allows 23 ♕xa1 f6 24 g4 (24 d7 is also possible) 24 ... ♗e4 25 ♖h2 with the idea of g5 and ♖f2.

22 ... c4!
This seems the most effective counter, sealing the fate of the bishop on b5. As before, both 22 ... a6 and 22 ... ♖d8 lead to very obscure positions.

23 d7
If 23 ♗xe5 ♗d3+ 24 ♔g1 ♕xe5 25 ♖a2 ♗d4+ wins, or 23 ♖a2 ♗d3+ 24 ♔g1 (24 ♔e1 ♗c3+ 25 ♗d2 ♘g4+ mates) 24 ... ♗d4+ 25 ♔h2 a6 26 ♗xc4 ♕xc4 27 ♖d2 ♗c3 retains the extra material.

23 ... ♗d3+
24 ♔f2
If 24 ♔g1 a6 25 ♗g5 f6 26 ♗xc4 ♕xc4 27 ♗xf6 ♕d4+ 28 ♔h2 ♕f4+ 29 ♔g1 ♗d4

mate.

24	...	a6
25	♖e1!	

A worthy last ditch effort.

25	...	axb5
26	axb5	

So that if 26 ... ♗xa1 27 ♕xa1!! and White wins after all.

(a) 27 ... ♖d8 28 ♖xe5;

(b) 27 ... ♖xa1 28 d8♕+;

(c) 27 ... ♕b6+ 28 ♔g3 ♖xa1 29 ♖xe5 ♖a8 30 ♗h6+ and 31 ♖e8+ mating.

However, Black's next finally brings this complex game to a definite conclusion.

26	...	♕b6+

White resigned, for if 27 ♔g3 (27 ♗e3 ♕f6+), Black can now play 27 ... ♖xa1 (having guarded d8) with an easy win.

0-1

A fascinating and theoretically important game. I am indebted to the winner's superb notes in *Pergamon Chess Magazine* for the above comments.

Verdict ✳ ✳ ✳ ✳

> **Milner–Barry**
> (French Defence)

1 e4 e6 2 d4 d5 3 e5 c5 4 c3 ♘c6 5 ♘f3 ♕b6 6 ♗d3 cxd4 7 cxd4 ♗d7 8 0-0 ♘xd4 9 ♘xd4 ♕xd4

One of the sharpest lines against the French, popular in postal play. After 10 ♘c3 there are two possibilities: 10 ... ♕xe5 11 ♖e1 ♕b8 12 ♘xd5 ♗d6 13 ♕g4 ♔f8 14 ♗d2 h5 15 ♕h3 ♗c6 16 ♘e3 ♘f6 17 ♗c3. Alternatively, 10 ... a6 11 ♕e2 ♘e7 12 ♔h1 ♘c6 13 f4 ♘b4 14 ♖d1 ♘xd3 15 ♖xd3 ♕b6 16 ♗e3 ♗c5 17 ♗xc5 ♕xc5. Here White can either play the immediate 18 ♖ad1 planning f5 or 18 f5 (met by 18 ... d4) or even 18 ♕g4. These positions should appeal to lovers of gambit play.

Verdict ✳✳✳

```
┌─────────────────────────────┐
│                             │
│      Modern Defence         │
│                             │
└─────────────────────────────┘
```

The Modern Defence, like most hypermodern openings, is not generally associated with gambit play. One interesting idea is the following.

Hodgson - Norwood
British Ch 1989

1	e4	g6
2	d4	♗g7
3	c3	d6
4	f4	♘f6
5	♗d3	0-0
6	♘f3	c5
7	dxc5	♘bd7!?

This is an idea of mine. I first employed it in the 1972 Skopje Olympiad against Orestes Rodriguez of Peru. Black has sufficient compensation for the pawn.

8	cxd6	exd6
9	0-0	♘c5
10	♕c2	♖e8
11	♘bd2	

Up to this point the players have been following the Lau - Hodgson, Wijk aan Zee II 1989, which continued 11 ... ♘xd3 12 ♕xd3 ♘xe4 13 ♘xe4 ♗f5 14 ♕xd6 ♖xe4 15 ♕xd8+ ♖xd8

16 ♔f2 b5 17 a3 a5 ½-½. Julian's intended improvement on this was to play on in the final position as White, for he believes that White has chances to exploit his extra pawn.

| 11 | ... | ♗d7! |

Much stronger than 11 ... ♘xd3. White has no constructive moves, so why resolve the position?

12	♘d4	♖c8
13	♔h1	♕e7
14	f5	♘fxe4
15	♗xe4	♘xe4
16	fxg6	hxg6
17	♘xe4	♕xe4
18	♕b3	♗e6
19	♘xe6	♖xe6
20	♗f4	

Black has regained the pawn, all his pieces are active, and his queen beautifully centralised. Nevertheless, White has no real weaknesses and threatens to equalise with ♖ad1 and ♕d5. Norwood finds an excellent manoeuvre to keep the initiative.

20	...	♖c5!
21	♗g3	♖f5
22	♖xf5	gxf5
23	♕d1	♗e5
24	♗xe5!?	

A courageous decision and typical of Julian's style. He saw that it was possible to bail out into an ending with 24 ♕f3 ♕xf3 25 gxf3 ♗xg3 26 ♖g1!). Instead, he chooses a continuation which, while entailing some risk, keeps his own winning chances alive. After all, Black's king might become exposed.

24	...	dxe5
25	♕d2	f4
26	♖e1	♕f5
27	♕d5!	

White takes the centre ground and, in doing so, holds up the pawns. In order to get them going again, Black must bring his king up the board.

27	...	b6
28	h3	♔g7
29	b4	♔g6

Threatening ... e4.

30 ♖e4

Probably necessary, though hardly pleasant. The attempt to give perpetual check fails: 30 ♕d8 f3 31 ♕g8+ ♔f6! and now 32 ♕d8+ ♔g7 or 32 ♕h8+ ♔e7 33 ♕h4+ ♖f6 look good for Black.

30 ... ♔f6

Criticised, but unfairly

so. 30 ... b5!? was suggested in the tournament bulletin. Indeed this would stop White creating the passed pawn on the queenside which later became menacing, but only because Black played inaccurately. Perhaps White should have preferred 29 c4 to exclude this possibility.

Note that 30 ... f3 fails to 31 ♖g4+ ♕xg4 32 hxg4 f2 33 ♕d1 e4 34 g3 e3 35 ♕e2 ♖f6 36 ♕d3+ ♔g7 37 ♔g2.

31 c4!

31 ♕d8+ ♔g7 32 ♕d5 does not lead to a repetition – 32 ... f3! 33 ♖g4+ ♕xg4 34 hxg4 f2 35 ♕d1 ♖h6+.

31	...	f3!
32	♖e1	e4!

The ending is winning for Black after 32 ... e4 33 ♕xf5+ ♔xf5 34 gxf3 e3.

33 ♖f1 ♖e5?

A mistake. After 33 ... ♔g6 Black has excellent winning chances. Both players were now in time trouble.

34	♕d4	♔g6
35	♕g1!	♔f6
36	♕d4	♔g7!
37	c5!	bxc5
38	bxc5	♔h7
39	c6	♖d5
40	♕e3?	

White throws it all away on the last move of the time control. After 40 ♕f2 the position is still unclear but a draw is the likely outcome. e.g. 40 ... ♕f4 41 c7! ♕xc7 42 gxf3 or 40 ♕f2 ♕g5 41 gxf3 (41 c7? ♖d2! 42 c8♕ fxg2+!) 41 ... ♖d2 42 ♖g1! Now Norwood finishes the game with a neat sequence.

40	...	♖d3
41	♕f2	fxg2+
42	♕xg2	♖xh3+
43	♔g1	♕c5+
44	♖f2	♕c1+
45	♕f1	♕g5+
46	♖g2	♕h5
	0-1	

A tremendous struggle.

Verdict ✳ ✳ ✳

Moller
---

1 e4 e5 2 ♘f3 ♘c6 3 ♗c4 ♗c5 4 c3 ♘f6 5 d4 exd4 6 cxd4 ♗b4+ 7 ♘c3 ♘xe4 8 0-0 ♗xc3 9 d5

See Giuoco Piano.

Morra-Smith
(Sicilian)
---

1 e4 c5 2 d4 cxd4 3 c3
The Morra-Smith Gambit promises White a long-term initiative in return for the pawn gambitted on the third move.

Adams - Watson
British Ch 1990

1	e4	c5
2	d4	cxd4
3	c3	

The Morra Gambit, a *rara avis* at Grandmaster level is a most useful shock weapon against William Watson. Watson eats, breathes, and sleeps the Dragon variation of the Sicilian, hence Adams's choice, wrenching him from his well worn theoretical orbit. The objective merits of the gambit are less clear.

3	...	dxc3
4	♘xc3	♘c6

An interesting way to counter the gambit is 4 ... e6 5 ♘f3 ♗c5!? which turned out successfully in Down - Chandler, Walsall 1992, 6 ♗c4 d6 7 0-0 a6 8 a3 ♘e7 9 b4 ♗a7 10 ♕e2 0-0 11 ♗f4 ♘g6 12 ♗g3 ♘c6 13 ♖fd1 e5 14 ♕d2 ♗g4 15 ♕xd6 ♗xf3 16 gxf3 ♕g5 17 ♕d2 ♕xd2 18

♖xd2 ♘d4 19 ♚g2 ♖ac8 0-1.

    5   **♘f3**   **e6**

The more normal 5 ... d6 is considered in the next game.

    6   **♗c4**   **♘ge7**

    7   **♗g5**   **f6**

    8   **♗e3**

If White plays the over-optimistic 8 ♘b5 hoping for 8 ... fxg5 9 ♘d6 mate, then Black reacts with the immediate 8 ... d5.

    8   **...**   **♘g6**

    9   **0-0**   **♗e7**

    10   **♕e2**   **a6**

This creates a weakness on b6 upon which Adams immediately seizes. The simple 10 ... 0-0 might have been better, meeting 11 ♖fd1 (with the threat of ♗g6+, exploiting the pin on the d-file) with 11 ... d6.

    11   **♘a4**   **♕c7**

Of course not 11 ... b5?? because of 12 ♗b6 trapping Black's queen.

    12   **♘b6**   **♖b8**

    13   **♖ac1**

It is standard procedure where possible to place a rook opposite the opposing queen.

    13   **...**   **0-0**

    14   **♖fd1**   **f5**

Incautiously seeking to seize the initiative when, for his pawn, White's pieces dominate the board. It would be much better to play 14 ... ♚h8 avoiding the

baleful influence of White's king's bishop on c4.

    15   **exf5**   **♖xf5**

    16   **♕d3**

The double attack against the rook on f5 and the pawn on d7 can only be parried by 16 ... d5. In that case, however, White can win brilliantly with 17 ♕xf5 exf5 18 ♘xd5 ♕a5 19 ♗b6 ♕a4 20 ♗b3 (there may well be other solutions) forcing the return of the queen with heavy interest.

    16   **...**   **♚h8**

Even 16 ... ♖xf3 followed by ... ♘ge5 would put up more defence than this.

    17   **♘xd7**   **♗xd7**

    18   **♕xd7**   **♕xd7**

    19   **♖xd7**   **♘f8**

    20   **♖d2**   **♗b4**

    21   **♖e2**   **♖d8**

    22   **a3**

White has an immense advantage based on this bi-shop pair, Black's scattered pieces and the weak pawn on e6. It is hardly possible now for Black to avoid the loss of material.

22	...	♗c5
23	♗xa6	♗xe3
24	♖xe3	bxa6
25	♖xc6	♖b5

If 25 ... ♖d1+ 26 ♖e1 ♖xf3 27 ♖xd1 wins.

26	b4	a5

Black's last hope is to liquidate all the queenside pawns.

27	bxa5	♖xa5
28	g3	

A sensible precaution, often overlooked, ensuring that there are no accidents on the back rank.

28	...	♖dd5
29	♖c8	♔g8
30	♖b3	♔f7
31	♖b7+	♘d7
32	♘e5+	1-0

If 32 ... ♖xe5 33 ♖xd7 ♔g6 34 ♖cc7 and Black loses all his kingside pawns.

Matulovic - Sethi
Yugoslav Ch 1963

1	e4	c5
2	d4	cxd4
3	c3!?	

If accepted, and given correct defence by Black, the Morra Gambit may offer White sufficient positional compensation to hold the balance. Black can also infuse more life into his position, while renouncing the pawn, with 3

... ♘f6 4 e5 ♘d5 5 ♗c4 ♕c7 - see Milner-Barry - Stean which follows.

3	...	dxc3
4	♘xc3	♘c6
5	♘f3	d6
6	♗c4	e6

Avoiding the trap 6 ... ♘f6? 7 e5! dxe5 (not 7 ... ♘xe5?? 8 ♘xe5 dxe5 9 ♗xf7+) 8 ♕xd8+ ♘xd8 9 ♘b5 when Black is in desperate trouble.

7	0-0	♘f6
8	♕e2	a6?

A stupid waste of time, preparing to place his queen on an inferior square. Much to be preferred was 8 ... ♗e7 9 ♖d1 e5 10 h3 0-0 with a normal, solid position, although White has some counterchances on the queenside (11 b4!?).

9	♖d1	♕c7
10	♗f4	♘e5
11	♗xe5	dxe5
12	♖ac1	♗d7

If Black seeks to sidestep the coming combination with 12 ... ♕b8 13 ♗b5+! axb5 14 ♘xb5 leads to pretty much the same sort of position as occurs in the game.

13 ♗xe6!

A seemingly inspired sacrifice in that it is launched against a heavily defended square (e6), but its chief point is simply to clear lines for White's rook. If now 13 ... fxe6 14 ♘d5 ♘xd5 15 exd5! (15 ♖xc7 ♘xc7 gives Black too much wood for the queen) 15 ... ♕b6 16 ♘xe5 with a vehement attack. In particular it is impossible to defend adequately against the threats of ♕f3 or ♕h5+. Black could also try 13 ♗xe6 fxe6 14 ♘d5 ♕b8 but I cannot conceive that Black could survive after 15 ♘c7+ and 16 ♘xe5.

13	...	♗xe6
14	♘d5	♕b8

Or 14 ... ♘xd5 15 exd5!.

15	♘c7+	♔e7
16	♕d2	♘e8
17	♘xe6	fxe6

If 17 ... ♔xe6 18 ♕d7+ ♔f6 19 ♕f5+ ♔e7 20 ♖d7+.

18	♕d7+	♔f6
19	♘g5!	

The only way White can proceed is to open further lines for his rooks.

19	...	♔xg5
20	♕xe6	♘f6
21	♕f5+	♔h6
22	♖c3	

From now on the combination is easy to calculate. Black's last chance to complicate matters was with 22 ... g6.

22	...	♕e8
23	♖h3+	♔h5

Or 23 ... ♘h5 24 g4 g6 25 ♕f6! with mate by either ♖xh5 or g5.

24	g4!	♕xh3
25	g5+	♔h5
26	♕xh3+	♔xg5

As so often the defender has been forced to shed his queen in order to beat off the attack. In material terms Black is okay, but his pieces lack co-ordination and the continued vitality of White's queen and rook spell his imminent doom.

27	♕f5+	♔h6
28	♖d3	♘h5
29	♖h3	

The wheel turns again.

29	...	g6
30	♖xh5+	♔g7

Or the pawn epaulette, with 30 ... gxh5 31 ♕f6+.

31	♕xe5+	♔g8
32	♕d5+	♔g7
33	♕xb7+	♔f6
34	e5+	♔e6
35	♕c6+	1-0

Milner-Barry – Stean
Cambridge 1973

1	e4	c5
2	c3	♘f6
3	e5	♘d5
4	d4	cxd4
5	♗c4	♕c7
6	♕e2	♘b6
7	♗d3	♘c6
8	♘f3	g6
9	0-0	

Not 9 cxd4?? ♘xd4!.

9	...	dxc3
10	♘xc3	♗g7
11	♘b5	♕d8

12 ♘d6+! exd6

12 ... ♔f8 is safer.

13 ♗g5! ♘d4!
14 ♘xd4 ♕xg5
15 exd6+ ♔f8
16 ♘b5 ♗f6
17 ♘c7 ♖b8?!

Safer may be 17 ... ♔g7 leaving the useless rook to its fate.

18 ♖fe1 ♔g7
19 ♘e8+ ♖xe8
20 ♕xe8 ♘d5
21 ♖ad1 b5
22 ♗e4 ♘b6
23 h4?

Having played very well so far, White suddenly goes wrong. The unprententious 23 b3! leaves Black well and truly trussed up. The idea behind the text move is to bring a rook to e7 (the immediate 23 ♗f3 fails to 23 ... ♗b7!) but time is not important here.

23 ... ♕xh4
24 ♗f3 ♕c4
25 ♖d2 0-1

Schrentzel - Barash
Ramat Hasharon 1990

1 e4 c5
2 c3 d6
3 d4 ♘f6
4 dxc5 ♘c6

A kind of 'counter' Smith-Morra Gambit!.

5 ♕d3

5 f3 d5!.

5 ... d5

6 exd5 ♘xd5
7 ♕g3 ♗f5

Black gets some play for the gambit.

8 ♘d2 e6
9 ♘gf3 ♗xc5
10 ♕xg7 ♖f8
11 ♘c4 ♗e7!

Idea ... ♗f6, and ... ♘xc3.

12 ♗h6 ♘f6
13 ♖d1 ♕xd1+

The best chance. If 13 ... ♕c7 14 ♕g3.

14 ♔xd1 ♖d8+
15 ♔c1

15 ♗d2 ♖g8 16 ♕h6 ♘g4 17 ♕f4 ♘xf2+ 18 ♔e1 ♘xh1 is unclear.

15 ... ♖g8
16 ♕xg8+ ♘xg8
17 ♗e3 ♘f6
18 ♘ce5

White wants to prevent ... ♘g4 but probably 18 ♗e2 was better.

18 ... ♘d5
19 ♗b5 ♘xc3
0-1

Verdict ✳✳✳

Muzio
(King's Gambit)

1 e4 e5 2 f4 exf4 3 ♘f3 g5 4 ♗c4 g4 5 0-0

One of the most famous names in the mythology of gambit lore is that of Muzio. His variation is the quintessential sacrifice orgy in the King's Gambit. However, according to *The Oxford Companion to Chess*, Muzio was more of a reporter than an inventor.

"Muzio d'Alessandro, who lived in Naples in the early 17th century, told Salvio (qv) that he had seen it played by Geronimo Cascio, a first-class player. Sarratt appears to have misunderstood this and to have made popular the idea that Muzio was the inventor."

**Staunton – Amateur
London 1845**

1	e4	e5
2	f4	exf4
3	♘f3	g5
4	♗c4	g4

Players who feared the Muzio were content to continue with 4 ... ♗g7.

| 5 | 0-0 | |

Clearly White's most

sensible course, aiming to profit from Black's weakness on the f-file, albeit at the cost of a piece. Contemporary theory suggests that it should lead to equality. There are some exotic (and unsound) alternatives: the Ghulam-Kassim Gambit (5 d4); the Lolli Gambit (5 ♗xf7+) and the McDonnell Gambit (5 ♘c3), the last of which is the most respectable of the off-beat deviations at this point.

| 5 | ... | gxf3 |
| 6 | ♕xf3 | ♕f6 |

The thematic starting position in the Muzio. Black's last move is very definitely best since it not only barricades the f-file but also impedes the formation of a white pawn centre with d4. The defects of the defence by 6 ... ♗h6? were shown up vividly in a game Keene - Townsend, London 1961, played at the odds of White's queen's knight 6 ... ♗h6? 7 d4 ♕f6 (too late; Staunton here reckoned the only move was 7 ...♘c6) 8 e5 ♕f5 9 g3 ♕xc2 10 ♗xf7+! ♔xf7 11 ♗xf4 ♗xf4 12 ♕xf4+ ♔g7 13 ♕f7+ ♔h6 14 ♖f5 ♕xf5 15 ♕xf5 ♘c6 and White won rapidly.

7	e5!	♕xe5
8	d3	♗h6
9	♘c3	c6!?

After decades of analysis the main line has finally settled on 9 ... ♘e7 10 ♗d2 ♘bc6 (10 ... 0-0 11 ♖ae1 ♕c5+ 12 ♔h1 ♘g6 13 ♘e4 ♕c6 14 ♕h5 ♔g7 15 ♗c3+ f6 16 ♘xf6 ♖xf6 17 ♖e7+ ♔f8 18 ♕xh6+ ♔xe7 19 ♕g7+ ♔e8 20 ♗xf6, with advantage) 11 ♖ae1 ♕f5 12 ♘d5 ♔d8 13 ♗c3 ♖e8 14 ♕e2 ♕e6 15 ♕f3 ♕f5 16 ♕e2, and the game is equal.

Another way to draw while setting a trap, is 13 ♕e2 ♕e6 14 ♕f3 ♕f5=. The trap is 13 ... b5? (given as strong in *MCO*!) 14 ♘xe7 ♕c5+ 15 ♖f2 ♘xe7 16 ♗c3 ♖e8 17 ♗xf7 ♖f8 18 ♗d4!+-.

10 ♗xf4

A more enduring attack results from 10 ♗d2 e.g: ... ♕d4+ 11 ♔h1 d5 12 ♖ae1+ ♔d8 13 ♘xd5 cxd5 14 ♗c3. Staunton in his analyses always recommended 10 ♗d2 as best here, and it was only against opponents much weaker than himself that he ventured the text move.

10 ... ♕d4+?

In a later game against an amateur (c. 1850) Staunton's opponent played the better 10 ... ♕xf4 with the continuation 11 ♕h5 ♕d4+ 12 ♔h1 d5 (This exposes him to further sacrificial attacks. After 12 ... ♔d8 13 ♕xf7 ♔c7 14 ♖ae1 White may well

control the greater part of the board and recover one piece, but Black's position is so impervious that it is doubtful if White has sufficient compensation) 13 ♕xf7+ ♔d8 14 ♖ae1 ♗d7 15 ♗xd5 cxd5 16 ♘xd5 ♕g7 17 ♕h5 ♕g6 18 ♕h4+ ♔c8 19 ♖f6! ♕g7 20 ♕c4+ ♘c6 21 ♖xc6+ ♗xc6 22 ♖e8+ ♔d7 23 ♖xa8 ♕e5 24 ♕g4+ ♔d6 25 ♖d8+ ♔c5 26 ♕b4+.

11 ♔h1 ♗xf4
12 ♖ae1+ ♘e7

Here 12 ... ♔d8 might provide Black with a more resilient position.

13 ♖e4 ♕g7
14 ♕xf4 d5

The point of Black's defence, but ...

15 ♗xd5! cxd5
16 ♖xe7+!?

Obviously superior was the more materialistic 16 ♘xd5 ♘bc6 17 ♘c7+, with a rook and a strong attack for two pieces.

16 ... ♔xe7
17 ♘xd5+ ♔e6

If 17 ... ♔d7 18 ♕c7+ ♔e6 19 ♘f4+ ♔f5 20 ♘h5+ winning.

18 ♕e4+ ♔d7

After 18 ... ♔d6 19 c4 ♘c6 20 ♖f6+, Black could obtain more than sufficient material compensation with 20 ... ♕xf6, but his king would be horribly exposed.

19 ♕e7+ ♔c6
20 ♕c7+ ♔xd5
21 c4+ ♔d4?

The final error. He had to play 21 ... ♔e6 when White's only line is 21 ... ♔e6 22 d4! (planning 23 d5 mate) 22 ... ♕xd4 23 ♕xf7+ ♔d6 24 ♖f6+ ♕xf6! (24 ... ♔c5 25 ♕e7+ ♔xc4 26 b3+ ♔b5 27 a4+ ♔a5 28 ♕e1+ ♔b4 29 ♕e5+ b5 30 ♕c7+) 25 ♕xf6+ ♔c7 26 ♕xh8 ♘c6 27 ♕xh7+ ♗d7 and White's passed pawns represent an element of great strength in this position.

22 ♕d6+ ♔e3
23 ♕f4+ ♔xd3
24 ♖d1+ ♔c2
25 ♕d2+ 1-0

Verdict ✳✳✳

> **(Double) Muzio**
> (King's Gambit)

1 e4 e5 2 f4 exf4 3 ♘f3 g5 4 ♗c4 g4 5 0-0 gxf3 6 ♕xf3 ♕f6 7 e5 ♕xe5 8 ♗xf7+

Strange as it may seem, this is the best version of the Muzio. After 8 ... ♔xf7 9 d4 ♕f5 (if 9 ... ♕xd4+ 10 ♗e3 ♕f6 11 ♘c3 ♘e7 12 ♘d5 ♘xd5 13 ♕xd5+ ♕e6 14 ♖xf4+ ♔g8 15 ♕g5+ ♕g6 16 ♖xf8+ ♔xf8 17 ♖f1+ and White wins) 10 g4 ♕g6 11 ♗xf4 ♘f6 12 ♗e5 d6 13 ♗xf6 ♗xg4 14 ♕g2 ♖g8 15 ♔h1 ♗f5 16 ♕d5! is ±. A good example of White's chances in the Muzio.

Verdict ✳✳✳✳

> **(Wild) Muzio**
> **(aka Young)**
> (King's Gambit)

1 e4 e5 2 f4 exf4 3 ♘f3 g5 4 ♗c4 g4 5 ♗xf7+ ♔xf7 6 0-0 gxf3 7 ♕xf3

An unreliable version of the Muzio, much less promising, for example, than the Double Muzio.

Verdict ✳✳

Unless you feel in a very adventurous mood!

1 e4 ♘c6 2 d4 d5 3 ♘c3 dxe4 4 d5 ♘e5

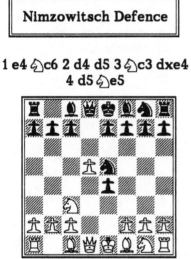

Nimzowitsch's Defence still exerts a lure over natural tacticians. The gambit 3 ♘c3, which invites Black to shut in his queen's bishop with 3 ... e6, leads to challenging play for both sides.

Milner-Barry – Mieses
Margate 1935

1	e4	♘c6
2	d4	d5
3	♘c3	dxe4

4	d5	♘e5
5	f3	

Safer alternatives to this gambit continuation are 5 ♕d4 and 5 ♗f4, e.g. 5 ♗f4 ♘g6 6 ♗g3 a6 7 ♗c4 ♘f6 8 ♕e2 ♗f5 9 0-0-0 (Boleslavsky).

5	...	exf3

Black demonstrates excessive confidence in his ability to defend the resulting position. More circumspect and better would have been 5 ... e3, refusing the poisoned chalice.

I have pointed out so often in this book that ... e3 is frequently the prudent response to an f3-gambit by White.

6	♘xf3	♘xf3+
7	♕xf3	♘f6
8	♗f4	a6

The threat was now 9 ♘b5.

9	h3	g6

If 9 ... ♗f5 10 ♗xc7 ♕xc7 11 ♕xf5 regaining the pawn, though this could hardly have been worse than the text.

10	g4	♗g7

| 11 | 0-0-0 | ♗d7 |

If 11 ... 0-0 12 ♕g3 ♘e8 13 h4 when White gains a huge attack against the black king, much as in the game.

12	♕g3	♖c8
13	♗e2	0-0
14	h4	c6
15	h5	♘xd5
16	hxg6	

White's attack is on the point of crashing through. If now 16 ... hxg6 17 ♕h4 ♖e8 18 ♕h7+ ♔f8 19 ♗h6. Or 16 ... ♘xf4 17 ♕xf4 fxg6 18 ♗c4+ ♔h8 19 ♖xh7+ ♔xh7 20 ♖h1+ ♗h6 21 ♕xh6 mate. In this variation 18 ... e6 is a superior parry to the check but after 19 ♕e3 the threats of ♗xe6+ and ♖xd7 followed by ♗xe6 are impossible to meet.

16	...	♗xc3
17	♕h4	♘f6
18	g5	♕a5
19	gxf6	h5

A last vain effort to check the impetus of the attack.

| 20 | gxf7+ | ♔xf7 |
| 21 | ♗xh5+ | 1-0 |

Verdict ✳✳✳✳✳

Nimzo-Indian Defence

The Nimzo-Indian Defence generally leads to calm positional play, but there are still opportunities for sharp players to introduce gambit ideas.

Shirov - Eingorn
Rilton Cup 1989

1	d4	e6
2	c4	♗b4+
3	♘c3	♘f6
4	f3	

This is a variation which has only recently become fashionable. It can lead to colossal complications, and for that reason if no other, it has become one of Shirov's favourites.

4	...	d5
5	a3	♗e7
6	e4	c5

A gambit which is probably not fully adequate.

7	cxd5	exd5
8	dxc5	♗xc5
9	e5	♘fd7
10	♕xd5	0-0
11	f4	♕b6
12	♘f3	♗f2+
13	♔e2	♘c5

14	b4	♖d8
15	bxc5	♗xc5
16	♕e4	♕b3
17	♗d2	♖xd2+
18	♔xd2	♕b2+
19	♔d3	♕xa1

20 e6

Black must have believed that he was forcing events, the more so since White's king seems ludicrously exposed on d3. Yet now, with his own king in the thick of events, Shirov launches the decisive attack.

20	...	fxe6
21	♘g5	g6
22	♕e5	♗e7
23	♘xe6	♔f7
24	♕g7+	♔e8
25	♘c7+	♔d8
26	♕h8+	♔d7
27	♘xa8	♕xa3
28	♔c2	1-0

Verdict ✳ ✳

**Korchnoi - Karpov
World Ch. Baguio 1978**

1	c4	♘f6

2	♘c3	e6
3	d4	♗b4
4	e3	0-0
5	♗d3	c5
6	d5	b5

Repeating the sharp method adopted earlier in the match. This may not in fact be the best move. The paradoxical 6 ... h6 bypasses the possibility of ♗xh7+ and leaves White with some anxiety about his centre, e.g. 7 e4 exd5 8 exd5 ♗xc3+ 9 bxc3 ♖e8+ 10 ♘e2 d6 and the position is about equal.

7	dxe6	fxe6
8	cxb5	a6

Varying from 8 ... ♗b7 played in the seventh game.

9 ♘ge2

Improving his strategy in the seventh game when he developed this knight on f3.

9	...	d5
10	0-0	e5
11	a3	axb5
12	♗xb5	♗xc3
13	bxc3	♗a6
14	♖b1	♕d6
15	c4	d4
16	♘g3	

By now it was clear that Karpov's handling of the opening had been suspicious to say the least. I would even go so far that Black was already lost. Not only was he a pawn down, but his own centre pawns were immobile and there were a number of weak squares in his camp, such as f4.

16	...	♘c6
17	a4	♘a5
18	♕d3	♕e6
19	exd4	cxd4
20	c5	♖fc8
21	f4	

21 ♗g5 is a good alternative but the text, ripping open lines against Black's insecure kingside, is quite sufficient to win.

21	...	♖xc5
22	♗xa6	♕xa6
23	♕xa6	

Better was 23 ♖b8+ ♔f7 24 ♖b5 displacing Black's king, keeping queens on the board and introducing unpleasant threats. Incredibly, Korchnoi did not even consider this obvious manoeuvre and from now on we witness his decline.

23	...	♖xa6
24	♗a3	♖d5
25	♘f5	♔f7
26	fxe5	♖xe5

27 ♖b5?

This is a blunder which allows Black to complicate things in White's time pressure. Again, the simple course would have been 27 ♘xd4 and White still has good chances to win.

Down in the press room I was beginning to become pessimistic.

27 ... ♘c4

A typical example of Karpov's eel-like skill after earlier unimpressive play. If now 28 ♘d6+ ♖xd6 29 ♖xe5 ♖d7 and the black knight on c4 is forking two pieces.

28	♖b7+	♔e6
29	♘xd4+	♔d5
30	♘f3?	

Better was 30 ♗f8 ♔xd4 31 ♗xg7 ♖ee6 32 ♖f7 ♔e5 33 g4 h6 34 ♖f5+ or 33 ... ♘e3 34 ♖1xf6 ♖xf6 35 g5 and wins. In view of this Black would have to play 31 ... ♘e4, White can then get rook plus pawns for two knights in much more favourable circumstances than the game. All this was proposed by Murey.

30	...	♘xa3
31	♘xe5	♔xe5
32	♖e7+	♔d4
33	♖xg7	♘c4
34	♖f4+	

Better was 34 ♖f7.

| 34 | ... | ♘e4 |
| 35 | ♖d7+ | ♔e3 |

36	♖f3+	♔e2
37	♖xh7	♘cd2
38	♖a3	♖c6
39	♖a1??	

Now the gremlins get at White's position. 39 h4 also lost to 39 ... ♖c1+ 40 ♔h2 ♘f1+ 41 ♔h3 ♘f2+. But simply 39 g4 should draw since after 39 ... ♘f3+ 40 ♖xf3 ♔xf3 41 h4 the ending is still drawn even if Black wins all of the White pawns.

| 39 | ... | ♘f3+! |

Very pretty. It is mate after 40 ♔h1 ♘f2+ or:

40	gxf3	♖g6+
41	♔h1	♘f2+
	0-1	

Verdict ✱✱✱✱

Orang-Utang

Orsini
(King's Gambit)

1 b4 e5 2 ♗b2 f6 3 e4!? ♗xb4

A promising gambit invented by no less than Bobby Fischer. Fischer - Gloger, USA 1964, continued 4 ♗c4 ♘e7 5 ♕h5+ ♘g6 6 f4 exf4 7 ♘f3 with attacking prospects.

Verdict ✳✳✳

1 e4 e5 2 f4 exf4 3 b3

This has utterly vanished; 3 ... ♕h4+ would already be excellent for Black. The lamentable concoctor of this nonsense was one Emilio Orsini (1839-98) who produced the Italian magazine *Nuova Rivisti degli Scacchi* from 1875-1893.

Verdict ✳

P

Paris

**1 g3 e5 2 ♘h3 d5 3 f4 ♗xh3
4 ♗xh3 exf4 5 0-0**

See Amar.

Pernau

1 e4 e5 2 f4 exf4 3 ♘c3

See Keres.

Peruvian
(Queen's Gambit)

**1 d4 d5 2 c4 e6 3 ♘c3 ♘f6
4 ♗g5 c5**

If Black could get away
with this then the Queen's
Gambit would be out of
business. Not surprisingly,
the Peruvian Gambit is, in
fact, considerably less reliable than its near cousin,
the Hennig-Schara (qv).

**Sadler - Donchev
Toulon 1989**

1	d4	♘f6
2	c4	e6
3	♘c3	d5
4	♗g5	c5

A dubious gambit line
liable to succeed only against the unprepared.

5	cxd5	cxd4
6	♕xd4	♗e7
7	e4	♘c6
8	♕d2	exd5

The normal line 8 ...
♘xd5 9 exd5 ♗xg5 10 f4
♗h4+ 11 g3 exd5 12 gxh4
♕xh4+ 13 ♔f2 ♕e7+ 14 ♔e2
♗e6 15 ♘f3 d4 16 ♘b5 0-0 17
f5! (Furman - Dzindzihash-
vili, USSR 1969) casts se-

rious doubt on Black's play. Donchev tries to improve Black's prospects by sacrificing a pawn rather than a piece.

9	♗xf6	♗xf6
10	exd5	♕e7+
11	♘ge2	♘e5
12	0-0-0	♘c4?

An over-optimistic attack which quite underestimates the force of White's riposte. Black had to castle instead.

13	d6!	♕d8
14	♕d5	♗e6
15	♕b5+	♕d7
16	♘d4	♘xd6
17	♘xe6	♘xb5
18	♗xb5	♕xb5
19	♘c7+	1-0

Black loses a piece. A punishing miniature.

Verdict ✳✳

Petroff

1 e4 e5 2 ♘f3 ♘f6

The main Petroff gambits are the Urusov, by transposition after 3 d4 exd4 4 ♗c4, and the Cochrane, 3 ♘xe5 d6 4 ♘xf7 (qv).

Philidor
(King's Gambit)

---

1 e4 e5 2 f4 exf4 3 ♘f3 g5 4 ♗c4 ♗g7 5 h4

Transposes directly to the Greco version of the King's Gambit (qv).

Philidor

---

1 e4 e5 2 ♘f3 d6 3 d4 f5

Philidor's Counter-Gambit bears more than a striking resemblance to the Greco Counter-Gambit (qv) and leads to similarly wild positions. Other Philidor gambits are the Lopez

Counter-Gambit and the Lockock (qv).

Atwood – Wilson
London 1798

1	e4	e5
2	♘f3	d6
3	d4	f5
4	dxe5	

Modern theory prefers 4 ♘c3, although there seems to be nothing wrong with the text.

4	...	fxe4
5	♘g5	d5
6	e6	♘h6
7	♘c3	c6
8	♘gxe4	

A positional sacrifice, which should, if successful, create favourable conditions for the appearance of bona fide combinations.

8	...	dxe4
9	♕h5+	g6
10	♕e5	♖g8
11	♗xh6	

A strong alternative is 11 ♗g5.

11	...	♗xh6
12	♖d1	♕e7

More active is 12 ... ♕g5, as occurred in the celebrated consultation game Staunton and Owen – Morphy and Barnes, London 1858. The continuation was 13 ♕c7 ♗xe6 14 ♕xb7 e3 15 f3 ♕e7 16 ♕xa8 ♔f7. Now White played 17 ♘e4 and lost, but in his notes Staunton later recommended 17 ♖d4! and concluded that White should win. In his book *Morphy's Games of Chess*, P W Sergeant later challenged this verdict, giving 17 ... ♖c8 18 ♗c4 ♗xc4 19 ♖xc4 ♕d7+ – but then comes 20 ♘e4! threatening both ♖b4 and ♕b7 and meeting 20 ... ♘a6? with 21 ♕xc8 ♕xc8 22 ♘d6+.

13	♗c4	b5
14	♗b3	a5

In the style of his time, Wilson neglects development and consolidation (14 ... ♗g7) preferring to defend himself by counter-attack plus threats to gain material.

15	♘xe4	

The introduction to a finely calculated combination whereby Atwood forces a decision in his favour. If now 15 ♘xe4 ♗g7 16 ♘d6+ ♔d8 17 ♕c5 ♘d7 18 ♕xc6 ♖b8 19 ♘xc8 winning or 15 ♘xe4 ♗g7 16 ♘d6+ ♔f8 17 ♕f4+ ♕f6 18 ♘xc8 ♕xf4 19 ♖d8+.

15	...	a4

Consistent with his previous intentions. It seems as if the defender in those bygone days was almost morally obliged to accept every sacrifice offered.

16	♘f6+	♔f8
17	♘xg8	♔xg8
18	♖d8+!	

18 ...   ♕xd8

Or 18 ... ♗f8 19 ♖xf8+
♕xf8 20 e7+ axb3 21 ♕h8+!
♔xh8 22 exf8♕+.

19 e7+   1-0

Tartakower wrote of the
antagonists in this rela-
tively simple game: "Con-
temporaries of Philidor –
who, however, was able to
give them considerable
odds – the contestants are
representative of the best
class of players of their
day."

Verdict ✳✳✳

Pierce
(Vienna)

**1 e4 e5 2 ♘c3 ♘c6 3 f4 exf4
4 ♘f3 g5 5 d4**

This will normally trans-
pose to the Hamppe–Muzio
(qv). One independent line
is: 5 ... g4 6 ♗c4 gxf3 7 0-0
♕g5 8 ♖xf3 ♘xd4 9 ♗xf7+
♔d8 10 ♖f2 ♕g7 11 ♗xf4 ♘e7

12 ♕h5 d6 13 ♗g5 ♘xc2 14
♖af1 ♕e5 15 ♗g8 ♕c5 16 ♔h1
♔d7 17 ♖xf8 ♘g6 18 ♖d8+
♔c6 19 ♗d5+ 1-0 Motwani –
Kula, Berlin 1991.

So, gambit play is still
alive and well, in Berlin at
least!

Verdict ✳✳✳

Poisoned Pawn
(French Winawer)

**1 e4 e6 2 d4 d5 3 ♘c3 ♗b4 4
e5 c5 5 a3 ♗xc3+ 6 bxc3 ♘e7
7 ♕g4 cxd4**

Black offers a gambit of his entire kingside pawn constellation in order to loosen up the position and expose White's king.

Spassky - Korchnoi
Candidates Final,
Belgrade 1977

1	e4	e6
2	d4	d5
3	♘c3	♗b4
4	e5	c5
5	a3	♗xc3+
6	bxc3	♘e7
7	♕g4	cxd4
8	♕xg7	♖g8
9	♕xh7	♕c7

After 9 ... ♕a5, which looks plausible, White can virtually refute the black gambit with 10 ♖b1 ♘bc6 11 ♘f3 ♗d7 12 ♖xb7 Short - Timman, Amsterdam 1988. Alternatively in this line, 10 ... ♕xc3+ 11 ♗d2 ♕c7 12 f4 ♘bc6 13 ♘f3 ♗d7 14 ♘g5, Alexander - Botvinnik, England vs USSR 1946. White won both games.

10	♘e2	♘bc6
11	f4	♗d7
12	♕d3	dxc3

White should now play 13 ♕xc3 0-0-0 14 ♖b1 d4 15 ♕d3 ♘d5 16 g3 f6 17 exf6 ♘xf6 18 ♗g2 e5 19 fxe5 ♘xe5 20 ♕b3 ♗c6 21 ♕e6+±. Nevertheless, although in theory White stands better, this line, where White must

constantly defend against the black initiative, is not for the faint-hearted.

13	♗e3	d4

Korchnoi had specially prepared this sharp line as a psychological weapon. Black seizes the initative at the cost of one or two pawns - extremely uncongenial for Spassky who prefers attack to defence.

14	♗f2	0-0-0
15	♘xd4	♘xd4
16	♕xd4	b6
17	♗h4	♗b5
18	♕e4	♗xf1
19	♖xf1	♖d5
20	♗xe7	♕xe7
21	♖f3	♔b8
22	♔f1	♖d2
23	♖f2	♖gd8
24	♕f3	♖xf2+

Exchanges, in general, help the defender, but in a wide open position they serve to expose the defending king still further.

25	♔xf2	♖d2+
26	♔g3	♕d8
27	♕e4	♕g8+
28	♔h3	♕h8+
29	♔g3	♕g7+
30	♔h3	♖d8

Threatening mate. Now Black's queen and rook develop amazing versatility and hammer White from all directions.

31	g4	♖h8+
32	♔g3	♕h6
33	♕g2	♕h4+

34	♔f3	♖d8
35	♕g3	♕e7

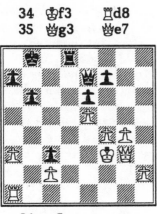

36 g5

A fatal error – after 36 ♖e1 it might be possible for White to hang on by means of a very exact defence.

36	...	♖d2
37	♔g4	♕b7
38	♕xc3	♖g2+
39	♔h3	♖f2
40	♔g4	♕e4
	0-1	

Verdict ✳✳✳

Poisoned Pawn
(Sicilian Najdorf)

---

1 e4 c5 2 ♘f3 d6 3 d4 cxd4 4 ♘xd4 ♘f6 5 ♘c3 a6 6 ♗g5 e6 7 f4 ♕b6 8 ♕d2 ♕xb2

The Poisoned Pawn variation of the Najdorf Sicilian. It was a favourite of Bobby Fischer and one of the most cut-throat variations available. Many erudite volumes have been devoted to its complexity.

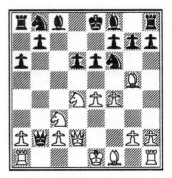

**Ivanchuk – Kasparov
Linares 1990**

1	e4	c5
2	♘f3	d6
3	d4	cxd4
4	♘xd4	♘f6
5	♘c3	a6
6	♗g5	e6
7	f4	♕b6
8	♕d2	♕xb2
9	♖b1	

Also possible is 9 ♘b3, as used by Boris Spassky in his 1972 World Championship match against Bobby Fischer.

9	...	♕a3

Now White can also try 10 e5 or 10 ♗e2 but the text move has been the most fashionable continuation for some time.

10	f5	♘c6
11	fxe6	fxe6
12	♘xc6	bxc6
13	♗e2	♗e7

14	0-0	0-0
15	♖b3	♕c5+
16	♗e3	♕e5
17	♗f4	♕c5+
18	♔h1	

18 ♗e3 would lead to a draw by repetition. However, this would have been quite contrary to the Linares fighting spirit and would also have been an admission that White's opening play lacked bite.

18	...	♘g4
19	h3	

If 19 ♗xg4 then 19 ... e5 regains the piece in view of the f-file pin.

19	...	e5
20	♘a4	♕a7
21	♗c4+	♔h8
22	hxg4	exf4
23	♘b6	d5!

Believe it or not this is Kasparov's improvement on a previous game (Spraggett – A Sokolov, St. John Candidates 1988) where Black had played 23 ... ♖b8 and went on to lose.

24	exd5	cxd5
25	♗xd5	♖b8
26	♘xc8	♖bxc8
27	♖h3	♕b6
28	♖e1	♗g5
29	♖e6	♕d8
30	c4	♖b8
31	♕d3	♗h4
32	♗e4	♕g5
33	♗xh7	

It is difficult to say whose king is the more ex-

posed.

33	...	♖fd8
34	♕c2	f3

This thrust, by ensuring the penetration of Black's rook to d2, gains material.

35	♖xf3	♖d2
36	♕e4	

If 36 ♕f5 ♖d1+ 37 ♔h2 ♕c1 with a devastating attack.

36	...	♖d1+
37	♔h2	♖e1

This wins a bishop. If now Black tries to execute the same attack as in the previous note by means of 37 ... ♕c1 then 38 ♖e8+ ♖xe8 39 ♕xe8+ may well give perpetual check.

38	♕f5	♖xe6
39	♕xe6	♔xh7
40	♕e4+	g6
41	♖h3	

The last chance would be 41 ♖f7+ thought it is by no means clear that this would save the game. After the text though, Black can swiftly evade the checks and White has to recognise that the game is up.

41	...	♔g7
42	♕d4+	♔g8
43	♕e4	♕f6
	0-1	

An extraordinarily difficult game.

Verdict ✳✳✳✳

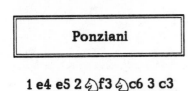

Ponziani

1 e4 e5 2 ♘f3 ♘c6 3 c3

The black gambiteer should rejoice when facing the Ponziani, since it is an open invitation to enter the line 3 ... ♘f6 4 d4 ♘xe4 5 d5 ♗c5!? 6 dxc6 ♗xf2+ 7 ♔e2.

Black now has two possibilities: 7 ... d5 8 cxb7 ♗xb7 9 ♕a4+ c6 10 ♘bd2 f5 11 ♘xe4 fxe4 12 ♔xf4 0-0 13 ♗e3 exf3 meeting 14 gxf3 with ... e4 or 14 g3 with ... ♕c8, planning ... c5 and ... ♗a6 to weaken White's light squares. In Wayte -

Ranken, 1885 Black went on to win. Equally exciting is 7 ... bxc6 8 ♕a4 f5 9 ♘bd2 0-0 10 ♘xe4 fxe4 11 ♕xe4 ♗b6 12 ♔d1 d5 13 ♕xe5 ♗f5!

Verdict ✳✳✳

Pterodactyl

1 e4 g6 2 d4 ♗g7 3 c4 c5 4 ♘f3 d6 5 ♘c3 ♕a5 6 d5 ♗xc3+ 7 bxc3 ♘f6

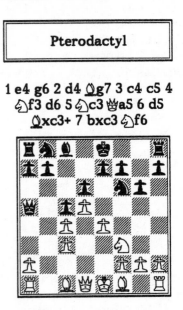

This challenging opening used to be my main Black defence, e.g. 8 ♘d2 ♕xc3 9 ♖b1 ♘xe4 10 ♗b2? ♕xd2+ 11 ♕xd2 ♘xd2 hitting the rook on b1 and winning two safe pawns, Rogers - Keene, Adelaide 1983. However, I ultimately realised that 10 ♖b3! ♕d4 11 ♘xe4 ♕xe4+ 12 ♖e3 with ♗b2 to follow is a dangerous gambit, possibly terminal for Black.

Verdict ✳✳✳✳✳

Q

Quaade

1 e4 e5 2 f4 exf4 3 ♘f3 g5
4 ♘c3

D. L. Quaade, a Dutch-man, was, like Evans, a 19th Century sea captain. He it was who advocated 4 ♘c3. Paul Keres analysed this maritime inspiration thus: 4 ... g4 5 ♘e5 ♕h4+ 6 g3 fxg3 7 ♕xg4 g2+ 8 ♕xh4 gxh1/♕ 9 ♕h5 ♗d6 10 ♕xf7+ ♔d8 11 d4!±.

Stronger is 7 ... ♕xg4! 8 ♘xg4 d5 9 ♗h3 dxe4 10 ♘f6+ ♔d8 11 ♗xc8 ♔xc8 12 ♘fxe4 gxh2 when White's open lines compensate for the gambit pawn.

Verdict ✳✳✳

Queen's Gambit Accepted

The Queen's Gambit Ac-cepted only really becomes a 'real' gambit when White strives for an early e4 and Black meets this in uncom-promising fashion.

Karpov - Ehlvest
Belfort 1988

1	d4	d5
2	c4	dxc4
3	e4	c5
4	d5	♘f6

The Queen's Gambit Acc-epted is a favourite defence of the Estonian Grandmas-ter. He had already used it to defeat Beliavsky in an earlier round from Belfort.

5	♘c3	e6
6	♘f3	exd5
7	e5	♘fd7
8	♗g5	♗e7

9	♗xe7	♛xe7
10	♘xd5	♛d8
11	♗xc4	♘c6
12	0-0	0-0
13	♖e1	♘b6
14	♘xb6	axb6

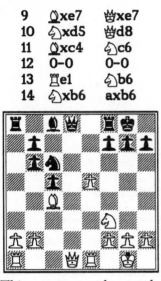

This apparently rather barren situation had arisen once before, in the game Miles – Seirawan, from the GLC/Phillips & Drew, London 1984. There Miles had chosen the insipid continuation 15 ♛e2 when 15 ... ♛e7 16 a3 ♗e6 led to dead equality and an inevitable draw. With his perception of small advantages Karpov now proceeds to demonstrate that the seemingly even less ambitious exchange of queens can yield White some initiative.

15	♛xd8	♘xd8
16	a3	♘c6
17	♖ad1	♗g4
18	e6	♗xe6
19	♗xe6	fxe6
20	♖xe6	♖fd8
21	♖de1	♖d3
22	h3	h6

23	♘e5	♘xe5
24	♖1xe5	♖f8

It gradually becomes clear that Karpov is pinning his hopes of victory on the weakness of the doubled pawns on the b-file.

25	♖xb6	♖d1+
26	♔h2	♖xf2
27	♖e7	♖dd2
28	♖g6	♖f7
29	♖xf7	♔xf7
30	♖b6	♖d7
31	♔g3	♔e7
32	♔f4	♔d8

Ehlvest has survived the first wave of Karpov's attack, but he is still pinned down by the vulnerability of his pawn on b7 and the more active placing of White's rook. In addition, White's king now enters the fray and begins to develop a ferocious activity.

33	♖b5	♖c7
34	♔e5	♔c8
35	♔d5	♔b8
36	g4	♖e7

Karpov is at last able to reap the fruits of his superb positional play, and the coming gain of a pawn proves swiftly decisive.

37	♖xc5	♖e2
38	♖b5	♔c7
39	♖b3	g6
40	♖c3+	♔b6
41	b3	h5
42	♖f3	hxg4
43	hxg4	♔a5

44	♖f7	♖g2
45	♖xb7	♖xg4
46	♔c5	♖g5+
47	♔c6	♔a6
48	b4	1-0

Beliavsky – Tal
Reykjavik World Cup 1988

1	d4	d5
2	c4	dxc4
3	e4	e5
4	♘f3	exd4
5	♗xc4	♗b4+
6	♘bd2	♘c6

Tal does not make a habit of using the Queen's Gambit Accepted. More often he is to be seen on the Black side of the Slav Defence or the Orthodox. Whenever he does accept the gambit he appears to get into difficulties. For example: Timman – Tal, 2nd match game 1985 continued 6 ... ♘c6 7 0-0 ♕f6 8 e5 ♕g6 9 ♘h4 ♕g4 10 ♘df3 ♗e6 11 h3 ♕e4 12 ♗d3 ♕d5 13 ♘g5 instituting a powerful attack. In view of this, it is a mystery why Tal ever becomes involved in this variation.

7	0-0	♘f6
8	e5	♘d5
9	♘b3	♘b6
10	♗g5	♗e7
11	♗xe7	♘xe7
12	♗d3	♗f5
13	♘fxd4	♗xd3
14	♕xd3	0-0

15	♖ad1	♕d5
16	♕e2	♕c4

White has been threatening the dangerous discovered attack 17 ♘f5. With his move Tal invites the trade of queens, but this exchange by no means alleviates all of his problems.

17	♕xc4	♘xc4
18	♖c1	♘xe5
19	♖xc7	♘d5
20	♖xb7	♖fb8
21	♖xb8+	♖xb8
22	♖d1	♘b4

Tal has sacrificed a pawn for active piece play in the endgame, but against Beliavsky's expert consolidation the compensation appears to be not fully adequate.

23	a3	♘bd3
24	♖d2	g5
25	♔f1	♖e8
26	♘a5	f5

This move sets a diabolical trap, worthy of a better fate. If now 26 ... f5 27 ♘xf5 ♘f3 28 ♖xd3 ♖e1+. Alternatively, 26 ... f5 27

♘xf5 ♘f3 28 gxf3 ♖e1+ 29 ♔g2 ♘f4+ 30 ♔g3 ♖g1+ again. After 27 ♘xf5 ♘f3 White's only move to stay on the board is the humiliating retreat 28 ♖d1, which however, leaves the rook exposed to attack after 28 ... ♘xb2. Unfortunately for Tal's brilliant concept, Beliavsky has a relatively easy win by ignoring the sacrifice.

27	b4	f4
28	b5	g4
29	♘ac6	f3
30	gxf3	gxf3
31	♘xf3	♘xf3
32	♖xd3	♘xh2+
33	♔g2	♘g4
34	♘xa7	1-0

Verdict ✳✳✳✳✳

┌─────────────────────────┐
│   **Queen's Gambit**   │
│   **Declined**   │
└─────────────────────────┘

1 d4 d5 2 c4 ♗f5!?

I predict a bright future for this highly unusual and little regarded defence to the Queen's Gambit. White appears to have a promising gambit himself in 3 cxd5 ♗xb1 4 ♖xb1 ♕xd5 5 e3 ♕xa2 6 ♘d3, but Black can strike back with 6 ... e5! a dangerous counter-gambit, e.g. 7 dxe5 ♘c6 with ideas such as ... ♗b4+ or ... 0-0-0 in the air.

Also interesting is the gambit alternative 3 ♕b3 e5!? 4 ♕xb7 ♘d7 5 ♘c3 exd4 6 ♘xd5 ♗d6 7 e4 Miles – Gobet, Geneva 1986. The fact that Shirov, one of the world's strongest grandmasters, is experimenting with 2 ... ♗f5 makes me think it contains plenty of mileage.

Verdict ✳✳✳

┌─────────────────────────┐
│ **Queens Gambit**   │
│   **Declined –**   │
│ **Cambridge Springs**   │
└─────────────────────────┘

Alekhine – Euwe
World Ch., Holland 1935

1	d4	d5
2	c4	e6
3	♘c3	♘f6
4	♘f3	c6
5	♗g5	♘bd7
6	e3	♕a5

The Cambridge Springs variation.

7	cxd5	♘xd5
8	♕d2	

The alternative here is 8 ♕b3 ♗b4 9 ♖c1 e5 and Black has a promising game.

8	...	♘7b6

8 ... ♗b4 9 ♖c1 e5 was tried in Kasparov–Smyslov, 9th match game, Vilnius 1984, but after 10 a3 ♗d6 11 dxe5 Black failed to equalise.

9	♗d3

As will be seen later, this is a gambit to exploit Black's lack of development. Anaemic is 9 ♘xd5 ♕xd2+ 10 ♘xd2 exd5 with equality in Karpov–Kasparov, World Ch., Moscow (47) 1984/85, but safer is 9 ♖c1!.

9	...	♘xc3
10	bxc3	♘d5
11	♖c1	♘xc3
12	0-0	

12 ♖xc3 loses the exchange after 12 ... ♗b4.

12	...	♗b4

13	a3

Continuing his gambit theme in order to bring the black queen within range of attack.

13	...	♕xa3
14	♖a1	♕b3
15	♗c2	♕d5
16	e4	♘xe4
17	♕xb4	♘xg5
18	♘e5	a5
19	♕a3	f6
20	♗g6+	

An interesting and dangerous looking manoeuvre, but Euwe refutes it. It is more difficult for Black to defend after 20 ♗b3 ♕d8 21 ♘c4 ♘f7 22 ♖fe1 when Black must play 22 ... ♖a6 and follow it with 23 ... ♕e7.

20	...	hxg6
21	♘xg6	

Black is now threatened with both ♘xh8 and ♕e7#; he delivers himself away from these threats in a most unusual way.

21	...	♘f3+!
22	♕xf3	♕xf3
23	gxf3	♖h5

Black now has a won game, but Alekhine fights on grimly and, being Alekhine, manages to find possible counter-chances, even in this deplorable position.

24	♘f4	♖f5
25	♘d3	♖xf3
26	♘c5	b6
27	♔g2	♖f4
28	♘b3	e5

29	dxe5	♗e6
30	♘c1	0-0-0
31	exf6	♖g4+
32	♔f3	♖f8
33	♔e3	♖xf6
34	f4	g5
35	♘d3	♗c4
36	f5	♖h4
37	♖ad1	♖xh2
38	♔e4	♖e2+
39	♔f3	♖e8
40	♔g4	♖d8
41	♘e5	

If 41 ♔xg5 ♖fd6 winning the knight.

41	...	♖xd1!

Simpler and more decisive than 41 ... ♗xf1 42 ♖xf1 ♖g8 43 ♘g6 and White wins the g-pawn with possible counter-chances; a highly improbable blunder would then be 43 ... ♖gxg6 44 fxg6 ♖xf1 45 g7 etc.

42	♖xd1	♗e2+
43	♔xg5	♖xf5+
44	♔xf5	♗xd1
45	♘xc6	a4
	0-1	

Verdict ✳✳✳

```
┌─────────────────────┐
│   Queens Gambit     │
│    Declined -       │
│     Orthodox        │
└─────────────────────┘
```

I once tried an obscure gambit in one of the long main lines of the QGD Orthodox. Conventional wisdom indicates the grindy 16 f5 b5 17 ♗b3 b4 18 ♖c5 ♗a6 19 ♖f4± but the gambit led to a remarkably swift knockout!

Keene – Lund
London 1962

1	d4	d5
2	c4	e6
3	♘c3	♘f6
4	♗g5	♘bd7
5	e3	♗e7
6	♘f3	0-0
7	♖c1	c6
8	♗d3	dxc4
9	♗xc4	♘d5
10	♗xe7	♕xe7
11	0-0	♘xc3
12	♖xc3	e5
13	dxe5	♘xe5
14	♘xe5	♕xe5
15	f4!?	♕e4
16	♗d3!?	♕xe3+
17	♔h1	♕e7
18	♕c2	f5
19	♖c5	g6
20	♖e5	♕f6
21	♗c4+	♔g7
22	♖fe1	b5
23	♗b3	h5
24	♖e7+	♔h6
25	♕c5	a5
26	♖c7	♖d8
27	♖ee7	♖h8
28	♖f7	♕xb2

Black even gobbles the traditional poisoned pawn.

29	♕f8+	1-0

Verdict ✳✳✳

Queens Gambit Declined – Slav and Semi-Slav

The Slav and Semi-Slav, despite their rather solid names, often lead to extremely sharp positions.

van Wely – van der Sterren
Dutch Ch 1991

1	d4	d5
2	♘f3	♘f6
3	c4	dxc4
4	♘c3	c6
5	e4	b5
6	e5	♘d5
7	a4	e6
8	♘g5?!	h6
9	♘ge4	b4
10	♘b1	♗a6
11	♘bd2	♘f4!

11 ... c3 12 ♘c4.

12	♕g4	♘d3+
13	♗xd3	cxd3
14	♘d6+	♗xd6
15	♕xg7	♗f8!

15 ... ♖f8? 16 exd6 ♘d7 17 ♘f3 ♕b6 18 ♗xh6.

16	♕xh8	♕xd4
17	0–0	♘d7
18	♘f3	♕g4
19	♗xh6	♕h5
20	♗g7	♕xh8
21	♗xh8	♗h6
22	♘f6	

22 g4 ♔e7 23 g5 ♖xh8 24 gxh6 c5 25 ♖fe1 c4.

22	...	♘xf6
23	exf6	d2
24	♖fd1	♖d8
25	h4	♗e2
26	♘g5	♗xg5
27	hxg5	c5
28	b3	c4
29	bxc4	b3
	0–1	

Verdict ✱✱

Karpov – Timman
Tilburg 1988

1	d4	d5
2	c4	c6
3	♘f3	♘f6
4	♘c3	dxc4
5	a4	♗f5
6	♘e5	e6
7	f3	♗b4
8	e4	♗xe4
9	fxe4	♘xe4
10	♗d2	♕xd4
11	♘xe4	♕xe4+
12	♕e2	♕h4+

The piece sacrifice Black has employed in this game has recently become popular though more usual now would be 12 ... ♗xd2+ 13

♔xd2 ♕d5+ 14 ♔c2 ♘a6 15 ♘xc4 0-0-0 16 ♕e5 f6 17 ♕e3 ♔b8!∞ as in Wells - Hector, London 1991.

13	g3	♗xd2+
14	♔xd2	♕e7
15	♕e3	♘a6
16	♗xc4	♘b4
17	♖ad1	♘d5
18	♗xd5	cxd5
19	♘d3	0-0
20	♖c1	♖fc8

Now Karpov rejects the murky back rank speculation 21 ♕xa7.

21	♖he1	b6
22	♕e5	♕d7

Black has three pawns for his sacrificed knight, combined with a solid position. Nevertheless he is somewhat lacking in active counterplay. Timman's coming attempt to liven up his chances is, in fact, what brings about his downfall.

23	b3	h6
24	h4	♕e7

The pin on the e-file now allows White to capture the black d-pawn. Timman

may have believed that White could not risk opening up the game with his king lodged in the centre, but he had under-estimated Karpov's expertise in consolidation.

25	♕xd5	♖d8
26	♕f3	♕b4+
27	♔e2	♕xb3
28	♖c7	♖f8
29	♖xf7	

This capture strips away come of the protection around the black king. If, in reply, 29 ... ♖xf7, then 20 ♕xa8+ wins.

29	...	♕xa4
30	♖f1	♕a3
31	♕b7	♖xf7
32	♖xf7	♕a1

The Dutch Grandmaster has been driven totally onto the defensive. Karpov's next move picks up a valuable pawn and ensures his victory.

33	♖xg7+	♕xg7
34	♕xa8+	♔h7
35	♕e4+	♕g6
36	♕f4	a5
37	g4	e5
38	♘xe5	♕c2+
39	♔e3	♕c1+
40	♔e4	♕xf4+
41	♔xf4	1-0

After 41 ... b5 42 ♘c6 a4 43 ♘b4 Black's passed pawns on the queenside are paralysed, and White wins.

Verdict ✱✱✱✱

Taimanov – Steiner
Saltsjobaden 1952

1	d4	d5
2	c4	e6
3	♘c3	c6

Steiner fearlessly ventures along a path that has been completely surveyed by Russian masters and one in which Black has met with resounding reverses over the recent years (amongst others in the game Bronstein – Kotov, Budapest 1950).

4	e4	dxe4
5	♘xe4	♗b4+

6	♗d2

Definitely offering to gambit. 6 ♘c3 is also possible.

6	...	♕xd4
7	♗xb4	♕xe4+
8	♗e2	♘a6

This continuation has been suggested by Euwe, but probably 8 ... c5 is Black's best defence.

9	♗d6!

Stronger than 9 ♗c3 which was the move formerly played and which, according to the latest analysis, yields White no advantage.

9	...	♗d7
10	♘f3	c5?

Now Black cannot manage to castle.

11	♘e5	♗c6
12	♘xc6	bxc6

Or 12 ... ♕xc6 13 ♗f3 ♕d7 14 ♗xb7! ♕xb7 15 ♕a4+ ♔d8 16 0-0-0 with a winning attack.

13	0-0	♘e7
14	♕a4	♘b4

15	♗xc5!

Taimanov plays the game with equal elegance and efficiency.

15	...	a5
16	♗f3	♕c2
17	b3	♖c8
18	♕xa5	♘d3
19	♗e4	♕e2
20	♗xd3	♕xd3
21	♖ad1	♕f5
22	♕a7!	1-0

Verdict ✳✳✳

Queen's Gambit Declined – Tarrasch

Marshall – Duras
San Sebastian 1991

1	d4	d5
2	c4	e6
3	♘c3	c5
4	cxd5	exd5
5	e4	

A dubious gambit. Marshall loved such things.

5	...	dxe4
6	d5	f5
7	f3	

7 ♗f4 ♗d6 8 ♗b5+ ♔f7 9 ♘h3 ♘f6 10 ♗c4 a6 11 a4 h6!∓ Bronstein - Marjanovic, Kirovakan 1978.

7	...	♗d6
8	♘h3	♘f6
9	♗b5+	♘bd7
10	fxe4	fxe4
11	♘g5	a6
12	♘e6	♕e7
13	0-0	

Force majeure dictates this frantic sacrifice. If 13 ♗xd7+ ♗xd7 with no problems for Black, as indeed 13 ♕e2 ♘e5.

13	...	axb5
14	♘xb5	♖a6
15	♗g5	h5

Stopping checks on h5.

16	♕b3	♘f8
17	♘xg7+	

This at last looks promising, but Duras has an ingenious defence lined up.

17	...	♕xg7
18	♗xf6	♗xh2+!
19	♔xh2	♖xf6
20	♕c3	♘d7
21	♘d6+	♔d8
22	♖xf6	♘xf6
23	♕a5+	♕c7

The point which Marshall might, perhaps, have overlooked is that White cannot interpose ♘f7+ since his knight on d6 is pinned to the king. Resistance is futile, as the *American Chess Bulletin* put it.

24	b4	b6
25	♕a8	♕xd6+
	0-1	

Verdict ✶✶

Queen's Gambit Declined – Vienna

Kasparov – Hjartarson
Tilburg 1991

1	d4	♘f6

2	♘f3	d5
3	c4	e6
4	♘c3	dxc4
5	e4	♗b4
6	♗g5	c5
7	♗xc4	cxd4
8	♘xd4	

The Vienna variation, sharp and dangerous for both sides. Black tries to destroy White's queen's wing, while White shreds Black's kingside. It was a great favourite from the white side with Kasparov's hero Alekhine, the World Champion for most of the 1930s and half the 1940s.

8	...	♗xc3+
9	bxc3	♛a5
10	♗b5+	♗d7
11	♗xf6	gxf6
12	♛b3	a6
13	♗e2	♘c6
14	0-0	♛c7
15	♖ab1	♘a5
16	♛a3	♖c8

White's next move is a theoretical novelty replacing the previously played 17 c4.

17	♖fd1	♛xc3

Since this is evidently all preparation by Kasparov, it was foolhardy of Black to take the pawn.

18	♛d6	♛c7
19	♘f5!	exf5
20	♛xf6	0-0

This is suicidal. But is there a defence! If 20 ... ♖g8 21 exf5 ♗e6 22 ♗f1 with the dreadful threat of ♖e1+. Alternatively in this line 21 ... ♛c6 22 ♛e5+ ♔f8 23 ♗f3!! ♛xf3 24 ♛d6+ ♔g7 25 gxf3 wins.

21	♖d3	f4
22	♖d5	h6
23	♛xh6	f5
24	♖b6	♗c6
25	♖xa5	♛h7

If instead 25 ... ♛xb6 26 ♗c4+ ♖f7 27 ♗xf7+ ♔xf7 28 ♖xf5+ leads to mate.

26	♛xf4	1-0

If 26 ... ♗xe4 27 ♛g5+ wins Black's queen after 27 ... ♔h8 28 ♖h6 or 27 ... ♛g7 28 ♖g6.

Verdict ✳✳✳✳✳

Queen's Indian Defence

The Queen's Indian Defence is one of the most solid choices of opening at Black's disposal. However, even here there are gambit possibilities for both White and Black.

Kasparov – Karpov
Moscow 1984

1	d4	♘f6
2	c4	e6
3	♘f3	b6
4	g3	

The continuation 4 a3 ♗b7 5 ♘c3 d5 6 cxd5 ♘xd5 used to be closely linked with Kasparov, but he has avoided it since his dramatic loss in the first game against Korchnoi, London 1983. A recent idea which might enliven White's prospects, is 7 e4!? ♘xc3 8 bxc3 ♗xe4 9 ♘e5, with threats such as ♗b5+ or ♕g4 and ♗c4. 9 ... ♕h4!? has been suggested as an antidote.

4	...	♗b7
5	♗g2	♗e7
6	0-0	0-0
7	d5!?	

A gambit which became popular after the Polugayevsky - Korchnoi match in 1980.

7	...	exd5
8	♘h4	c6
9	cxd5	♘xd5
10	♘f5	♘c7
11	♘c3	

Also worth considering is 11 e4 ♘e6 12 ♘c3 ♘a6 13 f4 f6 14 h4 ♘ac7 15 ♗e3 d6 16 ♕g4.

11	...	d5
12	e4	♗f6

13	♗f4	

Kasparov varies from his own game against Marjanovic, Malta Olympiad 1980, when 13 exd5 was played. That game continued: 13 .. cxd5 14 ♗f4 ♘ba6 15 ♖e1 ♕d7 16 ♗h3! with a powerful attack, but it was later discovered that 15 ... ♘c5 keeps Black afloat. It is generally believed that the variation with 7 d5!? and 8 ♘h4 was actually invented during the aforementioned Polugayevsky - Korchnoi match. But in his notes from *Sovietsky Sport*, Razuvayev draws attention to

the game Razuvayev - Ma-
karichev, Tbilisi 1978(!).
There Razuvayev continued
his attack with 13 ♕g4, and
the 15-year-old Kasparov
asked why not 13 ♗f4 ? Now
after a six year interval,
Kasparov gets the oppor-
tunity to pose the same
question to the World
Champion. Incidentally, it
takes some impudence to
try this out against Karpov,
since he has often worked
closely with Polugayevsky
in the past.

13	...	♗c8
14	g4	♘ba6
15	♖c1	

White has chances for
the initiative on all fronts.
If now 15 ... ♗xf5 16 gxf5
dxe4 17 ♗xe4 with serious
pressure against Black's
queenside pawns.

| 15 | ... | ♗d7 |
| 16 | ♕d2 | |

16 ♘d6!?.

| 16 | ... | ♘c5 |
| 17 | e5!? | |

Another bold concept.
Normal is 17 ♗xc7 ♕xc7 18
exd5, but after 18 ... a5! (to
stop b4) 19 d6 ♕d8 20 ♖fe1
♗xf5 21 gxf5 ♕d7 it is hard
to see how White makes
progress.

17	...	♗e7
18	♘xe7+	♕xe7
19	♗g5	♕e6

Not 19 ... ♕xe5 20 ♗f4.

| 20 | h3 | |

Seems natural enough,
but the wild alternative 20
f4!? was widely canvassed.
Presumably the idea is 20 ...
♕xg4 21 ♖f3 to be followed
by ♖g3 with combinational
possibilities against g7.

| 20 | ... | ♕g6 |
| 21 | f4? | |

Kasparov goes beserk!
He must play 21 ♗e7 ♖fe8
22 ♗d6 followed f4. Karpov
would probably have ass-
essed this as too risky for
Black.

21	...	f6
22	exf6	gxf6
23	♗h4	f5

Introducing what should
be a decisive counter-
attack.

| 24 | b4 | fxg4! |
| 25 | hxg4 | |

If 25 bxc5 gxh3 26 ♖f2
hxg2 27 ♖xg2 ♗g4 wins.

| 25 | ... | ♘d3 |

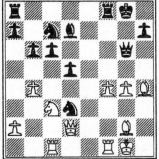

White's position sudden-
ly looks on the verge of
collapse. Kasparov strikes
back with an obscure sa-
crifice. If 26 f5? ♕xg4 27

♕xd3 ♕xh4 28 ♘xd5 ♘xd5
29 ♗xd5+ cxd5 30 ♕xd5+
♔h8 and Black wins.

26	♖f3!?	♘xc1
27	f5	♕g7
28	♕xc1	♖ae8
29	♕d2	d4
30	♘e2	♘d5
31	♘xd4	♔h8

If 31 ... ♖e4 32 f6!. Both
players, in desperate time
trouble, were moving in-
stantaneously here.

32	g5	♖e4
33	♗f2	♕e5
34	♖g3	♖f4
35	f6	♗e8
36	b5	c5
37	♘c6	♕a1+
38	♗f1	♖f5
39	g6!	♗xg6

Avoiding the diabolical
trap 39 ... ♖8xf6? 40 g7+
♔g8 41 ♕xd5+ ♖xd5 42 ♘e7+
♔f7 43 g8♕++-.

| 40 | ♖xg6 | ♖5xf6? |

Not 40 ... hxg6?? 41 ♕h6+
but 40 ... ♘xf6!, threatening 41 ... ♘e4 should win.
After 40 ... ♘xf6! 41 ♕h6
♘g4? fails to 42 ♕xf8+
♖xf8 43 ♖xg4 with a trio of
minor pieces for the queen;
41 ... ♘e4 allows the trick
42 ♗d4+! ♕xd4+ 43 ♘xd4
♖xf1+ 44 ♔h2 ♖8f2+ 45
♖g2!; but 41 ... ♘g8!! repul-
ses all threats.

| 41 | ♖xf6 | |

The sealed move. There
are three critical continuations here: 41 ... ♖g8+ 42

♔h2 ♘xf6 43 ♗h3 ♘e4 44
♕f4 ♕b2 45 ♕xe4 ♕xf2+ 46
♗g2 ♖g5 47 ♕e8+ ♔g7 48
♕e7+ ♔h6 49 ♕e6+ ♖g6 50
♕h3+ ♔g5 when White
must exchange queens with
a tenable ending. Better is
44 ♕e2! ♕f6 45 ♗e1 preserving the white queen's bishop. Alternatively, 41 ...
♘xf6 42 ♕e1 ♕xa2 43 ♕e5
with counterplay.

| 41 | ... | ♕xf6 |
| 42 | ♕e1! | |

42	...	♖g8+
43	♔h2	♕f4+
44	♗g3	♖xg3
45	♕xg3	♕xf1
46	♕b8+	♔g7
47	♕g3+	½-½

Verdict ✳✳✳

**Queen's Pawn
Counter-Gambit**

---

1 e4 e5 2 ♘f3 d5

See Elephant.

Relfsson
(Scotch)

1 e4 e5 2 ♘f3 ♘c6 3 d4 exd4
4 ♗b5

Harmless. White will struggle just to regain his pawn. Black has a number of good replies: 4 ... ♘f6, 4 ... ♗c5 or even 4 ... ♗b4+.

Verdict ✳✳

Réti

1 ♘f3 d5 2 c4 e6 3 g3 ♘f6 4
♗g2 dxc4 5 ♘a3 ♗xa3 6
bxa3 0-0

Even the sedate Réti offers gambit possibilities, such as this one, tried more than once by Smyslov: 7 ♕c2 b5 8 ♘g5 c6 9 ♗b2 ♖e8 10 0-0 h6 11 ♗xf6 ♕xf6 12 ♕h7+ ♔f8 13 ♘e4 Smyslov – Holmov, Baku 1961.

Verdict ✳✳✳

Reynolds
(Queen's Gambit Declined – Slav)

1 d4 d5 2 c4 c6 3 ♘f3 ♘f6 4
♘c3 e6 5 e3 ♘bd7 6 ♗d3
dxc4 7 ♗xc4 b5 8 ♗d3 a6 9
e4 c5 10 d5

Black has two interesting gambits in this position:

a) 10 ... e5 11 b3 ♗d6 12 0-0 0-0 13 a4 c4! 14 bxc4 b4 15 ♘e2 ♘c5 16 ♘g3 ♕c7 17 ♗e3 a5 and Black has a handy blockade.

b) 10 ... c4 11 dxe6 fxe6 12 ♗c2 ♗b7 13 0-0 ♕c7 14 ♕e2 ♗d6 15 ♘g5 ♘c5 16 f4 h6 17 ♘f3 ♘d3 18 ♗xd3 cxd3 19 ♕xd3 0-0 20 ♔h1 ♖ad8 with compensation for the pawn, Bareev - Shirov, Hastings 1991/92.

Arthur Reynolds (1910-1943), an English player of some imagination, published his analysis in 1939.

Verdict ✳✳✳

White has some chances but the gambit should not be sound after 8 ... ♗xe5 9 ♖e1 ♕e7 10 c3 ♘h5. *The Oxford Companion to Chess* remarks: "A grotesque monument to a rich man's vanity. Isaac Leopold Rice (1850-1915) financed many matches and tournaments restricted to this gambit, and gave prizes for other games in which it was used. White's sacrifice of a knight is neither good nor necessary."

One match sponsored by Rice was a set contest between Lasker and Chigorin, with Lasker taking White.

Verdict ✳

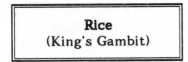

Rice (King's Gambit)	**Rosentreter** (King's Gambit)

1 e4 e5 2 f4 exf4 3 ♘f3 g5 4 h4 g4 5 ♘e5 ♘f6 6 ♗c4 d5 7 exd5 ♗d6 8 0-0?

1 e4 e5 2 f4 exf4 3 ♘f3 g5 4 d4 g4 5 ♗xf4

The Rosentreter, advocated in 1882 by the German army captain Adolf Rosentreter (1844 - 1920) has the curious point that White may try to castle queenside in some lines, pretty rare in the King's Gambit!

Keene - Milner-Barry
London 1980

1	e4	e5
2	f4	exf4
3	♘f3	g5
4	d4	g4
5	♗xf4	gxf3
6	♕xf3	d6

There is not much theory on this. Some sources give 6 ... d5 7 ♘c3!∞ and that is all.

7	♗c4	♕h4+
8	♗g3	♕f6
9	♕d3	♗e6
10	♘c3	♘e7
11	♖f1	

Here 11 0-0-0 ♗h6+ and ... 0-0 is also very specula-tive for White.

11	...	♕g5
12	♗f4	♕h4+
13	g3	♕h5
14	♘b5	♘a6
15	♗xd6	c6

Black should accept the sacrifice. Failure to do so gives White a won endgame in due course.

16	♗e5	♘g6
17	♗xh8	♗xc4
18	♕xc4	♘xh8
19	♖f5	♕g6
20	♖e5+	♔d7
21	♘c3	♗d6

22	♖f5	♕h6
23	e5	♖e8
24	♘e4	♕e3+
25	♕e2	♕xe2+
26	♔xe2	♗e7
27	♖h5	♔e6
28	♖f1	c5
29	♘f6	♗xf6
30	♖xf6+	♔d7
31	c3	cxd4
32	cxd4	♘c7
33	♖xh7	♘e6
34	♔e3	1-0

Verdict ✳✳✳

Rousseau
(Giuoco Piano)

1 e4 e5 2 ♘f3 ♘c6 3 ♗c4 f5

This gambit is named after Eugene Rousseau, a strong Parisian player of the mid-19th Century, who emigrated to New Orleans.

Black hopes for 4 ... exf5? giving up the centre, but 4 d4! exd4 5 e5 or 4 d4! fxe4 5 ♘xe5 ♘xe5 6 dxe5 keeps White safely on top.

Verdict ✳✳

Rubinstein
(Four Knights)

1 e4 e5 2 ♘f3 ♘c6 3 ♘c3 ♘f6 4 ♗b5 ♘d4

Rubinstein's invention 4 ... ♘d4 is the stock equaliser for Black in the Four Knights. The idea is to slice

the Gordian knot of White's pressure with a gambit, rather than submit to the long, slow pressure attendant on the copy cat response 4 ... ♗b4.

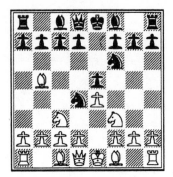

Bogolyubov - Rubinstein
Match 1920

1	e4	e5
2	♘f3	♘c6
3	♘c3	♘f6
4	♗b5	♘d4

This was Rubinstein's patent method of taking the sting out of the Four Knights Opening. For many years theory said White could not accept the gambit, but Nigel Short disproved this in games from his 1991 match against Jon Speelman. In any case, after the copycat 4 ... ♗b4 White can maintain the pressure well into the middlegame, for example 5 0-0 0-0 6 d3 d6 7 ♗g5 ♗xc3 8 bxc3 h6 9 ♗h4 ♗d7 10 ♖b1 Short -

Speelman, Candidates 6th match game 1991.

5 ♘xe5

It is this line, in fact, that Nigel Short revived in his Candidates match against Speelman with 5 ♗a4, deferring the capture of the pawn on e5, viz. 5 ... ♗c5 6 ♘xe5 0-0 7 ♘d3 ♗b6 8 e5 ♘e8 9 ♘d5 d6 10 ♘e3 c6 and now Nigel played 11 c3 in the 8th game and 11 0-0 in the 9th game.

5 ... ♘xe4

After this game 5 ... ♘xe4 was abandoned in favour of 5 ... ♕e7, for example: 6 f4 ♘xb5 7 ♘xb5 d6 8 ♘f3 ♕xe4+ 9 ♔f2 ♘g4+ 10 ♔g3 ♕g6 11 ♕e2+ ♔d8 12 ♖e1 ♗d7, Spielmann – Rubinstein, Baden Baden 1925, a game that Black went on to win on account of his bishop pair and superior pawn structure.

6	♘xe4	♘xb5
7	♘xf7	♕e7
8	♘xh8	♕xe4+
9	♔f1	♘d4
10	h4	

A surprise. Not only does White's king obtain a flight square, if it should be wanted, but his h-pawn becomes a trenchant weapon, whilst his motorised king's rook threatens to get into action via h3.

10	...	b5
11	d3	♕f5

12 ♗g5

Supported by the advance of the h-pawn, the white bishop is now comfortably settled in the enemy camp.

12	...	g6
13	♕d2	♗g7

At last the venturesome knight is caught, but by now the white rooks have gained power.

14 ♖e1+ ♘e6

15	h5	gxh5
16	♖xh5	♗xh8

After the text move Black has become the stronger in material; but the disorganised position of his pieces will cause his ruin.

17 ♕b4

The queen enters the fray by means of some very fine manoeuvres.

17	...	c5
18	♕h4	♔f7
19	♗d8	♕g6
20	♖h6	♕xh6
21	♕xh6	♘xd8
22	♕h5+	1-0

Verdict ✳✳✳✳

Ruy Lopez

The Ruy Lopez, in common with many other 'Open' games, is a treasure-trove of gambits. Apart from the Open Variation, gambits can also be found in the Closed, Bird's, Cordel and many other lines, as well as the famous Marshall Attack and Jaenisch-Schliemann.

Karpov - Korchnoi
World Ch 1978

1	e4	e5
2	♘f3	♘c6
3	♗b5	a6
4	♗a4	♘f6
5	0-0	♘xe4
6	d4	b5
7	♗b3	d5
8	dxe5	♗e6
9	♘bd2	

Varying from 9 c3 which was played in the second and fourth games.

9	...	♘c5
10	c3	g6

A new provocative and weak move. This unwise innovation was improvised by Korchnoi at the board and formed no part of our preparation. The move is partly motivated by our theory that Karpov does not like to gambit pawns, but the gambit which the text allows is more murderous than speculative.

Despite the weakness of Black's move, Karpov must have been disappointed to be denied the chance to play his innvation 11 ♘g5! after the standard move 10 ... d4. But he was to get his opportunity in his next game with White.

11	♕e2	♗g7
12	♘d4	

12	...	♘xe5?

Consistent, but suicidal. Black only wins a pawn but at the cost of allowing his kingside to be smashed and losing the right to castle - far too high a price.

13	f4	♘c4

13 ... ♘ed3 is a small improvement, but it is also not very promising, e.g. 14 f5 ♘xc1 15 ♖axc1 gxf5 16 ♘xf5 0-0 17 ♗c2 with a fierce attack in prospect.

14	f5	gxf5
15	♘xf5	♖g8

Making the best of a bad

job. In some lines Black sneaks some counterplay on the g-file.

16 ♘xc4

A simple solution, quite in Karpov's style, but 16 ♗c2 is probably more deadly.

16 ... dxc4

Korchnoi thought for thirty-five minutes over this move, which showed that something had gone seriously wrong. 16 ... bxc4 was also bad, e.g. 17 ♗c2 ♚d7 18 ♘xg7 ♖xg7 19 ♕e5 ♕g8 20 ♖f2 f6 21 ♕xf6 ♖f7 22 ♕d4 ♖xf2 23 ♕xf2 ♖f8 24 ♕xc5 ♗h3 25 ♗e4 dxe4 26 ♗g5 and wins. This is only a sample variation but it illustrates the unhappy plight of Black's exposed king. If instead 16 ... ♘xb3 17 axb3 dxc4 18 bxc4 bxc4 19 ♗h6 and Black will be mown down in the centre.

17 ♗c2

Best. If 17 ♘xg7+ ♖xg7 18 ♕e5, forking two pieces, 18 ... ♖xg2+ 19 ♚xg2 ♕d5+ 20 ♕xd5 ♗xd5+ followed by ... cxb3 gives Black counterplay.

17 ... ♘d3?

By now it is just a question of choosing the lesser evil, which would have been 17 ... ♕d5 18 ♗h6 ♗xh6 19 ♘xh6 ♖f8.

18 ♗h6!

Korchnoi freely admitted

he had overlooked this move.

18 ... ♗f8?

Two better chances were 18 ... ♗h8 or 18 ... ♗xh6 19 ♘xh6 ♖g6 20 ♘xf7 ♕e7 though both are fairly forlorn.

19	♖ad1	♕d5
20	♗xd3	cxd3
21	♖xd3	♕c6
22	♗xf8	♕b6+

If 22 ... ♚xf8 23 ♘d4 wins a piece.

23	♚h1	♚xf8
24	♕f3	

The position now looks like a Muzio King's Gambit where White has not had to sacrifice a piece.

24	...	♖e8
25	♘h6	♖g7
26	♖d7!	

Simple but pleasing. 26 ... ♗xd7 allows 27 ♕xf7+ ♖xf7 28 ♖xf7+.

26	...	♖b8
27	♘xf7	♗xd7
28	♘d8+	1-0

Verdict ✳✳✳✳✳

S

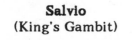

Salvio
(King's Gambit)

1 e4 e5 2 f4 exf4 3 ♘f3 g5 4
♗c4 g4 5 ♘e5

After 5 ... ♕h4+ 6 ♔f1
♘c6 7 ♘xf7 ♗c5 8 ♕e1 g3 9
♘xh8 ♗f2 Black has seized
the initiative. Alessandro
Salvio (1570–1640) was an
author and Doctor of Law
from Naples, one of the
leading players and perhaps
even the best analyst of his
day. His gambit, however,
has not stood the test of
time.

Verdict ✷

Scandinavian Defence

1 e4 d5

See Centre-Counter De-
fence.

Schliemann/Jaenisch
(Ruy Lopez)

1 e4 e5 2 ♘f3 ♘c6 3 ♗b5 f5

See Jaenisch/Schliemann.

Scotch

The Scotch, certainly as far
as World Championship
play is concerned, languish-
ed unused for around a century until Kasparov unex-
pectedly revived it against
Karpov in two games from
Lyons in their most recent
contest. Since then it has
become all the rage.

In common with many other commentators I had believed that the Scotch derived its name from a correspondence game between Edinburgh, White, against London, Black, played between 1826 and 1828. That game began 1 e4 e5 2 ♘f3 ♘c6 3 d4 ♘xd4 4 ♘xd4 exd4 5 ♕xd4 ♘e7 6 ♗c4 ♘c6 7 ♕d5 and was won brilliantly by White in 60 moves. What I had not appreciated was that there had been an earlier game London, White, against Edinburgh, Black, played by correspondence between 1824 and 1825, in which the Scotch concept of 3 d4 was introduced for the first time. What the canny Scots realised was that White need not make a gambit of the opening after Black captures on d4. White can simply recapture maintaining material parity and a slightly freer position.

Kasparov – Karpov
World Championship
Lyons 1990

1	e4	e5
2	♘f3	♘c6
3	d4	

This was the first time Kasparov had played the Scotch Game in this match, indeed, it may be the first time he has ever played the Scotch. Prior to this game, this opening had only occurred twice in World Championship matches, Steinitz – Zukertort, 1886, where Black played 3 ... exd4 4 ♘xd4 ♗c5, and Steinitz – Chigorin, 1892, when Black played 4 ... ♕h4.

3	...	exd4
4	♘xd4	♘f6
5	♘xc6	bxc6
6	e5	♕e7
7	♕e2	♘d5
8	c4	♗a6
9	b3	

9 ♕e4 ♘b6 10 ♘d2 0-0-0 11 c5 ♗xf1 12 cxb6 ♗a6 13 bxa7 was Karpov's gambit in Timman – Karpov, London 1984. It is interesting that the a7-pawn seems to be Black's main weakness in this line, but because it is so far from the scene of the action it is often unimportant.

9	...	0-0-0
10	g3	

This move essentially commits White to gambitting a pawn.

The alternatives are:

10 ♗b2 ♕g5 11 ♘d2 f6 12 h4 ♕h6 13 0-0-0 ♗c5 14 ♕f3 ♘f4 15 exf6 gxf6 16 g3 ♘e6 17 ♕xf6 ♕h5 18 f4 ♖hg8 19 ♕e5 ♕xe5 20 ♗xe5 ♘d4 21 ♗xd4 ♗xd4 22 ♘e4 ♘f5 23 ♖d3 1-0 Hort – Unzicker, Bundesliga 1983.

10 ♕b2 ♘b6 11 ♗e2 ♖e8 12 ♗f4 g5 13 ♗g3 ♗g7 14 ♘c3 f5 15 f4 gxf4 16 ♗xf4 ♗xe5 17 ♗xe5 ♕xe5 18 0-0 Ljubojevic – Seirawan, Wijk aan Zee 1988 (0-1, 39).

10	...	♖e8
11	♗b2	f6
12	♗g2	fxe5
13	0-0	h5

This gambit looks like Kasparov preparation. He had now used 8 minutes to Karpov's 65.

| 14 | ♕d2 | ♘f6 |
| 15 | ♕a5 | |

This wins back the pawn, while simultaneously the white queen crashes through to attack the black king. Once the queen is on a7, White can consider various ponderous attacking plans such as a4 - a5 - a6 or ♘a3 - c2 - b4 - a6. However, both of these are very slow and White has to reckon in the meantime with a backlash against his own king.

| 15 | ... | ♗b7 |

| 16 | ♗a3 | ♕e6 |
| 17 | ♗xf8 | |

Kasparov declared on French television that he had analysed this position up to move 17 with his seconds, concluding that White stood better.

| 17 | ... | ♖hxf8 |
| 18 | ♕xa7 | ♕g4 |

An excellent counter-attacking move after which Kasparov thought for 53 minutes, a record for one move in this match equal with Karpov's in game 4.

Kasparov had probably overlooked this very fine move. It fulfils a dual function. In some cases the black queen can travel to d4 in order to trade queens and banish the white attack. On the other hand ... ♕g4 also supports the advance of Black's h-pawn to h3, consequently driving the white bishop to h1 and thus crowding the white king.

| 19 | ♘a3 | h4 |

20	♘c2	h3
21	♗h1	♘e4
22	a4	

If 22 f3 ♘xg3 23 ♖f2 (23 fxg4 ♘e2 mate) 23 ... ♕g6 24 hxg3 ♕xg3+ 25 ♔f1 c5 26 ♕xc5 ♗xf3 27 ♗xf3 ♖xf3 28 ♖xf3 ♕g2+ 29 ♔e1 ♕xf3 with sufficient compensation. Kasparov prefers to wrench the attack into his own hands with a sacrifice of the exchange.

Alternatively, 22 ♘e3 ♘c3 23 ♕xb7+ (not 23 ♘xg4 ♘e2 mate) 23 ... ♔xb7 24 ♗xc6+ ♔xc6 25 ♘xg4 when White has an extra pawn but Black's pieces are active and the h3-pawn is a thorn in White's flesh.

22	...	♘c3
23	♖ae1	♘e2+
24	♖xe2	♕xe2
25	♘b4	

25	...	d5

Since each player has 150 minutes to reach the time control at move 40, one can appreciate how seriously short of time Karpov was. It is all the more praiseworthy then that he plays for a win rather than going for the probable draw with 25 ... ♖f3 26 ♘a6 ♔d8 27 ♕b8+ ♔e7 28 ♕xb7 ♖xf2 29 ♕b4+ d6 30 ♖xf2 ♕d1+ with a forced draw by perpetual check.

26	cxd5

26 a5 is parried by 26 ... ♕d2.

26	...	cxd5
27	♗xd5	

If instead 27 ♘xd5 ♕a6 28 ♕c5 ♕d6 beats off the attack.

In the bulletin Spassky gave the fantasy variation 27 ♖c1 ♕d2 28 ♕c5 ♖e7 29 ♘xd5 ♗xd5 30 ♗xd5 ♖xf2 31 ♗e6+ ♔d8 32 ♗xh3 ♖xh2 33 ♖c2 ♕xc2 34 ♕d5+ leading to mate.

27	...	♗xd5
28	♘xd5	♕c2
29	♕a6+	♔d7
30	♘e3	♕e4
31	♖c1	♖b8
32	♕f1	♖xb3
33	♕xh3+	♔d8
34	♕h5	♔c8

There is a possible improvement here with 34 ... ♕f3 for if 35 ♕xe5 ♕xf2+ 36 ♔h1 ♕f3+ 37 ♘g2 (37 ♔g1 ♕xe3+) 37 ... ♕f1+ 38 ♖xf1 ♖xf1 mate. If White acquiesces in the exchange of queens he faces a difficult endgame.

35	♕d1

35 ...   ♖xe3

Kasparov had three min-
utes left and Karpov two,
so it is understandable that
Black did not wish to keep
the tension going with a
move like 35 ... ♕d3. The
text assures him of a draw
at worst and also rescues
Karpov from his clock
trouble.

36	fxe3	♕xe3+
37	♔h1	♕e4+
38	♔g1	♕e3+
39	♔h1	♕e4+
40	♔g1	♖d8
41	♕c2	½–½

Fascinating gambit play
from the two greatest mo-
derns!

Verdict ✳ ✳ ✳ ✳

Sicilian Defence

The Sicilian Defence is a
common battleground for
gambiteers, see, for ex-
ample the Poisoned Pawn

and the Wing Gambit. In
this section we look at
some very different gambit
strategies.

Kasparov – Piket
Tilburg 1989

1	e4	c5
2	♘f3	d6
3	d4	cxd4
4	♘xd4	♘f6
5	♘c3	g6
6	♗e3	♗g7
7	f3	♘c6
8	♕d2	0-0

Kasparov's choice indi-
cates that there will now
be a war to the death on
opposite wings, with White
trying to checkmate the
black monarch in as brutal
fashion as possible, and
Black seeking to return the
compliment.

9	♗c4	♗d7
10	h4	♘e5
11	♗b3	♖c8
12	0-0-0	♘c4
13	♗xc4	♖xc4
14	h5	

A regulation gambit in the Dragon.

14	...	♘xh5
15	g4	♘f6
16	♗h6	♘xe4
17	♕e3	♖xc3
18	bxc3	♘f6
19	♗xg7	♔xg7
20	♖h2	♖h8

Remarkably, all this is known to theory, at least up to Black's twentieth move. Alternatives are 20 ... ♖g8 21 ♘e2 ♕a5 22 g5 ♘h5 23 ♕xe7 with a tremendous position for White, as in the game Short - Ernst, Subotica Izt. 1987; or 20 ... ♕c7 21 ♕xe7 ♕xc3 22 ♕xd6 ♖c8 when Black does have some play for his sacrificed material. This latter course was the path suggested by Kasparov himself in his comments in the openings manual *BCO*. Piket's choice in the game is designed to shore up the fortifications around his king, but to my mind it looks too passive to have any real prospect of success.

21	♘b3	♗e6
22	g5	♘h5
23	f4	♖e8
24	f5	♕b6
25	♘d4	♕c5
26	♖e1	♗d7
27	♕f3	♗c6
28	♕e3	♗d7
29	♕f3	♗c6

30	♕f2	♔g8

After a slight period of hesitation, during which Kasparov permitted the position to be repeated, White has now found the right attacking formation: queen on f2 and rook on e3.

31	♖e3	♗d5
32	♖xh5	gxh5

The return sacrifice of White's rook for the black knight has utterly wiped out any vestige of protection for the black king. Meanwhile, somewhat paradoxically, in view of his own shattered pawns, White's king remains relatively immune from checks by the opposing queen.

33	♕h4	♕c4
34	♕xh5	♕f1+
35	♔b2	e5
36	♕h6	♔h8
37	g6	fxg6
38	fxg6	♖e7
39	♖f3	♕c4
40	♕f8 mate	

Verdict ✳✳✳✳✳

Hodgson – Nunn
Aaronson Open,
London 1978

1	e4	c5
2	f4	♘c6
3	♘f3	g6
4	♘c3	♗g7
5	♗c4	d6
6	0–0	♘f6
7	d3	0–0
8	f5!	

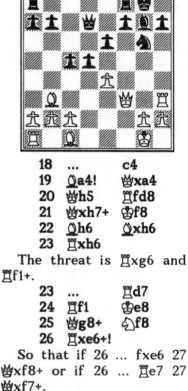

A Hodgson favourite, which was also used to great effect by Rumens on the Grand Prix Circuit. White has good practical chances and it would have been psychologically more sensible for the grandmaster to choose a different defence.

8	...	gxf5
9	♕e1	fxe4
10	dxe4	♗g4
11	♕h4	♗xf3
12	♖xf3	♘e5
13	♖h3	♘g6
14	♕g3	♕d7
15	♘d5	

Otherwise Black plays 15 ... ♕g4.

15	...	♘xd5
16	♗xd5	e6
17	♗b3	d5

Better ... b5, to neutralise White's bishop and then to gain space by ... f5.

18 ♕f3!

Brilliant play. The bishop sacrifice opens up the black king.

18	...	c4
19	♗a4!	♕xa4
20	♕h5	♖fd8
21	♕xh7+	♔f8
22	♗h6	♗xh6
23	♖xh6	

The threat is ♖xg6 and ♖f1+.

23	...	♖d7
24	♖f1	♔e8
25	♕g8+	♘f8
26	♖xe6+!	

So that if 26 ... fxe6 27 ♕xf8+ or if 26 ... ♖e7 27 ♕xf7+.

26	...	♔d8
27	♕xf8+	♔c7
28	♕c5+	♔d8
29	♖h6	1–0

Note the similarity to Fischer's Gambit.

Verdict ✳✳✳

Siesta
(Ruy Lopez)

1 e4 e5 2 ♘f3 ♘c6 3 ♗b5 a6
4 ♗a4 d6 5 c3 f5

certainly avoid the tempting 9 ♖e3 e4 10 ♘e1 ♗g5 11 ♘xd3 ♗xe3 12 ♘b4 ♗xf2+ 13 ♔xf2 ♛h4+ 14 ♔g1 ♘h6 15 ♕f1 ♘g4 16 ♕f4 ♖f8 17 ♕g3 ♖f1+ 18 ♔xf1 ♘xh2+ 19 ♕xh2 ♛xh2 0–1 Adams – Piket, Wijk aan Zee 1991.

7	...	e4
8	♘g5	

8 ♕e2 ♗e7 9 ♘fd2 ♘f6 10 h3 d5= is Capablanca – Marshall, Match 1909.

8	...	d5
9	f3	e3
10	f4	

If 10 ♗xe3 h6 11 ♘h3 ♗xh3. Euwe decides to surround Black's e-pawn under more congenial circumstances.

10	...	♗d6
11	♕f3	♛f6
12	♕xe3+	♘ge7
13	♗xc6+	

This surrenders the bishop pair and strengthens Black's centre. Better is 13 0–0 0–0 14 ♘f3.

13	...	bxc6
14	0–0	0–0
15	♘d2	

He had to play 15 ♘f3 planning ♘e5 to mask his weaknesses. After the dilatory text he is never given the chance.

15	...	♘g6
16	g3	♖ae8
17	♕f2	♗d3
18	♖e1	♖xe1+
19	♕xe1	♗xf4

The Siesta is yet another gambit invented by the amazingly fertile brain of Frank Marshall.

Euwe – Keres
The Hague/Moscow 1948

1	e4	e5
2	♘f3	♘c6
3	♗b5	a6
4	♗a4	d6
5	c3	

More popular nowadays is 5 0–0.

5	...	f5

The risky Siesta variation, employed by Capablanca to crush Réti.

6	exf5	♗xf5
7	d4	

Modern theory concentrates on 7 0–0 ♗d3 8 ♖e1. For example, 8 ... ♗e7 9 ♗c2 ♗xc2 10 ♕xc2 ♘f6 11 d4 exd4 12 cxd4 0–0 13 ♘c3±. This is a very simple plus for White, which is why the Siesta is under a cloud.

However, White should

20 gxf4

The decisive sacrifice which demolishes White's bastions. If now 20 ♕e6+ ♕xe6 21 ♘xe6 ♗e3+ 22 ♔h1 ♖f1+ wins.

20	...	♘xf4
21	♘df3	♘e2+
22	♔g2	h6
23	♕d2	♕f5
24	♕e3	hxg5
25	♗d2	♗e4
	0-1	

A dramatic miniature against a former champion who was also a noted theoretician.

Verdict ✳✳✳

Sjodin

---

1 d4 e6 2 ♘f3 f5 3 e4 Invented by the Swedish master, Bengt Sjodin, this colourful idea is clearly cognate with the Lisitsin and Staunton gambits. One wild game went thus: 3 ...

fxe4 4 ♘g5 ♘f6 5 f3 exf3 (5 ... e3!?) 6 ♕xf3 ♘c6 7 ♗d3 ♘xd4 8 ♕h3 d5 9 ♘xh7 ♘xh7 10 ♗xh7 ♘xc2+ 11 ♔e2 ♔d7 (11 ... ♕f6!) 12 ♖f1 ♘xa1 13 ♖f7+ ♔c6 14 ♕c3+ ♔b6 15 ♗e3+ c5 16 b4 d4 17 bxc5+ ♗xc5 18 ♕b2+ ♔c6 19 ♘c3!!. Paradise for the aficcionado of gambit play. If now 19 ... dxc3 20 ♗e4+ leads to mate or 19 ... dxe3 20 ♕b5+ is the same. 19 ... ♕b6 20 ♗e4+ ♔d6 21 ♘b5+ ♔e5 22 ♗f3 ♖h4 23 g4!! g5 24 ♗xg5 ♖xh2+ 25 ♔d1 ♖xb2 26 ♗f4 mate, Ginsburg - Young, Plymouth 1990.

A treasure trove for the hardened gambiteer.

Verdict ✳✳✳

Smith-Morra

---

1 e4 c5 2 d4 cxd4 3 c3

See Morra-Smith Gambit.

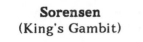

Sorensen
(King's Gambit)

1 e4 e5 2 f4 exf4 3 ♘f3 g5 4 d4 g4 5 ♘e5 ♕h4+ 6 g3 fxg3 7 ♕xg4 g2+ 8 ♕xh4 gxh1♕

This gambit is sound. 9 ♘c3! d6 10 ♘xf7 is ±. A better line for Black is to diverge from the above with 7 ... ♕xg4! 8 ♘xg4 d5 9 ♘e3 dxe4 10 hxg3 ♘c6 11 ♗g2. The similarities with the Quaade Gambit (qv) are self-evident.

Verdict ✳✳✳

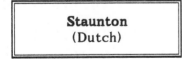

Staunton
(Dutch)

1 d4 f5 2 e4
The main line of the Staunton runs 2 ... fxe4 3 ♘c3 ♘f6 4 ♗g5 ♘c6 5 d5 ♘e5 6 ♕d4 ♘f7 7 ♗xf6 exf6

8 ♘xe4 f5 9 ♘g3 g6 10 0-0-0 with equality.

Verdict ✳✳✳

Steinitz
(Vienna)

1 e4 e5 2 ♘c3 ♘c6 3 f4 exf4 4 d4

Steinitz once said "The king is a strong piece", and his particular gambit tries to demonstrate this. However, there is no need for Black to go berserk to come to grips with the White monarch. The sensible procedure, advocated in my comments to move 4 of this game, is quite sufficient.

Steinitz - Zukertort
New Orleans 1886

1	e4	e5
2	♘c3	♘c6
3	f4	exf4
4	d4	d5?

Incorrect, as we now understand, 4 ... ♛h4+ 5 ♔e2 d6! 6 ♘f3 ♗g4 casts doubt on White's play.

5	exd5	♛h4+
6	♔e2	♛e7+
7	♔f2	♛h4+
8	g3!	

After this bold move to avoid the draw by repetition of position, Black's queen becomes even more exposed than White's king.

8	...	fxg3+
9	♔g2	♘xd4
10	hxg3	♛g4
11	♛e1+	♗e7
12	♗d3	♘f5
13	♘f3	♗d7
14	♗f4	f6
15	♘e4	♘8h6?

A blunder which permits a drastic termination.

16	♗xh6	♘xh6
17	♖xh6!	gxh6
18	♘xf6+	

Exploiting the pin on the king's file to fork Black's king and queen.

18	...	♔f8

And ...

1-0

Verdict ✳✳

Swiss
(Bird's Opening)

1 f4 f5 2 e4

2 ... fxe4 3 d3 exd3 4 ♗xd3 ♘f6 5 ♘f3 e6 6 ♘g5 g6 7 h4 gives White a strong attack. From's Gambit with f4 thrown in as an extra (Bird - Gelbfuss, Vienna 1873). Declining the pawn also fails to solve all of Black's problems, viz. 3 ... e3?! 4 ♗xe3 ♘f6 5 d4 e6 6 ♗d3 ♘c6 7 a3 ♘e7 8 ♘h3 b6 9 0-0 ♗b7 10 ♘d2 g6 11 ♘f2 ♗g7 12 c3 0-0 13 ♛e2 a5 14 g4 as in Pelikan - Alekhine, Podebrady 1936.

Verdict ✳✳✳

T

Tennison

1 ♘f3 d5 2 e4 dxe4 3 ♘g5

See Abonyi.

Torre Attack

The Torre Attack is another opening which generally leads to quiet positional play. However, if Black is adventurous (or careless) then White has some interesting gambit ideas.

Yusupov - Karpov
Candidates Semi-Final
London 1989

1	d4	♘f6
2	♘f3	e6
3	♗g5	c5
4	e3	

4 e4 is the dubious Wagner Gambit (qv).

| 4 | ... | b6 |

Falling, surprisingly, into an old trap which guaran-tees White a central preponderance. Karpov preferred 4 ... ♗e7 in game seven.

4 ... ♕b6 5 ♘bd2 ♕xb2 is a typical gambit for the variation, e.g. 6 ♗d3 d5 7 ♗xf6 gxf6 8 c4! ♕c3 9 ♗e2 dxc4 10 0-0 ♕a5 Vaganian - Razuvaev, USSR 1983.

5	d5!	exd5
6	♘c3	♗e7

Yusupov easily regains the gambit pawn, and the result is permanent domination of the important d5-square, plus possible pressure against the backward black d-pawn.

7	♗xf6	♗xf6
8	♘xd5	♗b7
9	c3	0-0

10	♗c4	a6
11	0-0	b5
12	♗b3	d6
13	♕d2	♘d7
14	♖fd1	♗xd5

White might do better now to recapture with the queen. Karpov's fine defence over the coming moves gradually eliminates White's edge.

15	♗xd5	♖b8
16	♕c2	♘b6
17	♖d2	g6
18	♖ad1	♕c7
19	♕e4	

This is premature, since it permits Karpov to reorganise his defences. Perhaps 19 h4!?.

19	...	♔g7
20	h4	♕e7
21	♕f4	♗e5
22	♘xe5	dxe5
23	♕g3	♖bd8
24	h5	♖d7
25	b3	♖fd8
26	e4	g5
27	♕e3	h6
28	c4	♖c7
29	♖d3	♘d7

The position is now more or less equal, or would have been, if Karpov had sealed up the left flank with 29 ... b4. The planned regrouping of his knight though, allows Yusupov to launch an extraordinary combination.

30 ♗xf7!!?

When Yusupov played this bold move a roar of approbation went up from the grandmasters in the press room, but this was quickly replaced with general puzzlement as to what precisely Yusupov had in mind as a follow-up. His idea is, in fact, extraordinarily profound though not, perhaps, absolutely water-tight.

30 ... ♔xf7

Karpov takes with the king in order to defend his pinned knight.

31 ♕d2 ♔e8

White's plans emerges: Black is totally pinned down, thus strikes can take place on the wings.

32 ♕a5 bxc4

With both sides in time trouble mistakes creep in. Here, for example, Karpov should defend with 32... ♖e6, while White, in turn, should have played 33 ♖d6.

33 bxc4 ♖cc8

Again 33 ... ♖c6 is necessary, though Black would be too paralysed to ever to think of winning.

34	♕a4	♖c7
35	♕xa6	♖b8
36	♕g6+!	♔f8

Both 36 ... ♕f7 37 ♕xf7+ and 36 ... ♔d8 37 ♖d6 are hopeless, so better end with horror than horror without end.

37 ♖f3+

1-0
A memorable game.

Verdict ✳✳✳✳

> **Traxler**
> **(aka Wilkes-Barre)**
> (Two Knights)

1 e4 e5 2 ♘f3 ♘c6 3 ♗c4 ♘f6
4 ♘g5 ♗c5

A crazy line which may just be playable.

Efimov - Shirov
Gausdal 1991

1	e4	e5
2	♘f3	♘c6
3	♗c4	♘f6
4	♘g5	♗c5
5	♗xf7+	♔e7
6	♗d5	♖f8

Anand - Beliavsky, Linares 1991, saw a different plan for Black: 6 ... ♕e8 7 d3 d6 8 ♗xc6 bxc6 9 ♗e3 ♕g6.

Also possible is 6 ... d6 7 c3 ♕e8 8 d4 exd4 9 cxd4 ♘xd4 10 ♘c3 ♕h5! 11 ♕d3 ♖f8 12 b4 ♗b6 13 ♘a4 ♘c6 14 ♘xb6 axb6 15 ♕c3 h6 16 ♘f3 ♗g4 17 ♗xc6 bxc6 18 ♘d2 ♕b5!∓ Karpov - Beliavsky, USSR 1983.

7   ♖f1

7 0-0 d6 8 c3 ♗g4 9 ♕b3 h6 10 d4 ♗b6 11 h3 ♘a5 12 ♕c2 hxg5 13 hxg4 c6 14 b4 cxd5 15 bxa5 ♗xa5 16 exd5± Estrin - Schmidt, corr. 1972.

7	...	♕e8
8	♘c3	d6
9	h3	♕g6
10	d3	h6
11	♘f3	♕xg2
12	♘h4	♗xf2+
13	♖xf2	♕g1+
14	♖f1	

Or 14 ♔e2 ♘d4+ 15 ♔e3 ♘g4+ 16 hxg4 ♕xf2 mate.

14	...	♕g3+
15	♔d2	♕g5+
	0-1	

Verdict ✳✳✳

> **Trompovsky**

1 d4 ♘f6 2 ♗g5 c5 3 d5 ♕b6
4 ♘c3 ♕xb2 5 ♗d2

A most promising gambit, which Black should probably sidestep. After 5 ... ♕b6 6 e4 e5 7 f4 d6 8 fxe5 dxe5 9 ♘f3 ♗d6 10 ♗c4 Pribyl - Hazai, Varna 1978,

White has easy play.

Black's best reply is 3 ... ♘e4! 4 ♗f4 ♕b6! 5 ♕c1 g6 6 f3 ♗g7 7 c3 ♘f6 8 e4 e6 9 ♘a3 0-0 10 ♘b5 ♘e8!=.

Verdict ✳✳✳

Two Knights

1 e4 e5 2 ♘f3 ♘c6 3 ♗c4 ♘f6 4 ♘g5 d5 5 exd5 ♘a5

This variation, popular in the late 19th Century, is hardly ever seen anymore except in postal games.

The main line is 6 ♗b5+ c6 7 dxc6 bxc6 8 ♗e2 h6 9 ♘f3 e4 10 ♘e5 ♗d6 11 d4 ♕c7 12 ♗d2 0-0∞. This is often accredited as being the soundest method of countering the ambitious 4 ♘g5.

Verdict ✳✳✳✳

Ulvestad
(Two Knights)

1 e4 e5 2 ♘f3 ♘c6 3 ♗c4 ♘f6 4 ♘g5 d5 5 exd5 b5

A striking idea, which looks as if it cannot be sound, but is nevertheless hard to refute. The main line is 6 ♗xb5 ♕xd5 7 ♘c3 ♕xg2 8 ♕f3 ♕xf3 9 ♘xf3 ♗d7 10 0-0 ♗d6 11 ♗xc6 ♗xc6 12 ♘xe5 ♗xe5 13 ♖e1±.

Less convincing is 6 ♗f1?! h6! 7 ♘f3 (7 ♘xf7 ♔xf7 8 dxc6 ♗c5 is every gambiteer's dream) 7 ... ♕xd5 8 ♘c3 ♕e6 9 ♗xb5 ♗b7 10 d3 0-0-0 11 ♕e2 ♕g4 12 ♗e3

♘d4 13 ♗xd4 exd4∓, Tiemann – Zmokly, corr. 1981.

Verdict ✳✳✳

Urusov (aka Petroff)

1 e4 e5 2 ♗c4 ♘f6 3 d4 exd4 4 ♘f3

Playable but harmless, e.g. 4 ... ♘xe4 (or 4 ... d5 5 exd5 ♗b4+ 6 c3 ♕e7+ 7 ♗e2 dxc3 8 bxc3 ♗c5) 5 ♕xd4 ♘f6 6 ♗g5 ♗e7 7 ♘c3 ♘c6 8 ♕h4 d6! 9 0-0-0 ♗e6 10 ♗d3 ♕d7 11 ♗b5 0-0 12 ♘d4 a6 13 ♗d3 h6 14 ♗xh6 gxh6=.

Verdict ✳✳

Vienna

The Vienna, like the King's Gambit, is a bountiful territory for the gambiteer, consult the index for other Vienna gambits.

Nunn – Hebden
Lara Open 1979

1	e4	e5
2	♘c3	♘f6
3	f4	d5
4	fxe5	♘xe4
5	d3	♘xc3

5 ... ♕h4+!? 6 g3 ♘xg3 7 ♘f3 ♕h5 8 ♘xd5 is an old trap favouring White, but the complex 5 ... ♗b4!? 6 dxe4 ♕h4+ 7 ♔e2 ♗g4+ is considered a drawing line and it would have been interesting to see what Nunn intended against this.

6	bxc3	d4

An active move more often favoured in practical play, but the more solid option is 6 ... ♗e7 and ... 0-0 followed by ... f6 or ...

f5.

7	♘f3	♘c6
8	♗e2	♗c5
9	0-0	dxc3+
10	♔h1	0-0
11	♕e1	♘d4

Chess Informant recommended this as equal, but Nunn analysed further and found an attacking idea.

12	♗d1	♘xf3
13	♗xf3	♗e6
14	♕g3	♔h8
15	♗e4	♗d5?

Losing – after 15 ... ♗e7 White has practical chances but nothing clear. Now Black gets wiped out.

16	♗g5!	♕d7

Black has to concede a tempo because after 16 ... f6 17 exf6 gxf6 18 ♗xd5 fxg5 allows 19 ♕e5+.

17	♗xh7!	♔xh7
18	♗f6	g5

If 18 ... gxf6 19 ♖f4 ♗e3 20 ♖h4+ ♗h6 21 ♕f4 ♗xg2+ 22 ♔g1 forces mate.

19	♕xg5	♗xg2+
20	♕xg2	♖g8
21	♕e4+	1-0

Verdict ✳ ✳ ✳

Wagner

1 d4 ♘f6 2 ♘f3 e6 3 ♗g5 c5
4 e4

An unsound handling of
the Torre Attack.

Marshall – Nimzowitsch
Berlin 1928

1	d4	♘f6
2	♘f3	e6
3	♗g5	c5
4	e4	cxd4
5	e5	h6
6	♗h4	g5
7	♗g3	

7 exf6 gxh4 8 ♕xd4 ♘c6
9 ♕xh4 ♕b6 intending ... d5,

...e5, ... ♗e6, ... 0-0-0.

7	...	♘h5
8	♕xd4	♘c6
9	♕e4	♗g7
10	♗b5	♕c7
11	♗xc6	♕xc6
12	♕e2	♕c5
13	0-0	♘xg3
14	hxg3	g4
15	♘fd2	♕xe5
16	♕xg4	♕xb2
17	c3	0-0
18	♘b3	♕c2
19	♖c1	♕g6
20	♕e2	d5-+

Verdict ✳✳

Wilkes-Barre

1 e4 e5 2 ♘f3 ♘c6 3 ♗c4 ♘f6
4 ♘g5 ♗c5

See Traxler.

Willemson
(King's Gambit)

1 e4 e5 2 f4 exf4 3 d4

No longer seen, since 3 ...
♛h4+ 4 ♔e2 d5! 5 ♘f3 ♝g4 6
exd5 ♘f6 is at least ∓.

Verdict   ✻✻

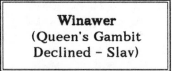

Winawer
(Queen's Gambit
Declined – Slav)

1 d4 d5 2 c4 c6 3 ♘c3 e5

This has become quite
respectable, though White
can probably maintain a
slight edge by refusing the
pawn, namely 4 cxd5 cxd5 5

♘f3 e4 6 ♘e5 and if 6 ...
♘c6 then 7 ♗f4 or 7 ♕a4±.

Verdict   ✻✻✻✻

Wing Gambits

A) 1 e4 c5 2 b4 (Sicilian)
B) 1 e4 c5 2 ♘f3 d6 3 b4
(Sicilian)
C) 1 e4 e6 2 ♘f3 d5 3 e5
c5 4 b4 (French)

A) This is quite a good
way of confusing the issue,
e.g. 1 e4 c5 2 b4 cxb4 3 d4
d5 4 e5! ♘c6 5 a3 ♕b6 6 ♘e2
♗f5 7 axb4 ♘xb4 8 ♘a3 ♖c8
9 ♘f4 ♗xc2 10 ♕g4 e6 11
♗b5+ ♘c6 12 ♘xd5∞ Mari-
otti - Kuzmin, Leningrad
1977.

Verdict   ✻✻✻

B) Gives White less free-
dom to manoeuvre, e.g. 1 e4
c5 2 ♘f3 d6 3 b4 cxb4 4 d4
♘f6 5 ♗d3 e6 6 0-0 ♗e7 7
♘bd2 d5 8 e5 ♘fd7∓ Corden
- Gligoric, Hastings 1969/70.

Verdict   ✻✻

C) Is an invitation to a
real slugfest, after 1 e4 e6 2
♘f3 d5 3 e5 c5 4 b4!? cxb4 5
a3 bxa3 6 d4 ♘c6 7 c3 f5 8
♗d3 ♗d7 9 g4! Mortensen -
Karlsson, Copenhagen 1985.

True gambiteers should adore the rich possibilities here.

Verdict ✳✳✳

Woozle

A little-known counter-attacking variation designed to dismantle the white centre. It was invented by a German expert, Stefan Bucker, who, for no obvious reason, called it the woozle.

I believe the best way to combat this slightly artificial Black plan is with a robust gambit!

Sarkar – Copeland
Times Schools' Final 1991

1	d4	c5
2	d5	♘f6
3	♘c3	♛a5
4	♗d2	b5
5	e4	b4
6	e5	bxc3
7	♗xc3	♛a4
8	exf6	♛e4+
9	♗e2	gxf6
10	♛d3	

This move results in a clear loss of tempo. More aggressive, and better, is 10 ♛d2 ♗b7 11 0-0-0 ♛xg2 12 ♗f3, with plenty of compensation for the sacrificed pawn in terms of open lines

and speedy development.

10	...	♛xd3
11	♗xd3	d6
12	♘e2	♗a6
13	♗xa6	♘xa6
14	a3	♖g8
15	g3	♘c7

Black has a clear plan of campaign, to undermine the White centre by means of ... e6.

16	♖d1	♖g5
17	♗a5	♔d7
18	c4	e6
19	f4	♖h5
20	♘c3	♖b8
21	♘e4	♖f5
22	♗c3	exd5
23	♘xf6+	♔c6
24	cxd5+	♘xd5
25	♘xh7	

This pawn hunt represents a very poor decision. White had to capture on d5.

25	...	♘xc3
26	bxc3	♗g7
27	0-0	♗xc3
28	g4	♖d5
29	♖xd5	♔xd5
30	♘g5	f6
31	♘f3	♔e4
32	f5	♔f4
33	♔g2	♔xg4
34	♘g1	♖b2+
35	♖f2	♖xf2+
36	♔xf2	♗d4+
37	♔g2	♗xg1
38	♔xg1	♔xf5
39	♔f2	d5
	0-1	

Verdict ✳✳✳

X

1 e4 e5 2 ♘c3 ♘f6 3 f4 d5 4 fxe5 ♘xe4 5 ♘f3 ♘c6 6 ♕e2 ♗f5 7 ♕b5 ♘c5 8 d4 a6 9 ♕e2 ♘e4 10 ♕e3 ♘xc3 11 bxc3 ♗xc2

After 12 ♕f2 ♗f5 13 ♘h4 ♗e6 14 ♗d3 White's development is well worth the gambit pawn, e.g. 14 ... ♕d7 15 0-0 ♘a5 16 ♘f5 0-0-0 17 ♕e2 ♕c6 18 ♖b1 a6 19 ♗d2 ♘c4 20 ♘c3 ♘xc3 21 ♗xc3 ♕xc3 taking a second pawn but opening a further file for White's attack. The game concluded 22 ♖fc1 ♕a5 23 ♕c2 c6 24 ♗d2 ♕c7 25 ♕a4 ♖d7 26 ♗xc6 1-0 Kan - Botvinnik, Moscow 1935.

Verdict ✳✳✳

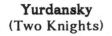

Y

Young

1 e4 e5 2 f4 exf4 3 ♘f3 g5 4 ♗c4 g4 5 ♗xf7+ ♔xf7 6 0-0 gxf3 7 ♕xf3

See (Wild) Muzio King's Gambit.

Yurdansky
(Two Knights)

1 e4 e5 2 ♘f3 ♘c6 3 ♗c4 ♘f6 4 d4 exd4 5 0-0 ♘xe4 6 ♖e1 d5 7 ♗xd5 ♕xd5 8 ♘c3 ♕a5 9 ♘xe4 ♗e6 10 ♗g5 h6 11 ♗h4 g5 12 ♘f6+ ♔e7 13 b4

The normal choices for White on the 10th move are 10 ♗d2 ♕d5 11 ♗g5 ♗d6 12 ♗f6 0-0 13 ♘xd4 ♘xd4 14 ♕xd4 ♕xd4 15 ♗xd4 burning out to equality, or 10 ♘eg5

0-0-0 11 ♘xe6 fxe6 12 ♖xe6 ♕f5! also = (Bogolyubov).

Not, however, 12 ... ♗d6 13 ♗g5 ♖df8 14 ♕e2 ♔d7 15 ♖e1! ♖xf3 16 ♕xf3 ♕xg5 17 ♕f7+ with a terrible attack.

Peter Konstantinovich Yurdansky (1891–1937) was champion of Moscow in 1913 and of the Red Army and Navy in 1927. His continuation of 10 ♗g5 is risky, but seeks to freshen up White's attacking chances.

Verdict ✳✳✳

Z

Zaitsev
(Closed Ruy Lopez)

Kasparov – Karpov
World Championship,
New York 1990

1	e4	e5
2	♘f3	♘c6
3	♗b5	a6
4	♗a4	♘f6
5	0-0	♗e7
6	♖e1	b5
7	♗b3	d6
8	c3	0-0
9	h3	♗b7

Karpov repeats his fa-
vourite Zaitsev variation,
the brainchild of Igor Zaitsev who was working as his
second at New York.

10	d4	♖e8
11	♘bd2	♗f8
12	a4	h6
13	♗c2	exd4
14	cxd4	♘b4
15	♗b1	c5
16	d5	♘d7
17	♖a3	f5

A bold idea which strikes
at the very foundations of
White's central pawns.

18	exf5	♘f6
19	♘e4	♗xd5
20	♘xf6+	

It is a remarkable testi-
mony to the depths to
which modern opening
theory extends that this
position is still known. A
game Horvath – Zobisch
played in Hungary two
years ago had seen 20 ♖ae3
in this position.

20	...	♕xf6
21	♗d2	♕xb2

22	♗xb4	♗f7!!

One of the most cunning
defensive ploys I have ever
seen. White has a multi-
tude of pieces attacked and
must return the material.
In contrast, the stereo-

typed 22 ... ♗xf3 23 ♖xf3 ♕xb4 24 ♖e6 would leave Black in all sorts of trouble on the light squares.

23 ♖e6

An amazing riposte, based on the perception that if Black ever takes the rook with his bishop the resultant opening of the b1 - h7 diagonal will prove fatal to the black king.

23	...	♕xb4
24	♖b3	♕xa4
25	♗c2	♖ad8
26	♖be3	♕b4
27	g3	a5

Black's massive armada of extra pawns means that he can consider sacrificing the queen in many circumstances in order to deaden White's attack. Here for example it is possible to play 27 ... d5 28 ♘e5 d4 29 ♖b3 ♗xc6 30 ♖xc4 ♗xf5 31 ♗xf5 ♖xe5.

28	♘h4	d5
29	♕e2	♕c4
30	♗d3	♕c1+
31	♔g2	c4
32	♗c2	♗xe6
33	♖xe6	

A natural recapture since White ends up with a queen check on e6 gaining some time to bring the knight into the attack as well.

33	...	♖xe6
34	♕xe6+	♔h8
35	♘g6+	♔h7
36	♕e2	♕g5
37	f6	♕xf6
38	♘xf8+	♔g8
39	♘g6	

Black's next move is a terrible blunder.

39 ... ♕f7

Black could have won with 39 ... d4 40 ♘f5 ♕c6+ 41 ♗e4 d3! 42 ♕f3 ♕f6.

40 ♘e7+ ♔f8

½-½

Verdict ✳ ✳ ✳ ✳

Zollner
(Sicilian Dragon)

---

1 e4 c5 2 ♘f3 d6 3 d4 cxd4 4 ♘xd4 ♘f6 5 ♘c3 g6 6 ♗e2 ♗g7 7 0-0 0-0 8 ♗e3 ♘c6 9 f4 ♕b6 10 e5

This is harmless - Black can accept with equanimity, thus 10 ... dxe5 11 fxe5 ♘xe5 12 ♘f5 ♕xb2! 13 ♘xe7+ ♔h8 14 ♗d4 ♕b4 15 ♗xe5 ♕xe7.

Verdict ✳ ✳

Index of Openings